CAPITALIST SOCIETY AND MODERN SOCIOLOGY

CAPITALIST SOCIETY AND MODERN SOCIOLOGY

H. Frankel

1970
LAWRENCE AND WISHART

SBN 85315 218 7

To Anna, Mark and Dora

Printed by
Unwin Brothers Limited
The Gresham Press, Old Woking, Surrey, England
A member of the Staples Printing Group
(HL 7928)

"To secure for the workers by hand or by brain the full fruits of their industry and the most equitable distribution thereof that may be possible, upon the basis of the common ownership of the means of production, distribution and exchange, and the best obtainable system of popular administration and control of each industry or service."

Labour Party Constitution.
Clause 4.

". . . the Welfare State is not the dictatorship of the proletariat and is not pledged to liquidate the bourgeoisie".

T. H. Marshall (1953)

FOREWORD

Argument about the nature of post-war British society started properly in the mid-nineteen fifties, with the publication of such books as Anthony Crosland's *The Future of Socialism* and the late John Strachey's *Contemporary Capitalism*, both of which sought to show that pre-war capitalism had been transformed out of all recognition. The controversy continued on into the 'sixties, with counter-arguments growing; but, so far as I know, except for certain major essays in such collections as *Towards Socialism* and *The Incompatibles*, the sociological arguments and evidence have not been brought together, from a Marxist view-point, in one book. This is what I have tried to do and readers will no doubt, after reading it, judge whether it has successfully answered the question, "Is Britain still a capitalist country?"

The book is addressed principally to thinking working men and women and I have tried to keep the language and the exposition as simple as possible. It seems to me that sociological jargon does not always—to use one of its favourite phrases—make for successful "communication" with ordinary people. Still, although I have tried to make my sentences more easily understandable than those of academic sociology, a fair amount of statistical material has had to be used to back the argument.

H. FRANKEL
December 1969

CONTENTS

I

ONE NATION?

Mr. Harold Macmillan's claim that the class struggle was obsolete put in a nutshell the view, propagated not only by Tories but by right-wing Labour theorists, that the old capitalism had gone for ever and with it the Marxist idea of class society. Crosland's *The Future of Socialism*, published in 1956, was something of a landmark in this attack on the Marxist conception of society.

> "I conclude", Crosland wrote, "that the definition of capitalism in terms of ownership, whether or not it was helpful 100 years ago, has wholly lost its significance and interest now that ownership is no longer the clue to the total picture of social relationships: and that it would be more significant to define societies in terms of equality, or class relationships, or their political systems. In any event, I personally think . . . that the proper definition of the word capitalism is a society with the essential social, economic and ideological characteristics of Great Britain from the 1830s to the 1930s; and this, assuredly, the Britain of 1956 is not. And so, to the question, 'Is this still Capitalism?', I would answer 'No'."[1]

The reader will note two admissions by Mr. Crosland.[2] He admitted that groups in society might be unequal in certain respects and that there might be "classes" even if society was no longer capitalist. He also committed the elementary logical sin of deducing what seems to be a reasonable conclusion from a false premise; that is to say, having defined capitalism in his own terms, he concluded that the system in 1956 was not capitalism according to his own definition, just as any racialist, asserting his own race to be inherently superior, then proceeds to "prove" to his own satisfaction that every other is inferior. In a later book,[3] he repeated that there were serious deficiencies in the present system in Britain.

> "Most wage-earners, happily, are now comparatively well-off. But poverty and distress are still wide-spread amongst non-producing

[1] Crosland, *The Future of Socialism*, p. 76.

[2] In 1969/70, as readers will know, one of the small élite of inner members of Mr. Wilson's Cabinet.

[3] *The Conservative Enemy* (1962).

dependants and those with exceptionally heavy responsibilities—the sick, the widowed, those with large families, and above all the 2½ million old people living below or near the poverty line . . ."[1]

In addition, the deficiencies in Britain's "social capital" were well recognised: the bleakness of most of our hospitals, the hopelessly overcrowded classes in many state schools, the shortage of university places, the nerve-racking road congestion, and so on. And following Professor Galbraith's similar strictures on the United States,[2] he concluded:

"These deficiencies have come to seem the more vulgar as the general level of prosperity rises. The huge increase in conspicuous private goods such as cars and household durables; the rash of ostentatious private office-building; the growth of the lavish teenage market; the rapid increase in mass consumer advertising—all these have heightened the contrast between 'private affluence and public squalor'."[3]

It seems odd that, after years of the "non-capitalist democratic" state, this contrast should not only exist but sharpen. But Crosland saw no contradiction here. Further, since the situation was so similar to that in the United States, did he believe that American society was no longer capitalist either? It would seem so.[4] It seems odd, finally, that the former leader of the Tory Party described the present situation in Britain even more glowingly.

"At any rate, here again we were all, in all parties, moving in a world that would have seemed incredible before the First World War and even between the wars. Wider distribution of wealth; the raising of the standard of the people in material comforts and opportunities; the determination to satisfy their spiritual ambitions by the provision of ever-increasing educational facilities; the ready acceptance of the care of the old and those who had fallen by the wayside, by humanising the pre-war systems of relief: all these radical developments, not merely of purpose but of performance, were approved by both parties. Politicians might differ on the means and methods, but they shared common aims.

"Unlike the period between the wars, there has been none of the

[1] *The Conservative Enemy*, p. 11.

[2] J. K. Galbraith, *The Affluent Society*.

[3] *The Conservative Enemy*, p. 12.

[4] *The Conservative Enemy*, p. 57.

bitter feelings which massive unemployment and poverty created *Disraeli's 'Two Nations' have grown gradually but steadily into one.*"[1]

Already, conscious socialists might well begin to be suspicious of a claim put in almost the same language by Tory leader and Labour theorist. Not only this, but especially during the nineteen-fifties almost all propaganda from the mass media, when it had a political or social aim, was designed to promote this idea. When the *Daily Mirror's* slogan was "Forward with the People", the implication was that high or low, rich or poor, irrespective of class distinction, all were members of a big family, the "people". When the *Daily Mail* claimed it was "for Queen and Commonwealth", this meant that, in the *Daily Mail's* opinion, Queen and Commonwealth were one and that no real difference existed between the Queen in Buckingham Palace, Windsor, Balmoral or Sandringham, the bank clerk in his suburban home, the manual worker in his council house, and the African peasant in his hut. "We are all in it together" might be taken as a motto: so could the appeal, "We must all work harder", made either by members of the Tory Government when Common Market talks failed early in 1963, or by the Labour Government during the sterling and balance of payments crisis beginning in 1964 (and not yet ended).

THE ACADEMICS AND PROPAGANDISTS IN THE 'FIFTIES

In the field of academic sociology, the situation was marked by a rash of conflicting theories of social structure. These ranged from a modified acceptance of the Marxist theory of class right through to subjective ideas and the concepts of élites and the "mass society". Criteria of social division included not only the more obvious indicators like income, birth and occupation, but education, language, way of life, what class you or your neighbours thought you belonged to, and who exercised power in society.

Thus T. H. Pear, a social psychologist, wrote:

> "The concept of class is insufficient to subsume the chief facts. Those of stratum, status and élite are useful for different purposes."[2]

Pear went on to say that he believed the importance of class to be diminishing and that of strata, status and élites to be increasing.

[1] H. Macmillan, *Winds of Change* (Vol. I of Autobiography)—my italics H.F.
[2] Pear: *English Social Differences.*

In *Studies in Class Structure*, the late G. D. H. Cole examined the various criteria and concluded that, though much could be said for the Marxist theory, no single criterion determined class. Cole's approach was echoed by D. C. Marsh,[1] who repeated that no criteria defined class exactly, but, like Cole, came down in favour of occupation as the best. Even the well-known Tory publicists, Lewis and Maude,[2] while defending the middle class, said they had as yet found no satisfactory definition of it, except as those who stood between the upper and lower classes. There were, finally, those very many writers who argued that, in view of the great rise in their standard of living, the working class had vanished, to become part of a much larger middle-class, which now included the bulk of the population of Britain.

The situation had, indeed, become so confused that one notable reviewer of a recent sociological book was stung to write:

> "... after half a century of Weberian sociology even morality is in a mess. It is no longer an issue of haves and have-nots, but of status categories, relative positions on a dozen different incommensurable ladders. What matters, we are told, is not whether you are a bloody capitalist or an honest working man, but whether you have passed the 11-plus and whether you have the sort of voice which would pass muster as that of an announcer on the B.B.C."[3]

Even a Polish Marxist separated from the capitalist scene could be influenced. In that year of national and international upheavals, 1956, Professor Ossowski wrote of the situation in the United States:

> "... today the immense national budget of the United States permits infinitely thorough-going intervention by the political authorities in the economic life of the country and enables them to exert considerable influence on the distribution of the national income *and the system of class relations*".[4]

In a number of important respects the evidence then seemed to be overwhelming. In the Western European capitalist democracies, the situation of the working class had enormously improved: mass unemployment had been abolished; the standard of living had risen considerably, including the well-publicised mass ownership of T.V., washing machine and "fridge"; educational opportunities for the children were much greater than ever before; barriers to advancement

[1] *The Changing Social Structure of England and Wales, 1871–1951*, ch. 8.

[2] *The English Middle Classes.*

[3] Edmund Leach, *New Statesman*, 8th July 1966.

[4] S. Ossowski, *Class Structure in the Social Consciousness* p. 185 (my italics H.F.).

and social mixing had broken down. As regards the upper classes, although the late Lord (Herbert) Morrison's remark that the rich had been taxed out of existence might be taken with a pinch of salt, most ordinary people would have accepted the proposition that the rich were now much less rich than before; and that the power of the upper classes and employers was much less now than pre-war, in view of the growth of the trade unions and the support given to the Labour Party. For in 1945 a Labour Government was elected for the first time with an overwhelming Parliamentary majority; and again in 1966. If we hadn't got the "classless society" yet, we were certainly well on the way; the British social system certainly wasn't capitalism. And all this, finally, by peaceful gradualism. Indeed, the English working class were today *less* revolutionary than they were in Marx's time. This surely proved the superiority of right-wing Labour theory and policy.

The popular propagandists had another weapon to hand to fling at the Marxists. Look at the Soviet Union! they said. Here you Marxists had your "classless society" so-called. Private ownership of the means of production, the basic cause of class division in society, had been abolished. Yet "classes" still existed. True, they were not based on property ownership, but on political criteria. Industrial managers, top artists and scientists, and government bureaucrats, enjoyed higher incomes and other privileges associated with an upper class. Above all, there was a governing élite, the Communist Party, which was in effect a ruling class more united and more powerful than any contemporary capitalist ruling-class—if, that is, there was a capitalist ruling-class at all!

This question was, therefore, not merely one of academic interest: it was important politically. If, first, Britain was not a capitalist society, then the Marxists were wrong and their call for the overthrow of the system was wrong. Indeed, if British society was progressing as the anti-Marxists claimed it was, then the Marxists were not only wrong but dangerous, in the sense that they wanted to upset a progressive development which was in the people's interests. Secondly, if Soviet society was not classless, then what the Marxists wanted (or if they didn't want it, at least they were working for it) was merely the substitution of a different sort of class society for the present one—a class system which, moreover, was more rigid than the one we had now. At best, the people would only be changing one type of class society for another; and since it was better to have the devil you know than the one you didn't, why bother?

2

THE CHIEF CRITICISMS

Anti-Marxists persistently argue that Marx's analysis of society was appropriate only for the period in which he lived.

They claim that he was wrong on the following counts:

1. He "polarised" society into two main classes, thus ignoring the middle class;
2. He predicted that the proletariat would be driven down to a "bare subsistence" and that poverty and misery would increase; whereas the opposite is the case;
3. He predicted that the middle class would disappear into the proletariat; whereas it would be truer to say that the proletariat has become part of a vast middle class;
4. He predicted the inevitability of proletarian revolution, but it is now further off in England than when he wrote;
5. He claimed that under socialism classes would disappear.

Let us take the first and third of these together. In those times, especially in England, the classic example of capitalist development, it was true to say that society was divided into two broad classes. Critics never tire of quoting the following famous passage in *The Communist Manifesto:*

> "Our epoch, the epoch of the bourgeoisie, possesses, however, this distinctive feature; it has simplified the class antagonisms. Society as a whole is more and more splitting up into two great hostile camps, into two great classes directly facing each other—bourgeoisie and proletariat."

Marx, in other words, "polarised" society into two main classes in continuous conflict. As if to emphasise this, they add, he forecast the disappearance of the middle-class, in a further famous passage later in the *Manifesto:*

> "The lower strata of the middle class—the small tradespeople, shopkeepers and retired tradesmen generally, the handi-craftsmen and peasants—all these sink gradually into the proletariat . . ."

Obviously this is not the case today: small tradespeople, shopkeepers, and all the rest, have not only not disappeared, but, in Western Europe anyway, are flourishing and even prosperous. Details of this type of refutation of Marx will be given later; but even without the details the case is clearly very strong.

But Marx's work is no bible, even if some of us Marxists have mistakenly taken this attitude in the past. What has to be done is threefold: first, to accept where necessary that history has falsified Marx's predictions; secondly, to observe where changes are necessary in the theory and practice of Marxism. If any other theory and practice, such as that of right-wing Labour, is truer and more in the interests of the people and of socialism, then we should accept that theory and practice. Thirdly, we should also see whether the critics give only a part of the Marxist picture.

Now *The Communist Manifesto* was a political clarion call. At the turbulent end of the first half of the nineteenth century, revolutions were sweeping Europe. Even in conservative England the Charter demanding universal suffrage, annual parliaments and the rest, obtained nearly half a million signatures. Engels wrote: "The Manifesto was published as the platform of the Communist League. . . . Drawn up in German in January 1848, the manuscript was sent to the printer in London a few weeks before the French revolution of February 24th."[1] Marx was then not quite 30, Engels only 27. This magnificent document has remained the classic short statement of the aims of the communist movement; but can anyone say that it must be perfect in every line, every prediction?

As the friendly American critics, Bendix and Lipset, put it:

> ". . . Marx and Engels often felt compelled by the exigencies of the social and political struggle, to cast their ideas in extremely pointed formulations. Had they been scholars of the traditional type, they might have avoided at least some of the dogmatic interpretations of their work, though they would have had far less success in spreading their ideas and getting them accepted. Much of the difficulty in obtaining a concise view of Marxian theory stems from the fact that it was meant to be a tool for political action."[2]

It is a fact, which many anti-Marxists conveniently ignore, or remain unaware of,[3] that Marx later altered his prediction that the

[1] Engels, in the 1888 Preface.

[2] Bendix and Lipset, "Karl Marx' theory of social classes," in *Class, Status and Power* (ed. Bendix and Lipset).

[3] But some, e.g. Dahrendorf, are well aware of this, though they still oppose Marx.

lower strata of the middle class would disappear. The last chapter of the third volume of *Capital* remained unfinished at Marx's death. Edited by Engels, the material it contained was written during the 1860s before the rise of imperialism in the last thirty years of the century. At that time the fusion of the landed aristocracy with finance capital had not taken place and Marx still separated "capitalists" from "landlords". Later Marxists, including Lenin, rectified this. Indeed, Engels in a letter to Bebel dated 24th July 1885, already noted this position. "Here the new franchise will overthrow the whole former party. The alliance between the Whigs and Tories into one great Conservative Party having as its basis the *entire* body of land-owners, which has hitherto been split up into two camps, and including all the conservative elements of the bourgeoisie: banking, high finance, trade, a section of industry . . ."[1] However, Marx in the 1860s was already aware that the division of society was complex, for in the final, unfinished chapter, entitled "The Classes", he wrote:

> "In England, modern society is indisputably developed most highly and classically in its economic structure. Nevertheless the stratification of classes does not appear in its pure form, even there. Middle and transition stages obliterate even here all definite boundaries, although much less in the rural districts. *However, this is immaterial for our analysis.*"[2]

Critics need to note the last sentence. It meant that for Marx the fundamental division of society still lay between capitalists and proletariat. But he recognised that the existence of "middle and transition" strata brought confusion. He spoke of the ". . . infinite dissipation of interests and positions created by the social division of labour . . ."[3]; and well do we know that in England! He also had a few words to say on some alternative *criteria* of class, when he wrote that classes were not determined by ". . . the identity of their revenues and their sources of revenue".[4] That is to say, because doctors, for instance, received their income by way of fees from patients, this did not constitute doctors a class. Nor would it mean that all workers who were paid monthly by cheque from the state Exchequer, i.e. civil servants, were a class.

But let us even go back to *The Communist Manifesto*. Remembering that it was written in a hurry, some self-contradiction was understand-

[1] *Selected Correspondence of Marx and Engels*, p. 423.
[2] *Capital*, Vol. III, Ch. 52 (my italics H.F.). [3] Same. [4] Same.

able. For, further on, Marx and Engels contradicted the earlier, flat statement about the lower middle strata sinking entirely into the proletariat. They wrote, first:

> "The lower middle-class, the small manufacturer, the shopkeeper, the artisan, the peasant, all these fight against the bourgeoisie, to save from extinction their existence as fractions of the middle class . . ."

And secondly:

> "In countries where modern civilisation has become fully developed, a new class of petty bourgeois has been formed, fluctuating between proletariat and bourgeoisie, and ever renewing itself as a supplementary part of bourgeois society."

The anti-Marxist critics must, therefore, stand condemned for presenting only part of the picture. The other quotations show that the young Marx and Engels broadly meant that, between the two major classes, the middle class, an amorphous, fluctuating mass, struggled for existence, while parts of it sank into the proletariat, less fortunate members of the bourgeoisie fell down into it and some successful sections of the proletariat rose to strengthen it. Nevertheless, the broad trend was towards that "polarisation" which modern right-wing theorists declare has not taken place.

The second major theme of anti-Marxism is on the issue of "pauperisation". In *The Communist Manifesto* appears the passage:

> "The modern labourer, on the contrary, instead of rising with the progress of industry, sinks deeper and deeper below the conditions of existence of his own class. He becomes a pauper, and pauperism develops more rapidly than population and wealth."

Again, in *Capital*, Marx wrote:

> "While there is thus a progressive diminution in the number of the capitalist magnates, . . . there occurs a corresponding increase in the mass of poverty, oppression, enslavement, degeneration and exploitation . . ."[1]

The general tenor of *Capital*, especially Vol. I, is along these lines, namely, that the capitalists ruthlessly exploit the proletarians, driving them down to the bare level of subsistence, to the level where they

[1] *Capital*, Vol. I, ch. 24.

can just keep working and reproducing to supply more fodder for the capitalist machine.

But, cry the critics, this is obvious nonsense today: poverty—at least mass poverty such as was known even in the 1930s—has disappeared. The brutal exploitation of men, women and children ended long ago. However, granted Marx again could not foresee the position today, whatever that position may be, and we have as yet to examine it, the critics again ignore another feature of exploitation which Marx discerned. If we continue the passage last quoted, we find Marx adding:

> "... but at the same time there is a steady intensification of the wrath of the working class—a class which grows ever more numerous, and is disciplined, unified, and organised by the very mechanism of the capitalist method of production."

In other words, it must be conceded that Marx saw that the proletariat fought back. In fact, that the working class does not passively submit to this exploitation, was and remains one of the essentials of Marxism. Capitalist pressure forcing the proletariat to the lowest levels of poverty and misery is fought and may be pushed back. The net result must, therefore, depend as long as capitalism lasts on the relative, organised strengths of bourgeoisie and proletariat. And this point in fact cropped up later, in different forms. For example, in *Capital* Vol. II, Marx repeatedly spoke of "normal average wage", being the wage paid under specified conditions. And, more particularly, in Vol. III, he concluded:

> "The actual value of his labour-power differs from this physical minimum; it differs according to climate and conditions of social development; it depends not merely upon the physical, but also upon the historically developed social needs, which become second nature. But in every country and at any given period this regulating average wage is a given magnitude."[1]

Elsewhere, Marx added, the cost of education was part of "subsistence". And, a final important addition, the analysis of capitalist production was conducted on the assumption of "free competition"; but Marx also discussed the distortions due to "imperfections", i.e. due to the growth of monopoly in its various forms, though he died long

[1] *Capital*, Vol. III, ch. 24 (also Vol, I. ch. 6).

before monopolism really got going.[1] However, the "imperfectly competitive" capitalist system was, in Marx's eyes and in the eyes of all Marxists, still capitalism, whether the "imperfections" were and are due to combinations of capitalists or to combinations of workers. Increase in wages due to trade union pressure, or following price rises, did not, in Marx's view, substantially alter the final distribution between capitalists, landlords, and proletarians. These points need to be stressed against the distorted emphasis on Marx's remarks about "bare subsistence".

As regards the absence so far of "proletarian revolution" in England, little can be said here, although we shall return to it later. Put simply, England's primacy in industrialisation put her ahead of the rest of the world. Coupled with the seizure of a large empire, the mother country became swollen with vast wealth extorted from the colonies and from other countries of profitable investment. Engels repeatedly wrote about the way this monopoly position allowed the ruling class to buy off not only sections of the working-class leadership, but to a lesser extent the masses as a whole. In 1885 he wrote:

> "The truth is this: during the period of England's industrial monopoly the English working-class have, to a certain extent, shared in the benefits of the monopoly. These benefits were very unequally parcelled out amongst them; the privileged minority pocketed most, but even the great mass had, at least, a temporary share now and then. And that is the reason why, since the dying-out of Owenism, there has been no Socialism in England." But he added: "With the breakdown of that monopoly the English working-class will lose that privileged position; it will find itself generally—the privileged and leading minority not excepted—on a level with its fellow-workers abroad. And that is the reason why there will be Socialism again in England."[2]

That Marx and Engels hoped for and expected the proletarian revolution in England fairly soon is certainly true. Nevertheless, their later writings, especially Engels', showed they realised that the early industrialisation and its results could and did postpone the revolution. The revolution has still not taken place, although the General Strike came pretty near to it; but if not in England, because of its peculiar

[1] The more popular term monopoly is used, though strictly capitalism in the twentieth century is a mlxture of monopoly and oligopoly.

[2] Preface (1892) to *The Condition of the Working-Class in England in 1844*.

development, it has certainly occurred in other countries. It does *not* mean, as some critics claim, that the Marxist theory of inevitable revolution has been disproved. A particular non-occurrence of a predicted event cannot *dis*prove a theory, particularly if the event has occurred elsewhere. The non-occurrence of the proletarian revolution in England yet, when it has occurred in other countries, should be explicable in terms of counter-revolutionary factors. These factors have been mentioned briefly.

The object of the present chapter has been to clear away some of the bias in presentations of Marx's views. It has aimed to show that, despite some contradictory statements, Marx' and Engels' picture was of a *broad* two-class division of society based on the ownership of capital, with a fluctuating middle-class between. It aimed to show also that the "pauperisation" of the working class would be at least partly off-set by the proletariat fighting back; and how much depended on the relative strengths of the two classes, as well as the total wealth of the particular country and the accepted "level of subsistence".

3

THE CRITICS AND THEIR ALTERNATIVES

The claim that Marxism has been disproved by developments in the capitalist world is not new; indeed, it started as soon as the influence of Marxism began to spread. It would be useful to look back at some of these criticisms.

Very important changes took place during the last thirty years of the nineteenth century. Other West European nations were catching up in the industrial race with Britain. Britain ceased to be the workshop of the world, but (and this is important), remained the financial centre of the world. Between 1875 and 1895 growing industrial competition brought a fall in wages, but they did not fall as much as prices. *Real* wages therefore continued to rise. Between 1895 and the First World War, however, the situation worsened for the working class. While money wages rose, they failed to keep up with rising prices. This was a period of strikes and other class struggles. The situation was saved, for the ruling class, by the outbreak of war.

In view of the growing influence of Marxism, attempts were made to counter it. In Britain the Fabian Society came into being, influencing Eduard Bernstein, a theorist of the German Labour movement. In the academic sphere, Max Weber, by far the most significant of modern bourgeois sociologists, developed an alternative theory of the structure of modern society.

FABIANISM

The story of Fabianism and its enormous influence on the policy of the Labour Party is well known; and criticism tends correctly to emphasise its theory of "gradualism". Yet it was founded on a firm belief in socialism, in the need to eliminate the capitalist and in the public ownership of the means of production. This was, however, to be obtained by a gradual process of, on the one hand, permeating the minds of sympathisers and opponents alike with the ideas of socialism and, on the other, socialising the system bit by bit. In the *Fabian Essays in Socialism*, Bernard Shaw, who edited them, enthusiastically wrote: "... The resolution to make an end of private property is gaining force every day..." The Fabians were contemptuous of revolutionaries who, they said, were mere idealists and amateur dreamers compared with the bourgeois realists. Sidney Webb concluded:

> "... important organic changes can only be (1) democratic, and thus acceptable to a majority of the people, and prepared for in the minds of all; (2) gradual, and thus causing no dislocation, however rapid may be the rate of progress; (3) not regarded as immoral by the mass of the people ... and (4) in this country, at any rate, constitutional and peaceful."[1]

Webb was above all impressed by the growth and extent of State and local government intervention:

> "On every side he (the capitalist) is being registered, inspected, controlled, and eventually superseded by the community; and in the meantime he is compelled to cede for public purposes an ever-increasing share of his rent and interest."[2]

He rhapsodised over this, which later came to be known as "gas-and-water socialism"; and was absolutely sure that in this way the capitalists would be eliminated peacefully and socialism brought in without a hair of anyone's head being put out of place.

On the eve of the formation of the Labour Representation Committee, forerunner of the Labour Party, the up-and-coming J. Ramsay MacDonald repeated the view that socialism could be obtained through the assimilation of socialist ideas and not through class struggle. For, first, there were more than two classes and, even more, neither the bourgeoisie nor the proletariat was a united class. Denouncing capitalism for its moral and physical impoverishment of the people, he nevertheless regarded the Marxian thesis of the inevitability of socialism as "mere fancy". Socialism was inevitable only if intelligence made it so. The working class was every time outsmarted by the capitalists; so only when progressive steps such as factory laws, public health laws and municipalisation were followed out and joined together, would Socialism result. Land, he wrote, must be nationalised and industrial capital controlled by the community. But neither could this be carried out solely by the working class. "... the political movement ... must be a movement of the whole Society and not one of its functions—the working classes".[3]

[1] *Fabian Essays in Socialism* (1889): essay by S. Webb. [2] Same.
[3] J. R. MacDonald: *Socialism and Society* (1905).

The conclusion is plain. The Fabians and the founders of the Labour Party all subscribed to a complete change in the economic system to full public ownership of land and capital. Where they differed from the Marxists was in the method. They were sure municipal socialism would lead steadily to total socialisation without the need for a revolutionary takeover. They differed in their attitude towards the role of the working class, but all implicitly assumed that they, intellectuals of middle or lower-middle class origin, could lead the way and convert friends and enemies, proletariat and bourgeoisie, to acceptance of complete socialism.

BERNSTEIN

Bernstein's book, the bible of early "revisionism" as Crosland's was of the 1950s, was based on his letter to the German Social-Democratic Party in 1898. He went further than Fabianism for, like MacDonald, he rejected the Marxist theory of the inevitability of socialism in the sense of a system based on the common ownership of the means of production. While *The Communist Manifesto* was correct in its theory of social evolution, he wrote, it was wrong in respect of the time it would take for capitalism to collapse. (Here, it should be noted, Engels agreed.) Bernstein also attacked on the same points as contemporary critics: the class struggle had not sharpened, the middle classes had not disappeared and the concentration of ownership of capital had not developed uniformly—that is to say, it had developed in certain sectors but not over the whole field of industry and agriculture. Indeed, the *number* of capitalists had actually increased and, like the Fabians and later theorists Strachey and Crosland he confidently claimed, "... the privileges of the capitalist bourgeoisie (are) yielding step by step to democratic organisations".[1] This, he wrote, was especially the case in regard to factory legislation, democratisation of local government and the increasing freedom of trade unions and co-operatives. The "catastrophic" theory of evolution was out-of-date. Even Engels, Bernstein added, had, in 1895, called on the working class to adopt lawful rather than violent means to seize power.

Bernstein concluded with the following words:

"Unable to believe in finalities at all, I cannot believe in a final aim of socialism. But I strongly believe in the socialist movement,

[1] Same, Preface.

in the march forward of the working classes, who step by step must work out their emancipation by changing society from the domain of a commercial land-holding oligarchy to a real democracy which in all its departments is guided by the interests of those who work and create."[1]

On what evidence did the father of "evolutionary socialism" base his conclusion? First on details of share-holdings in big companies to illustrate the growth of share-ownership. In England the number of share-holders was then already more than a million. Incomes of £150–£1,000 a year (those of the middle and lower-middle classes and the "aristocracy of labour") were held by one-and-a-half million people. In France, out of eight million families, six million were working class, 160,000 were rich and as many as 1·7 million belonged to the middle strata. In these countries and in Germany, too, he claimed, the number with higher incomes was increasing faster than the number with lower incomes.

The reason for this growing prosperity was, he wrote, the great increase in the productive power of labour. The result was a huge increase in the production of commodities. And where could all these commodities go? Obviously the big capitalists could not consume them all. They went therefore to the growing middle-class, to the proletariat with its rising standard of living and its slow transformation into membership of the middle-class, all contrary to Marx's prediction.

Bernstein continued with data refuting Marx's theory that ownership of the means of production concentrated into fewer and fewer hands. On the contrary, he declared, far from this happening, it was the case that in 1896 a majority of workers in England, France and Germany were employed in small and medium-sized businesses and there were also large numbers of self-employed persons. Independent craftsmen would continue to exist side-by-side with big industry, because the latter required specialist workshops to carry out small jobs, the rich would always demand a small quantity of expensive goods made by craftsmen and small retail shops would always be needed.

The state of agriculture, according to Bernstein, revealed a similar pattern. Widespread ownership of peasant holdings characterised West European agriculture; and, astonishingly, the same was true of England where, in 1895, holdings of 5–120 hectares (12–300 acres)

[1] Same.

comprised 64 per cent of the cultivated area and their number was increasing. Only 13 per cent of cultivated land was contained in estates of over 200 hectares (500 acres). In Wales and Scotland the proportions held in these small-holdings were even greater—72 per cent and 92 per cent respectively of the cultivated land were in small-holdings of 2–100 hectares (5–250 acres). The *proletariat* everywhere, Bernstein concluded, comprised at most only half the population.

Finally, on crises and the inevitable collapse of capitalism, Bernstein referred to Engels' notes to the third volume of *Capital*, which admitted that "inevitability" was an unproved hypothesis. Indeed, Bernstein argued, by means of cartel organisations and through the enormous improvement in transport and communications, the world market was being better regulated. It was, therefore, far more important and indeed possible for workers to struggle for a better share of the world's goods than towards a mythical end to the present system. Hence Bernstein defined socialism as "... a movement towards—or the state of—an order of society based on the principle of association" between the various sections of society. With minor variations this could truthfully be said to be the guiding hypothesis of all right-wing politicians of the Labour and Socialist movements, and, indeed, of the Liberal and Conservative parties. The original aim, even of the Fabians, was dropped; the "gradual steps" were all that mattered.

Bernstein's theory was answered by Rosa Luxemburg and Karl Kautsky, leading German Marxists of the time, and by Lenin. If Bernstein was right, Rosa Luxemburg wrote, then socialism was a utopia and the socialist movement unnecessary. Or it meant that the socialist movement should regard its task as the support of capitalism and that it should therewith believe that capitalism could abolish its own contradictions. "In that case socialism ... becomes anything you want to call it ..." Kautsky observed that Bernstein's revisionism (and, for that matter, Fabianism) was true only if it were granted that the proletariat alone was growing in strength while the bourgeoisie was not. But obviously this was not so. Hence, "That which from a one-sided observation appears as a gradual peaceable growth into Socialism is then seen as the organisation of ever larger fighting bodies, as the development and application of ever more powerful resources for conflict, as a continuous windening of the battle field."[1] Kautsky developed and detailed this point in a passage of great power and importance.

[1] K. Kautsky: *The Social Revolution* (trans. Simons).

"Democracy is . . . indispensable as a means of ripening the proletariat for the social revolution. But it is not capable of preventing this revolution. Democracy is to the proletariat what light and air are to the organism; without them it cannot develop its powers. But we must not be so occupied with observing the growth of one class that we cannot see the simultaneous growth of its opponent. Democracy does not hinder the development of capital, whose organisation and economic and political powers increase at the same time as does the power of the proletariat. To be sure, the cooperatives are increasing, but simultaneously and yet faster grows the accumulation of capital; to be sure, the unions are growing, but simultaneously and faster grows the concentration of capital and its organisation in gigantic monopolies. To be sure, the socialist press is growing . . . but simultaneously grows the partyless and characterless press that poisons and unnerves ever wider popular circles. To be sure, wages are rising, but still faster rise the mass of profits. Certainly the number of Socialist representatives in Parliament are growing, but still more sinks the significance and efficaciousness of this institution, while simultaneously Parliamentary majorities, like the Government, fall into ever greater dependence on the powers of high finance."[1]

Finally, Lenin showed how Bernstein and his followers exaggerated the developments within capitalism on which they based their theory.[2] Lenin declared his belief in the inevitable collapse of capitalism by pointing to the deepening crises in America and Europe. As for parliamentary democracy doing away with the class struggle, Lenin, like Kautsky, pointed to the fact that simultaneously with the growth of democracy grew the struggle of the masses. Lenin finally made the important point that revisionism was a petit-bourgeois creed and that, in one form or another, it was bound to appear and re-appear. "It is quite natural that this should be so and this will always be so right to the unfolding of the proletarian revolution, since it would be a foolish mistake to think that a 'complete' proletarianisation of the majority of the population is necessary before such a revolution can be achieved."[3] Moreover, this battle of ideas would sharpen in the revolutionary period itself. How true those revolutionary comments are today we shall see later.

[1] K. Kautsky: *The Social Revolution* (trans. Simons).

[2] Lenin: *Marxism and Revisionism* (1908). [3] Lenin: same.

History temporarily shattered reformist complacency and brought out revolutionary ideas and action. The years up to the outbreak of the First World War were, as we noted before, full of class struggles by workers against deteriorating conditions of life. After the war came slumps, then a short period of prosperity in the middle 'twenties before the Great Depression. Fascism, which had taken over in Italy in 1922, now swept through Western Europe, abolishing unemployment only by sweeping the unemployed into the manufacture or use of armaments and dependent industries. At the same time the successful proletarian revolution in Russia became a spur to revolutionary activity. Among socialists, therefore, reformist theory certainly did not seem as impressive as Marxism. Typical of comments on the situation in Britain before the outbreak of the Second World War was the following:

> "We end, then, on a note of uncertainty. Thanks to the fall in world prices, the working classes of Great Britain had in the decade after the General Strike made some real advance in their standard of living—after a period of a quarter of a century during which, as a whole, they had made no advance at all. It is true that even during this period of stagnation there was going on a process by which the proportion of manual workers and 'proletarians' generally to the total population was being somewhat reduced and the proportion of salary-earners above the working class standard somewhat increased, and also that there was some shifting among the manual workers from worse to better-paid occupations. But neither these changes nor the real advance of the 'thirties in the general standard (but let us always remember the painful exception of the depressed areas) had altered to any substantial extent the class structure as between rich and poor. The two nations still confronted each other, as they did in the days of the Chartists, when Disraeli wrote *Sybil* to point the contrast."[1]

WEBER

The most original and influential bourgeois sociologist and originator of the most powerful alternative to the Marxist theory of society is undoubtedly Max Weber. The family, into which he was born in 1864, were Prussian textile manufacturers and merchants and his father became a Liberal politician of right-wing views. Young Weber wanted

[1] Cole and Postgate, *The Common People 1746–1938*, Epilogue.

to do well academically and when, in 1895, he delivered a lecture at the University of Freiburg in defence of imperialist Prussian *Realpolitik* (which meant German expansionism) and the royal Hohenzollern family, his hope was fulfilled: he was awarded a professorship at Heidelberg University the following year, being then only 32. In 1904 a long visit to the U.S.A. convinced him that here was the model of the "new society". "Here a political federation of states had led to a 'voluntary' union of immense contrasts", he wrote.[1]

When the First World War came, Weber, then aged fifty, thought it a "great and wonderful war". But within a year he changed his opinion dramatically, denouncing the machinations of the war-makers as being "the gamble of munition makers and agrarian capitalists". In 1918 Weber, who had made his name first by defending the Prussian monarchy, became a republican. He died in 1920, leaving behind a mass of sociological writings on a great many topics showing immense learning.

Linked perhaps with this change of political attitude was the tragedy of his recurring mental illness. His first breakdown took place in 1898, only three years after his professorial appointment. It was six years after this that he found hope in the United States. Rest and relaxation, however, failed to get him permanently well again; the breakdowns recurred. Also, his humanity sometimes moved him to defend those whose opinions he opposed; and this humanity and uprightness made strict adherence to the ideology in which he grew up difficult. The imperialist who lived to praise "individual liberty", the Prussian royalist who ended life as a "constitutional democrat", nevertheless remained consistent in one fundamental attitude; he was always anti-socialist. He agreed that socialism was possible, but only in the distant future. In any case, socialism would merely transfer bureaucratic management to the State.

Weber defined a "class" basically according to the Marxian criterion, namely, in relation to the ownership of property. " 'Property' and 'lack of property' are", he wrote, ". . . the basic categories of all class situations."[2] He went on to distinguish two types of property ownership and non-ownership, of goods and services. In general, of course, goods were offered by property owners and services (chiefly labour-power) by non-owners. However, since offers of goods and services,

[1] Max Weber, *Essays in Sociology*. Introduction by Gerth and Mills, p. 17, and succeeding pages from which other quotations are taken.

[2] Same.

whether by owners or non-owners, all went through the "market", class situation was equivalent to "market situation". The class or market situation determined the individual's supply of goods, living conditions and other *chances in life*. The ownership or non-ownership of property also meant power to *dispose* of goods and services. In this way Weber, like Marx, linked class and power in society.

Like Marx, also, Weber distinguished between class and class-consciousness. From a long-term historical viewpoint Marx argued that classes arose only with the realisation of class interest, i.e. with class-consciousness. Of course, he and Engels recognised that at certain periods and with certain people class-consciousness fell to a low level or even never appeared; but historically proletarian class-consciousness would inevitably grow. Weber, on the other hand, tended to emphasise the *negative* aspect. Repeatedly he stressed that a class need not develop class-consciousness, even at the low level of "workers murmuring against the boss".

Weber looked for an alternative to class and found it in the idea of "status".[1] For whereas an individual's *class* situation need not lead to his becoming class-conscious, he was always conscious of his *status*. Status groups were normally "communities", classes were not. Weber defined status as position in society determined by social estimation of "honour" and, although admitting its links with class, repeatedly set the two in opposition. Thus, class was associated with *production* (and acquisition) of goods, status with *consumption*. A man might own a great deal of capital, which would rank him high from a *class* point of view, but be excluded from the highest social circles, so that his *status* situation was lower than his class situation.[2] With status went style of life and restrictions on social intercourse. Status could, and often did, cut across class differences, especially in societies where the economic system of production and distribution was more rigid. It completely dominated the caste societies like that of India. In general, by emphasising that status gave rise to innumerable privileges, material advantages and "monopolies"—for example, wearing special costumes, carrying arms and holding certain offices—Weber tried to give status greater importance than class.

Stressing this opposition, however, led Weber into some confusion

[1] Same. Also Weber, *Theory of Social and Economic Organisation*, section "Social Stratification and Class Structure".

[2] It was true, however, that his descendants would, by going to the right school etc. ("being educated in the conventions"), be accepted in the higher circles.

when he tried to separate out his classes and status groups. First, he divided classes into "property" classes and "acquisition" classes, the former determined by the ownership or non-ownership of property, the latter by "their opportunity for the exploitation of services on the market".[1] This division enabled him to distinguish, for example, landowners from industrial and financial capitalists. "Property" classes could be positively- or negatively-privileged or, in common English, they could own or not own property. A positively-privileged property-class, according to Weber's own description, enjoyed a producing *and consuming* monopoly in buying the dearest goods and services, selling goods, accumulating property, capital, as well as expensive and socially advantageous education. Such a class, said Weber, lived on income from property. Clearly here class situation led to an over-all status position, though there might be an interval of time before property-ownership led to status and there might even be indi.idual cases where high status was never achieved despite great property-ownership.

Weber's analysis of "negatively-privileged" property classes showed a similar confusion. Such classes included slaves, proletarians, "debtors", "the poor" and the "middle" classes (shopkeepers and professional people). But, can we say that debtors, for example, constitute a separate class? In England during the nineteenth century there were very many debtors and thousands languished in the sort of jails so faithfully described by Dickens. Today, debtors as such have disappeared; instead, a tremendous amount of debt in the form of hire-purchase and rental is spread over a very large proportion of the population. Similarly with the poor who, we are often told, have disappeared, compared with their number between the two world wars. There is, however, still a great deal of poverty, as will be shown later. The point is that to call these people classes is to recognise that such "classes" are historically temporary and vague. Or, to put the matter another way, the spread of indebtedness over the whole population makes more proletarians and middle-class members also debtors. Weber's separation, in other words, has serious limitations when applied outside his own times. It would be better to describe poverty and indebtedness not as *criteria of classes* but as *attributes of groups* and sections of classes. In the language of the logicians, poverty and indebtedness are necessary but not sufficient conditions of class. (Sufficient conditions define something completely, necessary conditions only

[1] *Theory of Social and Economic Organisation.*

partly). It means here that attributes other than poverty and indebtedness are needed to define a class.[1]

We find, again, the separation of "acquisition classes" of doubtful value. As noted before, Weber defined an acquisition-class as "primarily determined by their opportunity for the exploitation of services on the market". A positively-privileged acquisition class manages productive enterprises and exercises influence on the economic policy of political and other organisations. This class typically consists of entrepreneurs,[2] and the monopolised "liberal" professions, i.e. those professions like the law and medicine, in which then as today the practitioners' organisations exercise a "closed shop". On the other hand, negatively-privileged acquisition classes comprise all workers—skilled, semi-skilled and unskilled. Today, Weber's term "acquisition class" bursts apart because of its own contradictions. For, by his definition, workers are negatively privileged, but where they belong to trade unions, especially those which "monopolise" the workers' side of negotiating machinery, they are positively privileged. Even the lowest-paid workers are positively privileged in this sense, because they are to some extent in protected positions through the operation of Wages Councils, the Conditions of Employment Act and other legislation.

Weber's third type of class was "social class". Now the term itself suggests that it was based on a social estimation of "honour", i.e. a Weberian status group. Yet Weber defined it as a "class". "Social classes" seemed to be sections of society whose boundaries were boundaries of social intercourse determined by the class relations of *production*—that is, as Weber saw them. So his "social classes" included the working class, the lower middle-classes (shopkeepers and owners of small handicraft workshops), the intelligentsia without independent property, commercial and other officials (today probably at the "executive" level) and civil servants. Here, therefore, was a real plurality of classes, showing again how Weber looked for factors making for separation of the population. On the other hand, here the working class (manual workers) was seen as a whole, in contrast to the way he split it up into three "acquisition" classes. These contradictions lead students to ask many questions: When and under what conditions is the working class a unity and when split? Does this contradictory

[1] See later discussion on modern sociological investigations.

[2] A term meaning strictly persons who undertake enterprises, now widely used in economics to cover businessmen generally, but not landowners who are simply landowners and nothing more.

position occur simultaneously? Which description is superior? And if none is superior to the others, isn't the result just a useless mish-mash?

Finally, Weber introduced the idea of "strata". A stratum is any group of individuals enjoying a particular type and level of prestige. Of course, prestige usually arises from occupation; for example, a university teacher, whose salary can be less than a successful salesman's, nevertheless enjoys much higher prestige. Weber added that other characteristics enjoyed particular kinds and levels of prestige. These were the very important "hereditary charisma" and political or bureaucratic authority. Charisma was the word Weber employed for what might be called aura, particularly mystical aura surrounding witch-doctors and some political leaders. Charisma is therefore a quality deriving partly from the aura surrounding a certain occupation and partly from personal characteristics of the individual. Political or bureaucratic authority likewise enjoys prestige. If we take the case of, say, members of Parliament, clearly they do not constitute a class, nor are they quite big enough to be a status group (since others enjoy similar ways of life); they can therefore be regarded, in Weber's classification, as a unique stratum of society enjoying prestige due to their position in the hierarchy of political authority. The more well-established the system, the more distinct are the strata. Indeed, the more *feudalistic* the system, the more *entrenched* are the *strata*, in contrast to acquisition classes, which are favoured by the more fluid *market* economy. Strata are largely controlled by conventional rules of conduct, for example, modes of speech and dress.

As regards political parties, Weber claimed that they did not simply reflect class interests, as Marxists naively supposed. Certainly parties were possible only within organised (or, using Weber's term, societalised) communities. But they were partly class and partly status organisations; and sometimes neither, i.e. they cut across class and status divisions; for example, nationalist parties. They might be ephemeral or long-lasting; but the important fact about them, that is to say their aim, is *power*.

What exactly is meant by "power"? A party may be in power, but is the power vested in the whole party—that is to say, has each member an equal share of power? If not, which part of the party? Weber had already shown, or thought he had shown, that parties did not necessarily represent class, or even status, interests. It was left to his follower, Michels, to take the next step of identifying the interests of the party (and of any organisation) with the interests of the ruling caucus, thus eliminating the *class* basis of politics.

As was to be expected, Weber devoted much thought to the question of bureaucracy, for he saw its most authentic example in the Prussian state. His analysis brought out a number of the characteristics of bureaucracy. It was impersonal. It cut across democracy in the sense that, although the party in power might change, the bureaucracy continued, its personnel hardly changing. Once established, bureaucracy was hard to destroy. Yet he admired bureaucracy, because it promoted "rational" and "matter-of-fact" government. It worked, he admitted, in the interests of the bourgeoisie. For, in the modern business state, the ruler could not carry out his decisions through personal friends or servants, as he could do in the past. With the separation of public from private money, the modern bureaucrat had to act "impersonally", there was no patronage but considerable social esteem. The bureaucrat was usually appointed and had to pass examinations and interviews. His salary had to be enough to discourage bribery. Bureaucracy also centralised income and expenditure. "The bureaucratic structure goes hand in hand with the concentration of the material means of management in the hands of the master."[1] This occurred in capitalist enterprises, public organisations, and the armed forces of today. Bureaucracy was based on the *levelling* of economic and social differences; for if modern society were based on the encouragement of all possible differences, the work of the bureaucrat would be limitless and so would the size of the bureaucracy. Hence, it accompanied mass democracy, which saw every individual as simply a voter, or as a citizen with limited and clearly defined rights and privileges. Similarly, Weber argued, democratic mass parties inevitably became bureaucracies, dominated by caucuses, the theme to be fully elaborated by Michels. For democratic rule was not the same as rule by the masses, the "governed". On the contrary, the governed were all levelled: a conclusion which the exponents of the "mass society" were to take up. Hence bureaucracy, although it accompanied mass democracy, was also its enemy; and the masses fought it by insisting upon such procedures as periodic elections and the power of recall. The result, to return to Weber's original claim, was to make bureaucracy an entity in itself. It gave rise to the idea of the State as an impersonal third party standing over and above the contending parties and individuals below. In Weber's complicated phraseology:

[1] Same: "Bureaucracy".

"This conceptual separation presupposes the conceptual separation of the 'state' as an abstract bearer of sovereign prerogatives and the creator of 'legal norms' from all personal 'authorisations' of individuals."[1]

However, Weber added, there were times when bureaucratic rule was insufficient to meet the demands of the situation. When these demands, as in times of revolution or mass disorder, went beyond ordinary and normal routine, bureaucratic government, which went by established rule and precedent, was not enough. What the situation demanded was "charismatic" leadership, the leadership that could sway masses. Such leaders were men and women possessing exceptional physical and mental powers. They went, not by precedent, but by intuition. They made their own rules and remained in power only by justifying them. Such leadership had continually to "prove" itself in deeds, in action. It worked by revelation. So a modern follower of Weber would instance both Lenin and Hitler as charismatic leaders whose differing aims, for the purpose of this analysis, would be regarded as irrelevant.

Even this relatively short account of Weber's sociological ideas makes impressive reading. Of the real existence of his different types of social stratification there can be no doubt. There are classes, status groups and strata in every so-called Western society at least. Even if they overlap, class as defined by property-relationship is not the same as status defined in terms of way of life, education and cultural pattern. The "working class" is not a coherent mass, but splits and unites and splits again and shows wide differences in status and prestige. Class interest is a vague notion, depending on the degree of common action and may in fact be visibly absent. Under fascism status, arising from the person's position in the hierarchy, seems to be the only form of social stratification. Some sort of stratification must exist in the socialist states too, since there are such differing groups as industrial workers, "peasants" on collective or co-operative farms, intellectuals and State and party officials. Also there are different levels in income, and hence different levels of consumption of goods and "ways of life" in all advanced societies, capitalist or socialist. The modern state is typically bureaucratic and the bureaucracy a distinct stratum of society, enjoying a distinct social esteem. Finally, parties are (societal) organisations, which can represent the interests of classes or status groups but need

[1] Same.

not necessarily represent either. Authority lies in the leadership and leadership in the mass democratic parties tends to lie with a caucus. Normally, the government is a matter of routine and the bureaucracy flourishes; but in times of social upheaval a charismatic leadership takes over. In either case the leadership or government tends to stand apart from and above the mass and its conflicts.

That Weber's observations of the various divisions of society contain, despite all criticisms, a very great deal of truth, no one can possibly deny. Certainly he gave the critics of Marxism a massive foundation for the continuous and persuasive attacks on Marx's simpler two-class theory. Weber hardly lived to see socialism, but his followers have diligently applied his ideas to socialist society, especially the Soviet Union. In most cases (especially in the United States) they formulated the line that socialist or communist countries are "totalitarian" states displaying to a marked extent some of the worst features of capitalist and modern "Western" societies.

STRACHEY

Many politicians and sociologists followed Bernstein and Weber along the road of criticism and rejection of Marxism. During the 'fifties the most influential of these in Britain were the ex-Marxist John Strachey and the present (1969) Minister for Local Government and Planning, Anthony Crosland. Both Strachey's *Contemporary Capitalism* and Crosland's *The Future of Socialism* appeared in 1956, when, after six years of a post-war Labour Government, the Conservatives were back in power. The fact that Britain had had six years of a Labour Government, with a substantial majority in Parliament, is, as will be seen, of the greatest importance in this whole argument.[1]

Strachey's argument was briefly this. The concentration of capital had gone so far in the United Kingdom that the big combines could affect prices so as to keep consumption and hence production steady. (In the old days, *competition* determined whether business prospered or shut down.) Labour had also concentrated and strengthened its powers. With the extensive nationalisation measures after the Second World War the State had become a third power in the land. With all

[1] A year earlier the British sociologist Bottomore published the first edition of his *Classes in Modern Society*. Here the main arguments on class structure in Britain, the United States and the U.S.S.R. were put from the orthodox point of view. Strachey and Crosland expanded these views and added political conclusions. Professor Bottomore has since changed his views radically.

three interested in maintaining stability and with economic theory and statistics to help them, the economy as a whole was much more susceptible to control. Communists believed, following Marx, that the workers were constantly forced down to subsistence level and even below it. On the contrary, wrote Strachey, the subsistence theory was only a tendency, not a law, and had been *overcome* in post-war capitalism operating in a "democratic political environment". Indeed, the standard of living in the United States was now the highest ever reached anywhere. What in fact had happened was "that the wage-earners, by political and trade unionist efforts, sustained over a century, have *forced up* their standards of life in the teeth of the economic tendencies of the system."[1] While it was true that the workers' share of the national product had not altered much over the past hundred years, the Marxian "law of increasing misery", which all contemporary Communists seemed to believe, had been disproved.

It followed that all institutions changed with the democratic climate of opinion. Crown, military and political institutions, "all of them, even when they retain their traditional forms, change their social content as and when they become filled with the impulses of that vast majority of the people" . . .[2] Indeed, he went on, democracy had gone so far that some Tories and extreme right-wingers claimed "democracy" was mainly to blame for the troubles of our time. The parties of the Left, Strachey declared, needed to give up their traditional suspicions and support the present trend, or faith in democracy might vanish. He concluded with a new definition of socialism as ". . . present-day techniques plus the standard of life that can be founded upon them plus a reasonable distribution of the national product, involving new forms of ownership for income-bearing property plus the democratic diffusion of power throughout the community"[3]

It is quite clear that Strachey had abandoned completely the Marxist theory of capitalism and the need to overthrow the system, which he had advocated so well in his books published in the 1930's, for the theory of gradualism, the orthodox theory of right-wing Social-Democracy. This theory, an extension of course of Fabianism, claimed that capitalism had been drastically modified and that the forces operating this modification were in effect capable, if they continued to act, of bringing the type of socialism which he defined—a type *which did not require the abolition of the private ownership of the means of production.* Here he went beyond the Fabians to Bernsteinian revisionism. Even

[1] Strachey, p. 109. [2] Same, p. 177. [3] Same, p. 292.

though capitalism in its last stage was hostile to it, democracy would go furthest, though it might take longest. Strachey considered that events in the United States showed the same trend as those in Britain. As has already been mentioned, Strachey wrote all this after the defeat of the Attlee Labour Government, in which he had become War Minister. This in no way diminished his faith in right-wing Labour theory and practice. What his conversion meant—as Rosa Luxemburg explained in regard to the Bernstein revisionists—was that Strachey had come to terms with post-war British society.

CROSLAND

Crosland's approach[1] was wider-ranging and altogether more formidable. It covered almost every aspect of the British economic, social and political system and is probably still the most thorough attempt to justify right-wing Labour theory and practice.

Crosland, like Strachey and others, began his attack on Marxism with the claim that capitalism had changed beyond recognition. "Marx", he wrote, "has little or nothing to offer the contemporary socialist, either in respect of practical policy, or of the correct analysis of our society, or even of the right conceptual tools or framework."[2] Like Bernstein and Strachey, Crosland singled out particularly the theory of "ever-increasing misery" of the working-class and Marx's predicted collapse of capitalism. But Crosland was not content merely to make general statements; he brought forward some formidable statistics to support his case. Compared with 1870, British national income in 1938 was three and a half times as high and *real* wages two and a half times as high. Furthermore, while up to 1939 the share of wages in the national income was fairly static, since World War II the share had risen. Since 1945 capitalism had been in a condition of full employment, stability and growth. Where, then, was the impoverishment of the proletariat and the collapse of capitalism?

The second Marxist assumption, wrote Crosland, was that society was controlled by a capitalist ruling class. Certainly, before the last war the capitalist class did have economic power and, backed by right-wing governments, used it ruthlessly, for example, when it closed the shipyards and put almost every Jarrow worker on the dole. "Today the capitalist business class has lost this commanding position."[3] Power had passed now mostly to public authorities and "... govern-

[1] *The Future of Socialism*, also *The Conservative Enemy* (1962).
[2] *The Future of Socialism*, p. 20. [3] Same, p. 26.

ments now exercise this pervasive economic power . . . from motives other than a desire to prop up private business".[1] Nationalisation had shifted some economic power from capitalists to the "largely autonomous class of public industrial managers".[2] There had been a decisive movement of power in industry from management to labour since World War II, due to full employment. Unions were winning wage increases all the way, with even the Conservative Government (of that time) not resisting the claims. A "managerial revolution" had taken place in industry and the "maximum-profit-at-all-costs" motive had declined in importance. Private industry was very sensitive to public opinion and was becoming "humanised". Apart from steel and sugar, there had been practically no resistance to nationalisation. In Crossland's view, the bureaucratic power of the State, the Law, Church, Press, the nationalised industries and the trade unions "... are of greater significance than the economic power to control production and distribution . . ."[3] Of course, he concluded, Britain was still a society of social class; but it was at the same time without a ruling class in the Marxist sense.

In his later work, *The Conservative Enemy*, (1962), Crosland implicitly accepted the thesis put forward by the leading liberal American economist, J. K. Galbraith. In a book entitled *American Capitalism*[4] Galbraith set himself the task of reassuring his American (and other) readers that American capitalism was not really as bad as it was made out to be. Competitive capitalism was, he agreed, a myth: despite all efforts to prevent combinations among firms, despite all anti-trust laws, concentration in industry had reached the stage where a handful of giant firms was responsible for the major part of national production. But, at the same time, the buyer of commodities had hit back through consumer co-operatives; and so had the seller of commodities to the giant firms. Above all, the seller of labour-power, the worker, had hit back by combining into *his* giant corporation, the trade union. There was thus, today, a balance between giants: ". . . private economic power is held in check by the countervailing power of those who are subject to it. The first begets the second."[5] Of course, this assumed stability of condition: inflation strengthened the unions' hands, deflation weakened them. With the qualification that anti-monopoly legislation in Britain might need to be strengthened, Crosland accepted the countervailing power theory for Britain.

[1] Same, p. 29. [2] Same, p. 30. [3] Same, p. 40.
[4] *American Capitalism: the concept of countervailing power* (revised edition 1957).
[5] Same, p. 111.

Like other right-wing theorists,[1] Crosland emphasised the change in the condition of the people compared with before World War II. The high degree of "primary poverty" found in the '20s and '30s had now virtually disappeared, although Crosland agreed that this poverty level was drawn very low; that is to say, a lot of people could be poor today even if above the "primary poverty" line. Through taxation there had been a considerable redistribution of income: between 1938 and 1950 wages increased their share of the national income from 37 per cent to 44 per cent, while that of rent, dividends and interest fell from 24 per cent to a mere 15 per cent. These changes, he pointed out, were even greater if we considered incomes *after* taxation: *wages then had gone up from 39 per cent to 47 per cent and rent, dividends and interest down from 34 per cent to 25 per cent.*[2] True, said Crosland, this income had not gone from the rich directly to the poor, since (a) the working-class paid more in taxation than was paid out in social service benefits and (b) taxes from the rich were used to pay for "unallocable" benefits i.e. Defence, interest on the National Debt and a much bigger Civil Service. Nevertheless, whereas in 1938 the top one-sixth of tax-payers had average real income three and a half times that of the other five-sixths together, by 1948 this figure was down to only twice that of the rest, showing a marked reduction in inequality. It was true, he added, that since the return of a Conservative Government the rich had been regaining lost ground, but "When every allowance is made, the essential fact remains—that the rich are distinctly less rich, and the poor are much less poor."[3] This is like the story of the robber who decides to take only half his victim's money, then claims to be his benefactor. But more of that later on.

So Crosland came to the big question: was this system still capitalism? If capitalism were defined as the system described by Marx in the 19th century, namely, one of *laisser-faire*, in which industrial capital was mostly privately-owned, with great inequalities of wealth, dominated by an aggressively individualistic ideology and with intense class antagonisms—then clearly, he remarked, we were not living under capitalism. Furthermore, the system had altered markedly in other respects, for example in family relationships, sexual mores and population trends. In perhaps only one important respect had the system not changed and that was in respect of the ownership of the means of

[1] And not only right-wing, for example, the late G. D. H. Cole.

[2] These figures were taken from the official White Papers on National Income.

[3] Same, p. 53.

production. However, this, in Crosland's opinion, was irrelevant. For what, he enquired, *was* important? Marx showed that the real cause of proletarian misery and exploitation was their *alienation* (separation) from direct ownership of the means of production; and this could take place as much under a collectivist as under a capitalist system, for no worker in Russia actually personally owned the machinery he operated. Alienation, wrote Crosland, was a consequence not of the system, but simply of industrialism. It would, he wrote, be "more significant" to define societies in terms of (*a*) equality—that is to say, how well distributed were incomes, wealth and so forth or (*b*) (social) class relationships—that is to say, whether or not class barriers were difficult to surmount and the gaps between classes were very wide, or (*c*) their political systems, i.e. whether they were democracies or dictatorships. These distinctions made sense in the world today. But to talk of the Western countries as "capitalist" made little sense. His answer to the question "Is Britain still capitalist?" was therefore firmly, "No".

ELITISM AND THE MASS SOCIETY

This multiple anti-Marxist movement in bourgeois thought received additional help from the exponents of élitist and mass society theories.

The theory of elitism is chiefly associated with the Italian economist Pareto, but clearly follows Weber's description of the modern bureaucratic state.[1] Pareto, who wrote mostly in the earlier part of the twentieth century, argued that in existing society people could be put on a scale of achievement. For example, the top lawyer got top marks, the inmate of a poor-house zero. Those with top marks constituted an élite, an "aristocracy"[2] There was a governing and a non-governing élite. The rest of the population, the governed, were simply the non-élite. Pareto claimed that this division corresponded closely to social stratifications based on other criteria. If individuals were arranged according to intelligence, musical talent, moral character (!) or wealth, the statistical distributions would be similar, that is to say, the average would bulk heavily in the middle, while lower and upper ends would be thinly populated.[3] Even more, he contended that if individuals were arranged according to their degree of political and social power or

[1] See the excellent exposition by T. B. Bottomore *Elites and Society* (1964). I am indebted to this little book for much of this section.

[2] Pareto—*The Mind and Society* III, sections 2026–34. Valuable selections from Pareto's works are given in S. E. Finer's *Pareto's Sociological Writings.*

[3] Graphically represented as the Normal Curve.

influence, the distribution would correspond to the distribution of wealth. "The so-called upper classes are the richest. These classes represent an élite, an 'aristocracy'. . ."[1]

Pareto clearly regarded the most important division as that between the governing élite and the non-élite, the governors and the governed. Not a remarkable discovery, perhaps, since many, from Plato onwards, had argued as much long before. Pareto's specific contribution lay in his asserting that this pattern occurred in *all* societies, past, present *and* future. He argued that his position had nothing to do with morality—but repeatedly denounced "humanitarianism" and described socialism as a particular case of "spoliation" or robbery. There had always been a minority who had power and ruled and a majority who were ruled and had no power; and this would always be so. No wonder Italian fascism claimed him as its spiritual godfather.

Another Italian, Mosca, whose work first appeared earlier than Pareto's, put forward a much modified theory of élitism. Certainly a minority élite always ruled, and indeed, tended to develop always into a hereditary aristocracy which, contrary to Pareto, was not necessarily intellectually superior. But the system of representative government of the modern era provided a way for different social groups and forces to participate in the political system and hence to balance the influence of other groups and of the bureaucracy in particular. The result, according to Mosca, was that the élite came, as it were, to represent the interests of all the various groups in society. Furthermore, today the élite was heavily dependent, on the new middle-class of civil servants, managers and white-collar workers, scientists and engineers, and intellectuals generally. In this way Mosca rescued "Western democracy", which Pareto openly regarded as a necessary sham.

The argument between élite-theorists certainly reflected the differing views about how to run the capitalist system. In Pareto's version every ruling class obtained power by force and held it by force. When it started to manoeuvre, to show weakness, it was on its way out. He called this a change from "lions" to "foxes". Eventually a new set of young lions overthrows the old foxes and the whole cycle starts all over again. But Mosca, rushing to capitalism's defence, argued that "representative democracy" offered an open, peaceful path from non-élite to élite and that provided this openness was maintained, "democracy" could go on indefinitely. However, capitalist theory is one thing, practice another. In 1895, while editor of the journal of the Italian

[1] "Les Systemes Socialistes" quoted in Bottomore p. 8 (Penguin edition).

Chamber of Deputies, he wrote "... if the present crisis that is threatening our political systems and the social structure itself is to be surmounted, the ruling class . . . must become aware that it is a ruling class, and so gain a clear conception of its rights and its duties."[1]

Of course, "democratic" élitist theory cannot be so easily or lightly dismissed. The bourgeoisie is no tightly-knit and unified family group, as was the case with certain feudal ruling families; it does not combine in the same persons military, political and economic powers and there is continual internal competition and even conflict between its different sub-groups and individuals. It is, at least in theory, more open to recruitment from the lower orders, the non-élite. Open class warfare has been much reduced and governments take more heed, are more representative, of the views of all classes. In these and other respects already referred to, Mosca's model *seems* nearer to the real situation in the West than does Marxism with its predictions of (*a*) growing concentration of economic and political power in the hands of a smaller, extremely powerful ruling-class and (*b*) mounting class warfare.

But "democratic" élitist theory succeeds only at the cost of raising another query; that is, if the power of the bourgeoisie is so reduced, who are the government? Some élitists try to avoid the question of class interests by replying—those who have power. But obviously this answer is circular; it tells us nothing more than that those in power have power; and it certainly does not explain how governments come to or lose power. In one of the most important sociological books of post-war years,[2] the late C. Wright Mills, a leading exponent of the "power" theory, examined the constitution of the American upper-class but, after presenting a mass of detail, ended on an uncertain note. What he called the "power élite" did not, he thought, always constitute a single, tightly-knit group, but was made up of several groups, the economic, the political and the military, co-existing in a somewhat uneasy alliance. "... this instituted élite is frequently in some tension: it comes together only on certain coinciding points and only on certain occasions of 'crisis'."[3] Hence he did not regard the American power élite as a ruling class. "The simple Marxian view makes the big economic man the *real* holder of power; the simple liberal view makes the

[1] Mosca: *The Ruling Class* (trans. H. D. Kahn, edited & revised by A. Livingston 1939), p. 493.

[2] *The Power Elite* (1956).

[3] *The Power Elite*, p. 276.

big political man the chief of the power system; and there are some who would view the warlords as virtual dictators. Each of these is an oversimplified view. It is to avoid them that we use the term 'power élite' rather than, for example, 'ruling class'."[1] It will be observed that Wright Mills' understanding of the Marxist view was not strictly correct. But we shall return to this point later.

On the question of the rise and fall of élites, the academics had different answers. Pareto evolved a complicated theory which, briefly, resolved itself into a matter of group psychology: the "quality" of the élite declined and that of aspiring elements in the non-elite rose.[2] Although a theory of this type is mystical and leaves unanswered the question, why an élite becomes decadent at a particular historical period, at least it comes very near to Lenin's observation that in a revolutionary situation the ruling class is no longer able to govern. No ruling class or élite can rule for ever. Likewise Mosca supposed the rise of new "social forces" among the masses, although he rejected Marxism and, as a conservative, bitterly opposed the notion that socialism was a superior system and could produce more democratic rule. But he was frank about the defects in "respresentative democracy", especially its gross inequalities.

Later élitists concentrated much more on the question of conditions making for revolutionary change. In particular Brinton[3] distinguished the following: economic progress, inefficient governmental machinery, bitter class antagonisms, a politically inept ruling class and desertion of the ruling class by the intellectuals. Compared with Lenin's three pre-requisites for a revolutionary situation they differed through different class emphasis. Lenin's three were: the existence of conditions intolerable to the masses, a ruling class no longer able to govern and a strong revolutionary party. Brinton virtually ignored the necessity for a revolutionary party and overrated the role of the intellectuals. But at least sociologists now began to put the question of revolutionary change on their agendas and thereby admitted, unlike Strachey and, even more, Crosland, that the world had not yet settled down to an endless future of gradualism.

[1] Same, p. 277.

[2] "Revolutions come about through accumulations in the higher strata of society ... of decadent elements no longer possessing the residues suitable for keeping them in power, while meantime in the lower strata of society elements of superior quality are coming to the fore, possessing residues suitable for exercising the functions of government ..." *Mind and Society*, III, sec. 2057).

[3] C. Brinton, *The Anatomy of Revolution* (revised edition 1957).

BURNHAM AND THE "MANAGERIAL REVOLUTION"

An outstanding sociological feature of modern capitalism is the rise into prominence and positions of prestige of what some regard as the new élite of intellectuals, higher civil servants and business managers. "Intellectuals" is a wide term, and sociologists generally include within it writers and artists, scientists and technologists, social theorists and political commentators, whether self-employed or on the pay-roll of private business or public bodies. The other groups are self-explanatory. Since some higher civil servants and business managers fall under the umbrella of "intellectuals", clearly there is some overlap; but this fact is not important at this stage.

The importance of the role of the intellectuals is much debated. Some hold the extreme view that the intellectuals are the driving force of modern progress; and, although others disagree, most writers certainly regard the intellectuals as a considerable power in society today. After all, they say, look at all the leading revolutionaries of the present century (not to mention Marx and Engels in the last). Lenin, Trotsky, Mao and Castro, as well as most anti-colonial leaders, were all intellectuals. But deeper examination shows that the role and importance of intellectuals has varied widely between countries. A study of members of the French Chamber of Deputies from 1871 to 1958 showed that more than half of the six thousand deputies elected during that period were "intellectuals"—writers, teachers, lawyers, etc. In the United States, on the other hand, lawyers are certainly prominent in ruling circles, but intellectuals as a whole are not. Similarly, an examination of Labour Governments in Britain since the war shows that *certain* types of intellectuals become Ministers, but they are either lawyers or economists: artists, scientists and technologists are are on the whole conspicuously absent. Intellectuals are rare birds in Tory Governments, which are dominated by landowners and company directors.

In any case, intellectuals are noted for the diversity of their views. In Britain there are almost as many political theorists on the Right as on the Left. As Bottomore tells us, and as Marxists have long believed, there is a lot of evidence to show that intellectuals are strongly influenced by their class origins. For example, right-wing intellectuals in the Labour Party's leadership since the war—Attlee, Gaitskell, Wilson, Strachey, Crossman, Crosland, Stewart, Jay and Jenkins, to mention only the best-known, all come from the "middle class" and (excepting

Wilson) were educated at "public" schools. In any case, their roles in government are only incidentally intellectual; they act primarily as representatives of concrete political and economic interests. As for intellectuals as a whole, and not merely the few who may be in the government, Bottomore rightly points out that ". . . the very fact that they are increasingly engaged in such circumscribed, expert tasks, makes them less qualified for the position of a ruling élite, because they lack any distinctive group organisation or ideology".[1]

It isn't so easy to dispose of the other two groups, higher civil servants and business managers, or the political and industrial bureaucrats. Commonsense and experience confirm that these people wield enormous power through their positions and their know-how. How great is this power? Are they, separately or together, the real ruling class or the real political élite? Whose interests do they represent?

The most widely-known attempt to answer, yes, was made by James Burnham in his book, *The Managerial Revolution*. Although much less widely quoted today, the title and its meaning when first published caught on; and even if, as it is said, he exaggerated his case, the fact remains that very many people accept the idea that there has been something of a "managerial revolution" in all industrialised countries throughout the world. Critics of Marxism seized on the fact that he had been a Marxist: in fact he was first a Trotskyist, broke with Trotsky over defence of the Soviet Union, moved sharply to the extreme right and supported Goldwater in his presidential campaign.

Burnham's idea was not entirely new: this is said, not as a criticism, but to show his position in the chain of developing sociology. The basic idea was put forward much earlier by Veblen, in his book, *The Engineers and the Price System*. Writing when U.S. industrial capitalism was rapidly expanding, Veblen argued that while capitalism could not last, because it was inefficient, it would not be destroyed by the working class, nor would it be followed by the classless society. The chief opponents of capitalist mismanagement, in his view, were the technological specialists—the engineers—upon whose work the operation of modern industry depended and who were in the best position to take over.

> "They (the 'engineers') are thrown into a position of responsible directors of the industrial system, and by the same move they are in a position to become arbiters of the community's material welfare.

[1] *Elites and Society*, p. 77.

They are becoming class-conscious, and they are no longer driven by a commercial interest, in any such degree as will make them a vested interest in that commercial sense in which the syndicated (combined-H.F.) owners and the federated (i.e. unionised-H.F.) workmen are vested interests."[1]

Burnham adopted this idea, but dropped the word "engineers" in favour of "managers". "I mean by managers . . . those who already for the most part in contemporary society are actually managing, on its technical side, the actual process of production, no matter what the legal and financial form—individual, corporate, governmental—of the process."[2] But when Burnham came to name the various groups of managers, it became clear that his definition was much wider than and, in fact, qualitatively different from Veblen's. Burnham recognised four groups of "managers": those who actually did the managing, financial executives, finance-capitalists and stockholders. But, he added: "So far as the technical process of production goes, there need not be finance-capitalists or stockholders, and the executives of Group 2, stripped of many of their present functions, can be merged in the management of Group 1."[3] This generous recognition of the fact that finance-capitalists and stockholders are unnecessary for the production process had, however, a more far-reaching purpose in Burnham's reasoning. For he continued:

"Not only is this development conceivable: it has already been almost entirely achieved in Russia, is approached more and more nearly in (Nazi) Germany, and has gone a considerable distance in all other nations."[4]

Burnham did not accept the thesis that ownership of the means of production was now divorced from control. (See chapter 4.) Whoever *controlled* the means of production, he argued, i.e. the "managers", in effect *owned* them, in the sense that they (the managers) decided policy and could give themselves preferential treatment out of the firm's profits. Similarly in the political field the "managers", including the top bureaucrats, were the real bosses. The Stalins, Roosevelts and Hitlers could come and go, wrote Burnham, the managerial class stayed on. Totalitarianism, he prophesied, with an argument similar to Mosca's,

[1] Quoted in Bottomore, p. 78.
[2] *The Managerial Revolution* (Penguin edition), p. 81.
[3] Same, p. 87.
[4] Same.

would give way to democracy, because the managers couldn't do without the people.

In Burnham's opinion the major countries of the world were alike in three important ways: they were suppressing or had already suppressed the capitalists; they were curbing or had already curbed the aspirations of the masses towards a classless society; and they were beginning to compete for world supremacy. In his view, Nazi Germany, Soviet Russia and America under the New Deal were states in which these three fundamental features were either going on or were fully complete. Nazi Germany, which was quite clearly competing for world supremacy, had crushed the hopes of the masses for a classless society and was slowly curbing its capitalists. Soviet Russia was also beginning to compete for world supremacy, had crushed its capitalists and was in process of ending the hopes of its people for a classless society. New Deal America was certainly aiming for world supremacy, it had curbed the masses and politically defeated the capitalists. In this reduction of all three powers to a nearer and nearer sameness, Burnham got rid of all argument about the differences between socialism, capitalism and fascism. Every modern state was becoming a "managerial" state.

Of course, critics found it easy to pick holes in Burnham. His use of the term "manager" was unacceptably wide; he practically dismissed the role of political leaders; and the "managers" were *not* a cohesive (tightly-knit) group with consciously common aims. But anti-Marxist critics had little objection to the way the capitalists had vanished, or to Burnham's grouping of the (then) three major world powers, socialist and capitalist, into almost identical types. Burnham's popularity reflected the common view that, "basically", Russia and America, at least, were much the same; they were simply "big powers" trying to dominate the world and the differences between their systems, if any, were less important.[1]

Burnham's thesis derived much from Weber. As we pointed out

[1] A well-known recent American textbook of sociology trots this Burnhamism out, with an important omission: "The great revolutions of modern history—the French, the Russian, the Nazi—have all been alike in certain respects. In each case the revolutionary movement resulted in profound changes in the social structure of the society involved; the kinship system, the economy, religious organisation, the class structure, and of course the political system were all affected. Secondly, these changes were accompanied by much social mobility: many persons previously low in rank rose to great power and prestige, and many others once among the social élite were humbled. Thirdly, these changes did not take place without considerable violence amounting to civil war. Finally, though the process could always be traced to causes in the more remote past . . ., nevertheless the

before, Weber regarded the rise of the bureaucracy in the modern state as inevitable. Bureaucracy had its virtues; it brought order, efficiency and matter-of-factness into administration. But it was very hard to destroy; it could become excessively powerful; it could strangle democracy. Therefore he opposed socialism, because under it everything would be state-owned, the bureaucracy would become all-powerful and individual liberty would be lost.

This, in fact, was the claim made by Djilas, a former Yugoslav Communist theoretician, in his book, *The New Class*, which right-wing sociologists are very fond of quoting. Djilas made out a strong case that the political bureaucracy in a communist state was all-powerful by virtue of the fact that it controlled and therefore in reality owned the means of production, as well as the machinery for enforcing decisions. But he also made the important admission that the political bureaucrats were created by the Communist Party, which could therefore also remove them. What is the position in the "West"? Who creates the bureaucracy and what is its composition? Can it be more easily removed than the Soviet bureaucracy? These are questions we must try to answer later, but at this stage it can certainly be said that, while Weber was right to point out the dangers of bureaucratisation in the modern State, Burnham's attempt to equate the Soviet state system even with that of the United States—let alone Nazi Germany—is an extreme case of anti-science. Anti-science in sociology, politics and popular journalism is widespread. As "managerialist" theory it ignores fundamental differences and concentrates on certain resemblances, real though these may be. Just as the popular Press chatters glibly about "the two world giants"—except that the USA is always the "democracy" and the USSR always a "dictatorship"—so Burnham's theory finds the most important fact to be that both are ruled by bureaucratic elites and the masses have little or no say in how the country is run. But what class interests the elites or "managers" represent is a question Burnham avoided.[1]

revolutionary period at its height was marked by great changes taking place within a short span of time ..." (Johnson—*Sociology*, p. 333).

The omission, of course, is any reference to the United States—for good or evil. Orthodox contemporary American sociology is, perhaps, afraid of mentioning the fact that the United States, too, had a revolution once.

Later on, Professor Johnson remarks that Lenin "... was of a slightly different type from Hitler" (p. 335). Only slightly?

[1] The latest, refined version of the "managerial revolution" thesis comes from that pillar of the liberal American Establishment, Professor J. K. Galbraith. In his *The New Industrial State* (1967) and 1966 B.B.C. Reith Lectures, Professor Galbraith also argued that

A short step leads to the theory of Mass Society, possibly best described as a psychological theory of society. It adopts Pareto's division of society into an élite and a non-élite or mass. Masses are "large numbers of people who are not integrated into any broad social groupings, including classes".[1] Mass societies are those in which there is mass apathy, the people are concerned only with their own narrow, personal interests and mass movements arise. Kornhauser's version of the theory is conservative: he warns the "democracies" (above all the USA) that they are in danger of becoming mass societies. This is because the élites are allowing themselves to be pressurised by the masses and are in turn manipulating the masses too much by means of the mass media. Provided stronger leadership was exercised and more "democratic" participation by the organised masses encouraged, "liberal democracy" should continue to flourish. The class basis of society is swept aside completely in favour of this type of analysis, which, bearing in mind the social conditions underlying, say, the rise of German fascism, has much to say for it. But Kornhauser's solution to the ills of modern "democratic" society has nothing to say about changing its economic character.

Some sociologists on the Left, while taking economics into account, also adopt a form of Mass Society theory. The masses in the capitalist countries, they say, *are* concerned mainly with their own narrow, personal interests, they *have* become apathetic and are being manipulated by the ruling élites.[2] In this form the theory expresses the despair of many left-wing intellectuals at the non-revolutionary attitudes of the working masses of the advanced capitalist countries in the 1950s and early 1960s, when the British Tories were so jubilant about the never-had-it-so-good working classes. It tends to play down the economic contradictions within capitalist society and becomes rather obsessed with the almost mysterious "power" of the ruling class. It, of course, plays down the historic role of the working class, tending to adopt the right-wing view that the workers have become declassed.

socialist and capitalist states are converging towards the same model, dominated by the giant corporations' "technostructure". Adapting Shakespeare, one might write despairingly:

> "Why, man, they do bestride the narrow world
> Like a Colossus; and we petty men
> Walk under their huge legs, and peep about
> To find ourselves dishonourable graves."

[1] W. Kornhauser: *The Politics of Mass Society:* Conclusion.

[2] See, for example, C. Wright Mills' *White Collar* and *The Power Elite*, ch. 13.

FUNCTIONALISM AND TALCOTT PARSONS

At least the preceding theories admitted a division in industrialised societies between a governing class, bureaucracy, or élite and the rest, the mass. The school of American sociology which dominated post-war theory and began to be seriously challenged only in the last few years went further. It analysed society in such a way that Western capitalism appeared to be not merely classless, but without any splits at all. How did the theory of "structural-functionalism", to give it its full title, perform this vanishing trick?

Sociological functionalism was created largely by Talcott Parsons, the grand old man of American bourgeois sociology. In explaining the theories of the classical sociologists, Weber, Durkheim and Pareto, Parsons is extremely good, even if too long; but in developing his own, he writes in a style heavy with his own particular jargon. Yet the essence of his theory is fairly simple and straightforward. It is a type of idealism, owing much to the theories of the anthropologists Malinowski and Radcliffe-Brown, who called themselves functionalists before Parsons; to biology, particularly if interpreted idealistically; and to European bourgeois sociology, in particular the three "founding fathers" already mentioned.[1]

Functionalism's biological inheritance is the idea of the organism as an active unity. Every living thing is, of course, a unity, an organism; that is to say, it is a clearly defined object always in activity, taking in body-building and energy-producing substances, yet, through all its changes, remaining the same recognisable object. All its component parts and activities are essential to it: arms, legs, digestion, nervous activity, all are "functional" to the maintenance and stability of the system. These parts and activities (which together make up the "structure" and "function" of the organism) are not isolated from one another but interdependent. For example, were a hand missing, that part of the human being's central nervous system which receives and transmits messages to it could not perform its proper task and, conversely, if that part of the nervous system were paralysed, it could not activate the hand. Furthermore, messages from brain to hand depend on the efficient working of muscles, bones and blood supply and, indeed, to a great or lesser degree on every other structure and

[1] The "structural-functionalist" view, as we shall try to show later, reflects modern bourgeois society from a bourgeois point of view. Hence it is found in many other fields of intellectual activity. In the form of A. N. Whitehead's philosophy of organism it undoubtedly influenced the thinking of American scientists in many fields.

function of the organism. Finally, each structure of the organism may have more than one function. For example, the hand can wield a hammer, push a trolley or write with a pen. In short, every structure contributes (functions) in one or more ways towards the aims of the whole organism.

Anthropologists found that every act, object or belief served a particular purpose or function for the primitive community. "The functional view of culture", wrote Malinowski, "insists therefore upon the principle that in every civilisation, every custom, material object, idea and belief fulfils some vital function, has some task to accomplish, represents an indispensable part within a working whole."[1] For example, the family, the clan and sexual restrictions (taboos) were designed, according to Malinowski, to control mating, procreation and rearing of the young for the one aim of racial and cultural continuity. "Magic" ritualised the emotions blocked by nature and was functional also in giving the individual a place within the social order. In higher societies, religion laid down spiritual and moral ends. Malinowski distinguished the material from the non-material components of a culture. The former, which he called the "outer framework" of a culture, consisted of the materials which man put between himself and the rigours of nature. Pitting themselves against nature promoted social cohesion among primitive people; which in turn created new restrictions on the individual, for example, obedience to a leader. Both non-material and material culture activities, were however, functionally essential to the whole, the primitive society.

In contrast to Malinowski's "total" approach, Radcliffe-Brown's was positivistic and comparative. That is to say, while Malinowski viewed the culture as the determinant of every act and belief, Radcliffe-Brown starts off comparing the functions of a particular institution, say marriage, in a number of different societies in order to draw out the general function of marriage within all primitive societies. But both he and Malinowski were basically concerned with how the different customs, beliefs or rituals contributed to the stability and maintenance of societies. Indeed Radcliffe-Brown, following the conservative French sociologist, Durkheim, regarded social constraint as necessary: society *demanded* certain behaviour from the individual, who had to carry it out willy-nilly.[2]

[1] Article, "Anthropology", *Encyclopaedia Britannica*, 11th edition.

[2] For a useful discussion of the twin approaches by Malinowski and Radcliffe-Brown to the question of magical rituals, see Homans, *The Human Group*, ch. 12.

Parson's *The Structure of Social Action* appeared in 1937. Generally regarded as his best work, he expounded in it the ideas of Weber, Durkheim and Pareto, with the view to showing how their theories were steps towards an overall theory of societies. The main emphasis was upon the individual or "actor" in his situation, the "action" and the importance of values.

Of particular interest here was Pareto's transfer of the idea of "moving equilibrium" from technical to social science. The idea is very simply illustrated by a kettle of water. If the kettle is heated, we say that heat enters the system (kettle of water) which, on reaching the boiling-point of water, gives off steam. In engineer's language, heat is the input and steam (or steam-pressure) the output. The kettle of water remains a kettle of water, despite the input-output; but it is no longer static; it, or at least the water, is in constant motion. Thus the input of heat and the output of steam transform the previous static equilibrium of unheated kettle of water into the moving equilibrium of boiling kettle of water. Of course, eventually the water boils away, changing the system completely. Such changes, Pareto emphasised, take a long time; and, even then, filling the kettle only starts the same cycle all over again. Readers of Marxist philosophy will know about Engels' use of the change of water into steam as a simple illustration of dialectics. In Pareto's view the fundamental characteristic of nature and of society was not dialectical *change*, but systems of forces in *moving equilibrium*. These forces could be external or internal to the system. The more important internal forces of society could be "logical" or "non-logical". Logical forces or types of action were guided by reason, non-logical by what Pareto called "sentiment". Manifestations of sentiments he called "residues", because they were left over from *logical* actions. These non-logical "sentiments" and their "residues" were, Pareto argued, the most powerful forces moving men to action. These sentiments and residues were constants. Societies therefore, changed little in essentials. They were like kettles of boiling water, forever on the move through powerful forces, but always essentially of the same pattern.

How was the pattern maintained? "The real state of the system is determined by its conditions, which are of such a nature that if some modification in its form is introduced artificially, a reaction will take place tending to restore the changing form to its original state."[1] A person in equilibrium touched by a hot object will jump away to

[1] Martindale, *Nature and Types of Sociological Theory*, p. 466.

restore his equilibrium. The information to his nervous system causes a message to be "fed back" to his muscular system making him jump. This concept of "feed-back", as readers know, underlies the science of cybernetics and the construction of automatic control systems. The thermostat on a modern electric heater, switching it off as soon as the room reaches a certain temperature, "feeds back" this temperature to the switching mechanism. "Feed-back" is rapidly becoming part of ordinary, everyday English. Fundamentally, it is a mechanism for system self-regulation.

In 1945 Parsons emerged with the theory of "structural-functionalism".[1] His take-off point was still the individual units and their structural inter-relations. But from this point of view, he admitted, societies were static. However, it created the setting for solving the dynamical problems of societies. Of course, since every human society had a host of units and their inter-relations could be very numerous indeed, dynamical analysis could be incredibly complex. To provide the necessary criteria for determining the relative importance of these dynamical factors was, therefore, crucial to his analysis. Here the link was the all-important concept of *function*. The basic question regarding the factors was whether they contributed positively or negatively, that is, whether they were "functional" or "dysfunctional", to the stability of the system. Hence, he said frankly, his theory was "inherently teleological". "Function" was the regulator, the thermostat.

In *The Social System*, published in 1952, the theory was most fully expounded. As before, he started his analysis with his structural unit, the actor (one who "acts") and his action. A social system was composed of a plurality of actors in interaction, orientated towards that aspect of the social system which was the individual actor's "frame of reference" and motivated in terms of a tendency to the "optimisation of gratification" or to the "avoidance of deprivation". Rephrased in simpler language this means roughly that the actor is affected by that aspect of the social system which corresponds most to his desires. The theory, Parsons emphasised, was not concerned with the "internal structure" of the units (the actors): this was the province of psychology. Structural-functionalism was concerned only with the actor's external relations. Of course, internal structure or personality played a part in any social situation. So did other "systems", particularly the physical (land, climate, machines) and the cultural. But personality, physical and cultural systems were less important than the actors as units and

[1] *Essays in Sociological Theory*, esp. ch. 11 (1945).

their interactions, constituting the social system. Action, therefore, was the foundations of all social situations;[1] but actions, determined by the guiding lights of "optimisation of gratification" or "avoidance of deprivation", were selected from among alternatives. These selected actions composed the functions (or dysfunctions) of the system. The actor's relation to his situation, including other actors, "is defined and mediated in terms of a system of culturally structured and shared symbols".[2]

The individual is considered from two angles. As part of the social structure he has a certain "status" in society: and the part he plays is his "role". The two together constitute his "function" in the social system.[3] The tremendous complexity of even the simpler human societies arises from the fact that every individual actor occupies one or more statuses (one in the family, say, another in the tribe), while he may perform several roles at different times. But, as with the functionalist anthropologists, Parsons' view is that the individual's various status-roles are *determined by the system*. Thus the actors' motivations, as indicated in the last paragraph, are determined by the rewards and punishments available to the system. The collective "cuts across the individual actor as a composite unit". The actor, a status-role, becomes subordinate to the system. Most important in this equilibrium-system is the power of force of the system's norms and values, the guides to behaviour.

So Parsons took off, as before, from the bourgeois point of view of the individual in society. Individuals interact, and in doing so, create the "social system", but basically from the same motives which all bourgeois social philosophers have seen as the fundamental human

[1] *Tempter:*
You know and do not know, what it is to act or suffer
You know and do not know, that action is suffering,
And suffering action. Neither does the agent suffer
Nor the patient act. But both are fixed
In an eternal action, an eternal patience
To which all must consent that it may be willed
And which all must suffer that they may will it,
That the pattern may subsist, that the wheel may turn and still
Be forever still.
T.S. Eliot: *Murder in the Cathedral*

[2] *The Social System*, pp. 5–6.

[3] In socio-legal terms, an individual's role refers to his *obligations* and his status to his *rights* within the social system. "Thus, every social position is a status-role ... The role structure of a group is the same thing as its status-structure, because what is role from the point of view of one member is status from the point of view of the others" (Johnson—*Sociology* p. 16).

driving-force, self-interest. The "social system", modified by physical, personal and cultural "sub systems", determines all within it. Even more, every action contributes to the maintenance (equilibrium) of the "social system". Not economic (class) interests, but the "values" of the "system" especially its "moral" values, are the system's driving force.

Parsons' major contribution to sociological analysis was in detailing the ways in which the "individual gratifications" were harnessed to or repressed by the "value-patterns" available to system and actor for the end purpose of maintaining the stability of the system. For example, the system or the actor might be

(1) "self-orientated" or "collectivity-orientated"; that is to say, system or actor could have a value-pattern in which self-interest was put first (self-orientation) or the common good first (collectivity-orientation);

(2) "achievement" or "ascription"-based; that is to say, status-roles might be based on what the individual did (his performance) or on the position he was born to or placed in. Feudalism was an ascriptive system, capitalism an achievement system.

In all, there were five such "pattern variables", the permutations and combinations of which, Parsons claimed, determined *exhaustively* all possible status-roles and hence *all possible types* of societies.

In two later works written in collaboration with a couple of disciples,[1] Parsons applied his "pattern variables" not only to societies but to any system or sub-system right down to the individual firm and even departments of a firm. Certainly any detailed analysis of this kind could be useful within any bounded system or sub-system, covering as it did a very wide range of possible alternatives. But why did so many critics feel uneasy about it? The answer is simple.

Such a theory is a theory of absolute determinism. What do we mean by absolute determinism? We mean that it follows the philosophy expressed by the great French mathematician and astronomer of the eighteenth century, Laplace, who declared that if the dispositions and velocities of all the particles were known, the whole future of the universe could be predicted. It is mechanical science turned into universal philosophy. But, although mechanical science and its outlook, mechanism, can be brilliantly successful, as a universal philosophy it

[1] Parsons and Bales, *Working Papers in the Theory of Action*; and Parsons and Smelser *Economy and Society*.

ignores the emergence of novelty, the fact that, as time unrolls, qualitative as well as quantitative changes occur. Mechanism regards all change as quantitative, as merely additions (including permutations and combinations) of the same original units and, therefore, as strictly predictable in detail according to mechanical (i.e. quantitative) laws. Such a philosophy, as Christopher Caudwell so brilliantly showed,[1] is characteristic of the bourgeoisie, who believe that nature and society are theirs to control according to immutable laws, laws discovered by bourgeois scientists and philosophers.

Critics saw this defect in the form of the Parsonian emphasis on system-*maintenance* and the difficulty of dealing with social *change*. Parsons realised well enough the difference between quantitative and qualitative change. The first he called change *within* the social system, which left the system essentially unchanged (i.e. Pareto's "moving equilibrium"), the second change *of* the social system, meaning the ending of the old and creation of a new system (Pareto's change of cycle). But Parsons regarded a system as made up of units and their external relations only. Change, therefore, could only come externally, that is to say, from outside the units. For he had, additionally, written that the "internal structure" of the units was not functionalism's concern. Hence Parsons confessed that change internal to any system was difficult for his theory.

> "... the crucial characteristic of structural-functional theory is its use of the concept system without a complete knowledge of the laws which determine processes within the system".[2]

And later:

> "... a general theory of the processes of change of the social system is not possible in the present state of knowledge".[3]

Thus Parsons confessed that his theory could not explain the type of change which led to the collapse of the old and creation of a new system. Even change *within* a system could only be partially dealt with. How? Since Parsons regarded system-maintenance as his norm, it followed that any deviation must be pathological; the individual or group "guilty" of deviation must be either sick or criminal and be treated accordingly. Conformity to ruling values, "institutionalisation" and

[1] C. Caudwell, *The Crisis in Physics.* [2] *The Social System*, p. 483.
[3] Same, p. 486.

"internalisation" of value-patterns with a view to controlling deviance, were always, in his view, the chief problems of sociology.[1]

For him, as for other bourgeois theorists, the Marxist theory of social change was too simple and dogmatic. That when the forces of production conflicted with the relations of production social change took place, Parsons and others have found unacceptable; or, at least, as only one reason for change of the system and that, generally, not the most important. For accepting that it *was* the most fundamental reason would also imply that capitalism in any form must at some time collapse. Rather, Parsons argued, many factors caused social change, of which no one was dominant. So, although he gave many pages to an acute analysis of the effects of scientific and technological development on society, he avoided the obvious conclusion. But not when it came to applying his theory to the U.S.S.R.; for here he saw strong forces against stabilisation of the system. Especially he showed a certain wishful-thinking that the problem of Stalin's succession might destroy the Soviet Union.[2]

Parsons' whole emphasis lay on the overwhelming importance for any system of the "value patterns", especially of moral values. But in this he was guilty of just that sort of unacceptable "unicausality" of which he accused Marxism, that is, of ascribing overall importance in the creation and maintenance of systems to one particular factor. His emphasis on moral values is understandable. The individualism of capitalism, which has raised the United States to its supreme position in the Western world, is also in danger of destroying it. Also the world as a whole seems to be rejecting U.S. leadership and guidance more and more. As once he regarded the main danger to be fascism, so in the 1950's he believed it to be communism. As Parsons does not regard the basic cause of this trend to be fundamentally economic, he naturally believes that the "solution" must be for all those believing in the "free" world to hold on to (bourgeois) moral values.

Now it is a characteristic of idealism that it does away with the individual, or subordinates him to the whole. Every individual or thing becomes a factor (function, status-role or what you will) for the whole; the system becomes more, and more important, than all the separate units. Anti-Marxist writers have been extremely fond of accusing Marxists of placing the socialist system above the liberty of

[1] Same, p. 552. He puts his theory more briefly in "Some considerations on the theory of social change", *Rural Sociology*, 1961.

[2] Same, p. 532.

the individual—one aspect of the old ends-versus-means argument. Although Marxists are not historically guiltless in this respect, the criticism can surely be directed more against Parsons and the American bourgeoisie. One critic[1] pointed out that in 1935 Parsons had emphasised that man was an "active, creative, evaluating creature". But this was in the 'thirties, in the New Deal era. By 1951 Parsons had changed his tune. The individual will was still allowed, but "obscured and reduced to a hypothetical role". Optimum gratification had become more important; in other words, man, from being creative, had become merely a creature with appetites. But since appetite, like love, is blind, some higher end has to be imposed on man. Hence Parsons' frank admission that his theory was teleological; the system's ends were more important than the individual's gratifications. But this rests upon a wholly false assumption that man is only motivated by his appetites and that ends have to be imposed on him. By reducing man to a thing of appetite only, Parsons took the first step towards reducing man to just a "thing". A thing is a physical concept. Physics reduces things to geometrical concepts (points, lines, planes, solids) in space and time; or, in modern relativity physics, to similar concepts in space-time. Hence, in the final phase,[2] the unit of action (implicitly, a four-dimensional concept) ceases to be the living actor. Although he does not disappear altogether, his place for the purpose of *observing* a "system of action" is taken by the behavioural *role* and any activity of this role is considered as a change of *location* within a *social space*.

Caudwell's brilliant analysis of pre-war bourgeois thought applies equally to functionalism.[3] The bourgeois, Caudwell argued, sees the world from a bourgeois point of view. To him the capitalist system is eternal: no other is possible or, if possible, desirable. The bourgeois, however (like the worker), is increasingly alienated from the mode of production. To him it appears as a perpetual machine, in which all units including labour move according to their pre-determined "function". But the machine does not now appear to function smoothly; it exhibits distortions and dislocations (booms and slumps) and even (temporarily, in their eyes) breaks down altogether and is (temporarily) abandoned. The functioning of the machine (system) becomes a mystery. Now a machine is an object without life of its own. The bourgeois therefore abstracts the qualities which properly

[1] Scott, article in *American Sociological Review*, October 1963.
[2] Parsons and Shils, *Towards a General Theory of Action*.
[3] Especially *The Crisis in Physics* (1938).

belong to the world and man and are the result of the subject-object relation, and transfers these qualities to the subject, because for him the object is lifeless. Such qualities (aesthetic, philosophical, the qualities of mind) belong therefore only to the bourgeoisie, as they see themselves. Hence the bourgeois is convinced *his* thoughts, *his* ideas, are necessarily the only possible ones, and he tries to impose them upon the world. The values and norms of the bourgeois become the dominant factor within the system.

Now, since the bourgeois feels his world-view to be the only true one, the system must necessarily continue and factors other than bourgeois values must be less important. Despite some change, the system remains the same; there is movement, but the result is, or should always be, "moving equilibrium", which excludes change of system.[1] Anything which does not, as it should, function positively towards system maintenance is therefore morally wrong, or *dys*functional to the system. Lastly, since quality is abstracted from the system, the units (actors), who after all should be real people, find themselves in functionalism robbed of their humanity. In Parsons' own words, "personality" and "culture" are factors, but factors outside the system, foreign to it. The "actors" therefore appear lifeless puppets, motivated mainly by bourgeois values.

It follows that revolutionary change is due to vaguely sinister machinations of a "deviant sub-cultural group or movement" with an "ideology" in a social situation which (and no society can avoid this) exhibits "strains". Strains there may be, but never splits. Classes are bound to exist, for in any society there are always "winners" and "losers". Hence the need for "discipline" and "authority".[2] Revolutionary change, Parsons implies, is therefore evil. The proper answer is to relieve the strains, so that the featureless puppets can continue their dance to the tune of—what?

The answer was given by Merton, one of many American sociologists who observed defects in this harmonious but faceless theory. The great "value" in the U.S.A. today was, Merton declared with regret, simply —money; and an enormous propaganda machine was employed to put this across.[3] It deflected criticism of the social structure on to oneself, causing the lower strata to identify themselves with the top—

[1] "Change is never just 'alteration of pattern' but alteration by the overcoming of resistance" (*The Social System*, p. 491).

[2] Parsons: "Social Classes and Class Conflict" (in *Essays*).

[3] R. K. Merton: *Social Theory and Social Science*, ch. 4.

"everybody can get there"; and it provided very useful pressures towards conformity. If you didn't conform you wouldn't get there.

Thus the Parsonian functionalist "social system" is a capitalist myth. It is a dance of lifeless ghosts ("behavioural roles") in an abstract "social space". It is maintained by the "moral values" of the "free world". Any deviance within this perfect system, especially any sign of revolution, is pathological and must be sternly corrected by "discipline" and "authority". In this ideal, classes are natural and inevitable; but all are equal because they are equally "functional" and differences between them are of little importance. Stockbrokers and company directors are functional to "Western" society; therefore they are necessary for its maintenance as a going concern. A revolutionary is "dysfunctional"; therefore he and his influence must be curbed. In the ideal (i.e. "Western") society, there are no internal contradictions, no seeds of self-destruction; only "strains" to be relieved. And since "strains" are not qualitative but quantitative (changes within, not changes of, the system), the system is, in Caudwell's phrase, predetermined. And some American functionalists work out mathematical techniques for long-term forecasting of any "social system". Once the factors can be quantified the system's future can be completely predicted. The ghost of Laplace lives on in the U.S.A.

CONFLICT THEORY

There are other important criticisms of structural-functionalism. First, the idealistic emphasis of norms and values, real and important though they are, ignores *conflicting interests* in any society. For example, it is impossible to understand contemporary U.S. society without reference to business corporations, trade unions, capital, power, race and so on. These are the material substratum with which norms and values interact.[1] Functionalism is also too abstract, ignores history and cannot draw the question of personality into its scheme. Individuals are not dehumanised "actors" but persons. Marxists are often attacked (and implicitly by Parsons also) for subordinating people to system; but it was Marx who said that not man but *men* made history.[2]

Functionalism is not only teleological; it is also tautological, it says nothing new. For if some role or other factor is not functional, then,

[1] D. Lockwood, British Journal of Sociology, June 1966.
[2] C. Wright Mills, *The Sociological Imagination* (1959), ch. 2.

in functionalist theory, it is *dys*functional. All Parsons' dichotomies are similarly tautological: they merely say, in good old Aristotelian fashion, that if something isn't A it is not-A: if society isn't individualistically orientated it is collectivistically orientated; if it isn't good then it's bad.[1] To say that certain factors are necessary for a given system is to say very little; and unless the factors are put into some order of importance the theory can't be used for prediction. The theory can only say what is or is not functional for the system only after the event; it sets the question as to why the system is maintained, but does not answer it, or provide the means to answer it.[2] The most it says on this particular problem is that there is a feed-back from the system to the elements, keeping the elements, so to speak, in order. Existence of this feedback was, of course, recognised by anthropologists like Malinowski and by Marx, long before Parsons. But for Parsons the feedback is symmetrical, that is to say, the system does not discriminate between elements; for example, it ignores the fact that U.S. and other capitalist societies react more heavily upon the working class than upon the capitalists. It assumes that every system integrates all elements harmoniously (although there might be "strains"), ignoring the possibility that some would try to opt out, to be "autonomous". Such differences create tension and conflict, which would therefore be natural to the system. Indeed, far from attempts at autonomy being deviational or dysfunctional they might, if the society were destroyed by war or revolution, form the basis for recovery.[3] These comments point, in sum, to the abstractness and to the absence, or rejection, of conflict within society. Parsons' schema is, of course, an idealisation of "Western" capitalist society. It is an apology for the *status quo*.

Inevitably it led to a reaction. For just then, during the late nineteen-fifties, national and international problems were getting worse, the difficulties of capitalism were becoming aggravated; and the idea spread that conflict could not only not be pushed under the carpet but was a fact of life. In a book which became a bible or at least a manifesto of the anti-Parsonians, the German sociologist, Dahrendorf, declared that conflict was inherent in every social system.[4] If the conflict theorists were right, then not only Parsons but practically every writer we have been considering must be wrong, except Marx and the

[1] K. Davis, American Sociological Review, December, 1959.

[2] Hempel, article in *Symposium on Sociological Theory* (ed. L. Gross).

[3] A. Gouldner, article in *Symposium on Sociological Theory*.

[4] R. Dahrendorf: *Class and Class Conflict in Industrial Society*.

Marxists. If Dahrendorf was right, then sociology had gone full circle and returned to revolutionary socialism.

In an earlier paper[1] Dahrendorf declared that the Parsonian equilibrium or consensus[2] model was useful in certain respects, but that it was not the only possible one: the conflict model was at least as useful. Structural-functionalism, he wrote, was "complacently conservative"; it claimed that moral values were the system's most important, even determining, factor, yet never morally questioned any system, particularly the present "Western". In this criticism, Dahrendorf repeated Gouldner's charge that to have a "value-free" sociology, a sociology which refused to pass moral judgements, good or bad, on the society which it analysed, was a myth. Such a "value-free" theory was only a cover for justifying, or giving its blessing to, the society.[3]

Yet this beginning by Dahrendorf proved to be a mask. In fact, Dahrendorf opened his book with a lengthy attack on Marx's view of class and class conflict. Nothing in it was very new and much of it old stuff such as could be found in Bernstein and later right-wing social-democratic theorists. Like them, he accepted unquestioningly the opinion that the two main classes were becoming less rather than more polarised; the working class less homogeneous (divided more within itself), as was the ruling class (into capitalists, bureaucrats etc.); there was far greater mobility (movement) between classes; above all, less rather than greater extremes of wealth. In short, going even beyond Crosland, Dahrendorf thought that in post-war society, one could hardly talk of "classes" at all. As for the idea of social revolution, this was sheer utopianism, the very thing the young Marx and Engels had so vigorously attacked.

Where then, the reader might ask, was the conflict? For Dahrendorf made the point that to imagine society without conflict was equally utopian, but on the conservative side. His answer was that, though without *classes* in the Marxist sense, every society was split into various *interest groups:* shareholders, bureaucrats, company directors, wage earners, racial groups, religious groups, national groups and, most important of all, "authority" groups. It was through the clash of these

[1] American Journal of Sociology, September, 1958.

[2] "Consensus" because all members of the society consent to its norms and values. There is an obvious similarity to the idea of the General Will put forward by Rousseau.

[3] In a brilliant essay on the myth, the distinguished American sociologist, Alvin Gouldner, described it as "... the caste mark of the decorous ... the gentleman's promise that boats will not be rocked". (A. Gouldner: "Anti-Minotaur, the myth of a value-free sociology", in Horowitz (ed.): *The New Sociology.*)

different "conflict groups", of which class struggles were only a special case, that societies changed. And ". . . it is the decisive characteristic of the development of industrial societies since Marx that profound structure changes have occurred *without sudden, widely visible upheavals*".[1] Wars, slumps, revolutions and all seemed to disappear from Dahrendorf's line of vision as surely as from the consensus theorists'.

Conflict, says Dahrendorf, is over authority. Continuing his Weberian-type analysis he declares, using the functionalist distinction between latent and manifest functions, that a class is only a *latent* interest group, since, as Marx himself pointed out, it may not be aware of its class interests and, in fact, only becomes a class when it becomes aware of those interests. On the other hand, interest groups are those with *manifest* interests, having clearly defined structures, organisations and programmes or goals: *they*, says Dahrendorf, are the real agents of conflict and change. Political parties are particularly important cases of interest groups. Thus safely defining classes as only one kind of conflict grouping and then not always conscious of their own interests, Dahrendorf now feels able to reject Parsons' distinction between change *of* and change *within* a society. All conflict is now welcome, because in Dahrendorf's imagination industrial societies have developed without upheavals and will probably continue to do so. ". . . wherever there is life, there is conflict. May we go so far as to say that conflict is a condition necessary for life to be possible at all?"[2] A "classless" society is therefore, impossible because it would be without conflict. Marx is dead, long live conflict!

But, it could be said, whether Marx is alive or dead, surely Dahrendorf's theory makes him a conscious revolutionary, an advocate of change. Unfortunately, this isn't so. Far from it. First, like Strachey and Crosland, he believes we no longer live in a capitalist society, although there may be capitalists in it. He therefore calls our society "post-capitalist". Secondly, his concern is to limit conflict, especially industrial (i.e. class) conflict. This limiting comes about, he says, through the process of "institutionalisation".

"My thesis is that in post-capitalist society industrial conflict has become less violent because its existence has been accepted and its manifestations have been socially regulated. Today, industrial conflict is recognised as a necessary feature of industrial life. This recognition, as well as the establishment of regulatory institutions,

[1] Dahrendorf, same, p. 131, my italics. [2] Same, p. 208.

constitutes in itself a structural change which is due to no small extent to the effects of industrial conflict."[1]

What are the "regulatory institutions" curbing industrial conflict? They are unions and employers' associations, negotiating, conciliation and arbitration machinery, shop stewards and shop councils (especially well established in Western Germany) and the increasing participation of workers in the government of enterprises (in Western Germany a number of firms have workers' representatives on the boards of directors). Certainly, capital and wage-labour still exist in industry, but not outside the factory gates. In the world outside, owing to the steady erosion of class differences, society is no longer divided into a bourgeoisie and a proletariat. In the world outside there is—the reader can guess—yes, a "democratic political system".

In this picture, as with Crosland's, the economic, property basis of power vanishes. Unlike Parsons, who does not consider the question of power at all, because consensus means that (ideally) all members of a society freely agree on the society's aims, norms and values, Dahrendorf's conflict theory presupposes a hierarchy of interests, with some stronger than others. But since the most important groups are authority groups, that group exercising the greatest authority must, in Dahrendrof's picture, be the ruling class. Therefore he rejects both Marx and Burnham in favour of Pareto's "governmental élites".

> "Managerial and capitalist élites", he writes, "may be extremely powerful groups in society, they may even exert partial control over governments and parliaments, but these very facts underline the significance of governmental élites: whatever decisions are made are made either by or through them; whatever changes are introduced or prevented, governmental élites are their immediate object or agent; whatever conflicts occur in the political arena, the heads of the three branches of government are the exponents of the *status quo*."[2]

And later:

> ". . . the ruling class of the post-capitalist society consists of the administrative staff of the state, the governmental élites at its head,

[1] Same, p. 257. Incidentally, if Dahrendorf were right, there should be more conflict between rulers and ruled than *among* either rulers or ruled. But a study of 1,500 heads of families in Italy revealed greater conflict within the "dominant" heads than between them and their "subjects". (Lopreato: Authority and class conflict: *Social Forces*, September 1968.)

[2] Same, p. 302.

and those interested parties which are represented by the governmental élite."[1]

By this theory Dahrendorf does several things. First, even more than Pareto, he obscures the origin and economic basis of the ruling class. In other words, how does the state arise and why, and what major interests do the governmental élites represent? (The capitalist state arises, of course, to protect and foster capitalist rule.) Secondly, by diminishing the power of private property Dahrendorf is able, like other bourgeois ideologists, to transform capitalist society into what it is not. Thirdly, he also can attack socialism. For, he says, his analysis applies to the communist countries as well. There too, society is based on authority, the authority of the Party, which is the communist governmental élite. Only there the authority is nearly absolute, whereas in the "West", although he would not go as far as Riesman's claim that power is dispersed and there is no ruling class, democracy and periodical elections act, in Galbraith's phrase, as a countervailing power.

In contrast to consensus theory, according to which conflict is "dysfunctional", conflict theory says it is inherent in the system and may, indeed, be *positively* functional.[2] For the concern of both schools is to preserve the "Western" way of life, which has somehow stopped being capitalism—or so they say. So much have capitalism's internal contradictions forced sociologists to recognise them that Dahrendorf can say a society *without* conflict is impossible. Socialism, which the bourgeois theorists persistently call "totalitarianism", is denounced—because it aims to abolish conflict.

Dahrendorf writes:

> "Totalitarian monism is founded on the idea that conflict can and should be eliminated, that a homogeneous and uniform social and political order is the desirable state of affairs. . . . The pluralism of free societies (i.e. capitalism—H.F.) on the other hand, is based on recognition and acceptance of social conflict."[3]

Unfortunately, there are many Dahrendorfs. Many ordinary people hide their own despair and cynicism under phrases like "There will always be people at the top and people at the bottom", "You can't change human nature" and "You communists are idealists; you'll never stop people fighting one another". In doing so they adopt

[1] Same, p. 303.
[2] Coser: *The Functions of Social Conflict* (1956).
[3] Dahrendorf, p. 318.

bourgeois ideology. But this attitude is one-sided: "human nature" is not fixed in any one particular pattern and there are primitive as well as modern societies based on co-operation and not on crude economic competition. Again, Dahrendorf's picture assumes the possibility of the *permanent* containment of conflict, i.e. the permanent continuation of "Western" society. It is worth pointing out, too, that he and certain other conflict theorists use the word conflict rather than contradiction, because contradiction implies that at some stage the contradictions become so great that the system can no longer bear them and flies apart. This is what Dahrendorf hopes will never happen. That is why, in face of all the facts about wars, economic crises and revolutions, he blandly claims that the "Western" world has changed "without sudden, widely visible upheavals".

Conflict theory nevertheless provides a theoretical framework for sociologists who, working within the capitalist system, find it a weapon for progress. Conflict theorists, especially in the U.S., have helped the fight for trade union recognition, establishment of negotiating machinery, broadening of the functions of works committees and so on. Although their aim is the *resolution* of conflict,[1] nevertheless, in the U.S., where "resolution" of industrial conflict can sometimes be a long drawn out affair entailing a good deal of hardship to strikers and their families and where racial conflict is, as everyone knows, frequently bloody, the conflict theorists, with their call for "institutionalisation" and "tolerance" can often be very helpful. But in the present atmosphere of the U.S. it is very difficult to carry the logic of conflict theory to its conclusion, namely, that as the system is riddled with conflict, it ought to be replaced. So far, however, only a minority of sociologists, British and American, have thrown in their lot wholeheartedly with those seeking a new and better system of society.[2] Until most do so, it will still be possible to talk, as Professor John Rex has done,[3] of a convergence between consensus and conflict theorists on the common basis of defence of "western society" against "totalitarianism".

[1] Their American journal is actually called *The Journal of Conflict Resolution*.

[2] "... the majority of sociologists who dominate contemporary sociology, far from seeing themselves as reformers and addressing themselves to an audience of reformers, either have oriented themselves toward purely academic and professional audiences, or have attempted to find a hearing among decision-makers in public or private bureaucracies." (L. Coser: *Functions of Social Conflict*, 1956, p. 20.) But of course there has been something of a swing of opinion since Coser wrote.

[3] Article in *New Society*, 6th October 1966.

CONCLUSION

We have tried to describe the claims and arguments of some of the chief socio-economic theorists about the changes in Western capitalism. We have tried to show a thread running through most of them, a thread which is of a distorted view of capitalism.

Bernstein pointed to the apparent diffusion of share-ownership, the rise in working-class incomes, the continued existence of a sector of self-employed persons, the high proportion of agricultural small holdings and the unprovability (admitted by Engels) of the inevitability of the social revolution. But the period between the two world wars, especially the Great Slump, mass unemployment and the rise of fascism, put the revisionist views of Bernstein and the Bernsteinians in the doldrums.

During and after World War II the climate of opinion changed sharply. "Western" governments declared their intention to prevent a return to pre-war evils; and, in this spirit, the British coalition Government asserted its determination to maintain full employment, to institute comprehensive social services, including secondary education for all, to break down old social barriers and to abolish want and poverty. Six years of post-war Labour Government saw virtually full employment, no post-war slump as had occurred after the First World War, a Labour parliamentary majority of over 100, extensive nationalisation and a steadily rising standard of living among the working class. Strachey argued that all this refuted Marx. Post-war capitalism had developed its own controls and overcome the perennial cycle of boom and slump. As for Marx's prediction of increasing impoverishment of the proletariat, the exact opposite had taken place. Post-war capitalism had so altered that Crosland could argue that British democracy bore very little resemblance to Marxist capitalism. True, Crosland admitted, there were still great inequalities, but such great progress had been made under the Attlee Government in reducing them that the Labour Party could and would tackle the remaining inequalities, especially in wealth and in educational advantage. However, he opposed the abolition of all private ownership of capital. Private ownership of the means of production was not important today. What was important in estimating the justice or injustice of any society was the degree of inequality, the barriers between classes and the amount of democracy; and in all these Britain was more progressive than the Soviet Union.

Sociologists, transferring this economic picture to the social plane, argued that Marxian emphasis on class was out-of-date. Weber, the greatest bourgeois sociologist, claimed that social status (defined as based on the power to consume) was becoming more important than class position (which, for Marx, was based on ownership of the means of production). Weber also denied that modern society could be divided into two main classes. There were at least three modes of stratification, the social, the political and the economic; and one or the other became prominent, mainly depending on the economic situation.

Sociology became an examination of how to refute the Marxist case, how to find the source of political power in something other than ownership of capital. Weber found it in authority, of which authority arising from capital ownership was only one kind and that not the most important. The most important kind was bureaucratic, the authority arising from holding office; and the present epoch was characterised above all by the growth of bureaucracy. Not the capitalist but the bureaucrat was the most powerful figure of our time.

A school of thought begun by Pareto justified capitalist society by arguing that the division between rulers and ruled was inevitable and a classless society impossible. Elite theorists on the Left, especially C. Wright Mills, condemn present society on this ground but see little hope of anything else, at least in advanced industrial countries. Burnham's version of élite theory sweeps aside all significant differences between socialism and capitalism and describes the U.S.A. and the U.S.S.R. as "managerial" societies.

Elite theory breeds its other half, the theory of "mass society". This theory also ignores the Marxist class structure of "Western" society. The mass society theorists regard the non-élite, the governed, as lower orders pressing their views and demands upon an accessible élite, or as social atoms available for manipulation by élites—worst of all, by the leaders of totalitarian movements. The mass society theorists, stressing this contemporary danger, hold up "liberal democracy" as an ideal and a buttress against mass movements.

Finally, in the theory of functionalism, the sociologists simply concentrate on the contribution any individual or group makes to the society or societies of which he is a member. In so doing the functionalists regard maintenance of the system as primary and class antagonisms as regrettable deviations. There may be uppers or lowers, but all members of the society and their actions are simply judged on the basis of whether or not they are positively functional to the society.

Inevitably, functionalism produced a reaction. Conflict theorists return to the view that society is an arena of conflicting groups. They see these groups as inevitable in any scheme of society, not, as in Marxism, as historically temporary. Moreover, conflict is regarded as having positive value in stabilising society if such conflict is channelled into acceptable forms, for example, collective bargaining machinery.

Theory comes chiefly from the United States. British sociology inherits a radical tradition of its own. This radical tradition tends to shy away from theory and to concentrate on fact-finding investigations and issues of narrower importance.[1] The following chapters will show that the results of these investigations are shattering ammunition against the revisionist and bourgeois views of Western and particularly British society. Is Britain a bureaucratic, status-dominated, élitist, managerial, mass, consensus or post-capitalist society? Or, although these may all be features of Britain today, is it not still fundamentally a capitalist society as Marxists generally understand it? Attention will be concentrated on Britain, as in Crosland's and Strachey's books, because this country is a test case for both Marxists and anti-Marxists.

[1] But the younger British academics are arguing more about theoretical questions both in academic journals and in the theoretical publications of the Left.

4

THE CAPITALIST CLASS

ARE THE RICH NO LONGER RICH?

The bourgeois theorists, as the last chapter showed, based a large, perhaps even the largest, part of their claim about the transformation of capitalism on the post-war levelling of incomes. This levelling can be shown in different ways. First, the rates of income tax increased sharply during the war and stayed high during the period of the Attlee Government. Income tax was progressive, i.e. steeply graded, with standard rate of tax at 9/– in the £ and surtax at 10/6 in the £ for incomes over £20,000. By the financial year 1967/68 an individual with an income over £20,000 theoretically paid 19/6 in the £ at the top layer of his income. Income tax and surtax in 1967/68 reduced a top income to a mere fraction of what it was, as shown by the following table:

Income	*Income left after paying income tax and surtax*		
	Single persons	*Married couples without children*	*Married couples with allowance for 3 children*
£	£	£	£
5,000	3,485	3,535	3,687
10,000	5,715	5,804	6,075
20,000	7,337	7,446	7,784
50,000	9,962	10,071	10,409
100,000	14,337	14,446	14,784

High taxation is not, however, exclusive to Labour Governments. For example, in 1943, under the Churchill Coalition Government, a single person with earned income of £100,000 theoretically paid over £94,000 in tax, leaving him with a mere £6,000. It is true that the Tories reduced the rates of tax in the 1950s, so that by 1957/58 the £100,000 single person kept about £11,300; and this position was steadily improved until Labour came back into power in 1964. Although successive Labour chancellors of the Exchequer have increased the tax liability, the rich individual is still left with more than he retained during the war under the Churchill Coalition Government. Thus it must be said that very high rates of taxation of the rich are not exclusive to Social-Democratic governments, although Tories tend to reduce them in peace-time. But the fact remains that, especially since the beginning of World War II, high incomes have been heavily taxed.

The same applies to estate or death duties. In the 1930s the highest rate to be paid on any estate was 55 per cent and only for estates of over £2 million. In 1946 the top rate was raised to 75 per cent and since 1949 (Labour or Tory), all estates of over £1 million officially pay 80 per cent of their value in death duties. In this respect, therefore, both Tory and Labour administrations share the honour of leaving to heirs of the biggest estates only one-fifth of their original value.

Another way of looking at the redistribution of incomes is through the shares taken by wages, profits, etc., in the national income. In the 'thirties Clark[1] showed that the share of wages in the total of private income in Britain since the turn of the century fluctuated around 40 per cent. Bowley showed that it was 40 per cent as far back as 1880 and declined to 38½ per cent by 1913. Nor was there much progress after the First World War, despite concessions granted during the war through organised pressure by militant working-class action. By 1938 the share of wages was down to 37 per cent. But during and after the last war spectacular progress took place. Between 1938 and 1950 the share of wages leaped from 37 per cent to 44 per cent, salaries and professional earnings maintained their position, but the share going to rent, interest and dividends fell from 24 per cent to 15 per cent. Shares *after* tax had been paid were even better from the point of view of redistribution. For then wages took 47 per cent in 1950 compared with 39 per cent in 1938, salaries and professional earnings again maintained their position at 25 per cent, while rent, interest and dividends fell from 34 per cent to 25 per cent. According to the Oxford statistician, Seers, who calculated these percentages, the main fall occurred in incomes from property. Douglas Jay even calculated that the share of wages rose from 40 per cent in 1938 to 50 per cent in 1950.[2]

That there was a sharp improvement in the condition of the working class in this period it would be ridiculous to deny. But as regards the actual figures, two observations should be made. First, the item, "rent, dividends and interest" includes the earnings of farmers, sole traders and partnerships. Secondly, Seers himself[3] regarded the trend as due

[1] C. Clark: *Wages and Incomes since 1860* (1937).

[2] D. Jay: *Socialism in the New Society* (1962), p. 190.

[3] *Bulletin of the Oxford Institute of Statistics* (hereafter *Bull. Ox. Inst. Stats.*), February, 1956.

not so much to deliberate governmental policy of redistribution of wealth as to *temporary factors* like war-time dividend limitation and rent control. According to Seers, this movement stopped in 1950; and both Crosland and Jay claim that under the Tories things have gone the other way. However, the point is made that between 1938 and 1950 there was a sharp reduction in inequality in respect of the shares of the national income going to labour and to capital.

This shift is even more striking if we include price changes, as well as social service benefits, most of which (allegedly) go to the working-class. For then, Seers calculated, while the net working-class share rose from 37 per cent (1938) to 47 per cent (1949), the net share of "rent, interest and dividends" fell from 20 per cent (1938) to a mere 10 per cent (1949). "Thus the oustanding change was a transfer of 10 per cent of total disposable income from property-owners to the working class. Unearned income in 1949 took only one-tenth of the total . . . while wages, salaries, social service beneficiaries, and the armed forces took 80 per cent between them."[1] Note how the armed forces are lumped with the working class and the suggestion that social service benefits are virtually tax transfers from rich to poor. In fact, as Crosland himself admitted, the working class pays entirely for the social service benefits it receives. "As a general proposition, the working class pay enough additional in beer, tobacco, purchase taxes and other indirect levies to meet the increased cost of the food subsidies and health and education expenditures, while the increase in the direct taxes they pay covers the rise in their transfer money receipts."[2] In 1949, Crosland went on to admit, the working class, defined as those with incomes of less than £500 p.a., paid in taxes £139 millions more than they received in benefits. A later study by Peacock showed that for 1950/51 total taxation paid by the working class exceeded total social service receipts by an even bigger sum. Thus, even under the first post-war Labour Government, the taxation system appeared to make substantial demands on the working class in exchange (?) for the redistribution of income. The view is not quite so rosy; and we shall return to this problem later on.

But, when all is said, the fact remains that the rich are apparently very heavily taxed. A man like Sir Paul Chambers, former chairman of I.C.I., salary £50,000 p.a., is left with about £10,000. Of course,

[1] Crosland: *The Future of Socialism*, p. 52.

[2] Weaver, quoted in Crosland, p. 147. "Transfer money receipts" include such benefits as pensions and unemployment pay.

now that war-time restrictions are finished, Crosland admitted, the rich were regaining lost ground by access ". . . to sources of expenditure other than taxable income".[1] Although this admission revealed that some top income is not taxed, Crosland remained undaunted.

> Thus figures of net taxable income are not a wholly reliable guide to levels of expenditure; and a section of the rich, notably those with City and business connections, are able partially to avoid the effects of high taxation.
>
> "*But when every allowance is made, the essential fact remains—that the rich are distinctly less rich, and the poor are much less poor.*"[2]

WEALTH

That official statistics about taxation, incomes and wealth were unreliable occurred to a few investigators, apart from the many who could read and see with their own eyes. If a £50,000 a year company director was really left with only £10,000, or a £15,000 a year man with only £6,000, how could they live in the style in which so many were obviously living, since large houses were still occupied, staffed with servants, "gracious living" reappeared after the war (did it completely disappear during the war, with game and other luxury goods unrationed?), Rolls-Royces and Bentleys were seen in growing numbers, the gossip columns regularly described lavish "coming-out" parties, and wintering in the Bahamas was not unknown?

The first criticism was that "incomes", as measured by the Inland Revenue, omitted wealth or property, which is not taxable, except on the death of the holder. In a *Memorandum of Dissent to the Final Report of the Royal Commission on the Taxation of Profits and Incomes* (the Radcliffe Report), George Woodcock, H. L. Bullock and N. Kaldor argued that "income" should include all that "which embraces all receipts which increase an individual's command over the use of society's scarce resources—in other words, his 'net accretion of economic power between two points of time'."[3] In their view it meant that income must include inherited wealth and capital gains.

But had heavy taxation of high incomes forced the rich to fall back on their inherited wealth? And had higher estate duties worsened this trend, so that the rich were being soaked all ways? Certainly death duties were high and many estates were being sold to pay them; but if

[1] *The Future of Socialism*, p. 53. [2] Same, my italics. [3] *Final Report*, p. 355.

they were being sold, people were also buying them. And the capital value of all estates in Britain was going up year after year. In 1938/39 the value of all estates liable for estate duty was £550 million. In 1950/51 it was over £800 million and in 1960/61 over £1,240 million. George Woodcock and his colleagues were rightly suspicious of a system of inheritance taxation which caused estate values to rise so rapidly. In 1941/42 there were 459 estates worth £100,000 or more; in 1950/51 over 700 and in 1960/61 942. And the Board couldn't be certain about these figures because of a number of loopholes in the laws on death duties.

Meanwhile, the results of investigations carried out by the Oxford University Institute of Statistics were slowly becoming more widely known. Kathleen Langley investigated the ownership of private capital in 1950/51 (after 5 years of Labour Government). A serious limitation on official statistics about ownership of wealth was, she pointed out, that estate duty could be paid in instalments over a period of years. Nevertheless, she calculated that 43 per cent of all property holdings over £2,000 were owned by only 6 per cent of those owners. Taking only those estates worth £2,000 or more, she calculated that just over two per cent (56,000 persons) owned over £8,400 millions, an average of £150,000 each.[1]

A few years later came the most famous of all post-war studies of personal wealth.[2] Lydall and Tipping, the authors, also argued that income alone was not a true criterion of wealth. "Wealth gives power", they wrote, "indeed, it gives more power than income, because it is largely free of current commitment (and of current taxation)." Estate duty statistics were, they pointed out, grossly inadequate, not only for the reason given by Kathleen Langley, but because of the habit among the aged rich of distributing their wealth among the family before death. Allowing for these "trusts", they estimated that in early 1954

> three million persons (the top twelfth of the population) owned 78 per cent of all the personal wealth of Britain;
> the remaining 22 per cent of all personal wealth was distributed among the other eleven-twelfths of the population (32 million persons); the top 20,000 individuals, each owning more than £100,000, owned on average a quarter of a million pounds; the lower 16 million persons, each owning less than £100, had on average less than £50;

[1] *Bull. Ox. Inst. Stats.*, January 1954.
[2] *Bull. Ox. Inst. Stats.*, February 1961.

the top one per cent of British adults owned 43 per cent of total net capital; the top 10 per cent owned nearly 80 per cent of total net capital.

Stocks and shares were, they found, *almost entirely held by the top 10 per cent of the population.* While there *might* have been some reduction in the concentration of ownership compared with pre-war, it was hard to be sure, owing to the increasing number of trusts and the division of fortunes between members of each family during the owner's lifetime. Finally they said that concentration was much greater in Britain than in the U.S.A.: in the U.S. the top one per cent owned 24 per cent of all capital, compared with 43 per cent in Britain.

These shattering conclusions led to much rethinking on the Left and recriminations on the Right. Crosland produced *The Conservative Enemy* in 1962 and Douglas Jay his book in the same year. Both attacked the gross inequality of wealth, soft-pedalling the failure of the Attlee Government to do anything about it.

That the return of a Tory Government would worsen the situation was confirmed by two later surveys. A Cambridge economist, J. S. Revell, estimated that, in 1960, the top one per cent of British adults owned 42 per cent of total personal wealth, the top five per cent owned 75 per cent of the wealth and the top 10 per cent owned 83 per cent.[1] In 1966 *The Economist* published the results of its own investigation based on Inland Revenue returns on investment income[2]. According to this, the distribution of wealth in Britain in 1959/60 was as follows:

Range of Wealth £	*% of tax-payers*	*% of total wealth*	*Average wealth held* £
less than 3,000	87·9	3·7	107
3,000–10,000	5·1	12·0	6,000
10,000–25,000	4·9	29·0	15,200
25,000–50,000	1·2	16·6	36,250
50,000–100,000	0·6	15·1	68,250
100,000–200,000	0·2	10·6	136,400
over 200,000	0·1	13·0	334,100

Summarising this table, we find that 88 per cent of taxpayers owned only a little over £100 each; while just under one per cent of taxpayers at the top owned nearly 39 per cent, the top two per cent of taxpayers 55 per cent of the wealth, the top seven per cent, 84 per cent

[1] Given by Mr. Revell to Professor Meade and published in Meade's *Efficiency, Equality and the Ownership of Property* (1964).

[2] *The Economist*, 15th January 1966.

of the wealth and *the top 12 per cent of the population over 96 per cent of all wealth.*

Comparison between this and other estimates is not possible because of the different percentages, so, in the table below summarising the changes since 1938, *The Economist* estimates will be omitted.

% of population over 25	*% of total wealth* 1936/38	*1954 (Lydall and Tipping)*	*1960 (Revell)*
1	56	43	42
5	79	—	75
10	88	79	83

In less than ten years of Tory rule, then, half the change in ownership of wealth by the top 10 per cent of the adult population, due to special war-time and immediate post-war conditions, was cancelled out; and the top one per cent of the adult population (roughly 250,000 people) still owned over two-fifths of the entire wealth of the country. To give Strachey his due, he agreed that there had been little redistribution of wealth. No wonder he fell back on the phrase, "reasonable distribution of the national product". But what was all the other stuff about democracy worth if the top 250,000 individuals owned nearly half the wealth of the country? And it is simply laughable to say that the rich are distinctly less rich because the share of the wealth going to the top five per cent of the adult population went down from 79 per cent before the war to 75 per cent in 1960. No wonder that in his *The Conservative Enemy* Crosland agreed that the "gross maldistribution in property" had to be corrected.

But did the Wilson Government take any major steps in this direction? On the contrary, the movement has gone in the opposite direction. One startling indication of this was the enormous increase in share values during the 1967/68 share boom. In the first quarter of 1968, the index of share prices stood 60 per cent above its 1966 level. In round figures this means a rise in the value of shares since 1966 of £10,000 million, or *more than the whole annual Government expenditure on health, education and social security put together!* In 1962 Crosland even urged an annual wealth tax as in Sweden which, at 1 per cent, would bring in £500 million p.a. But this has not been introduced. Nor have the death duty laws been altered to stop avoidance of payment.[1] Nothing

[1] Judith Todd, herself a qualified accountant, describes, in her very witty little book, *The Conjurers*, some of the ways the estate duty laws enable the rich to pass on their estates virtually intact.

radical has in fact happened, although the 1969 Labour Party election manifesto included a possible wealth-tax.

Right-wing Labour spokesmen have an answer. "If", they say, "we had been in power all the time, this fantastic inequality would have been steadily reduced. After all, we have pledged and continue to pledge ourselves to do this." To which there are several answers. First, the greatest inequality doesn't necessarily go with Conservative governments: in the U.S.A., which has never had a declared social-democratic government, inequality of wealth is apparently less than in Britain, while inequality on a big scale still persists in Scandinavia, despite social-democratic governments and taxes on wealth. Secondly, it assumes that in Britain the Labour Party can stay in office, which three previous Labour Governments failed to do. Thirdly, the claim that a Labour Government will continue a process of equalisation is not borne out by the facts. Labour politicians deplore the gross inequality; so indeed does the Tory writer and M.P. Angus Maude;[1] but the actions of the Wilson Administration have increased it. Indeed Michael Stewart, Labour Foreign Secretary and former Minister for Economic Affairs, also recently deplored it but, apart from some minor additional taxation in the 1965 Budget, the Wilson Government continued to help increase company profits. While private wealth in the form of interest-bearing stocks and shares, i.e. capitalist ownership, is allowed and is, in fact, basic to the system, this inequality can not only not be abolished, it cannot even be substantially reduced. As *The Economist* put it in 1966: "... there is undoubtedly a permanent built-in tendency to inequality here", adding that even when the new capital gains tax is in full operation, it will still amount to a property tax of well under one per cent a year. No wonder the article was headed *The Indefensible Status Quo* and described British taxation as "a system which over the past 60 years ... has not only failed in its original aim of breaking up the big fortunes, but has also done far too little to help the building up of small ones".[2]

Automation and the further concentration of business ownership, both of which are proceeding rapidly, tend to worsen inequality of wealth, because by increasing productivity and reducing the work force, they lower the share of gross product going to wages and salaries. Making these points, Professor Meade speculates about the future thus:

[1] "Wealthy People", by A. Maude, in *Aspect*, April 1963.

[2] *The Economist* 15th January 1966. See also John Hughes, *New Statesman* 8th November 1966.

"There would be a limited number of exceedingly wealthy property owners . . there would have to be a large expansion of the production of the labour-intensive goods and services. . . . Let us call this the Brave New Capitalists' Paradise. It is to me a hideous outlook."[1] This type of "1984", "Brave New World" outlook on capitalism is a fair warning. As we observed earlier, Marx in later life saw the forces (mainly workers' action) tending to counter the "immiseration" of the proletariat, especially in periods of rapid technological change. So did Weber. But history is, in this respect, like a seesaw; and whatever the temporary changes, one thing is certain; under capitalism redistribution at best occurs when "national unity" is essential, i.e. during war and the immediate post-war period of "reconstruction"; at other times it will vary little and tend if anything to worsen.[2]

INCOMES

Here the right-wing case seems much surer. Each year the Board of Inland Revenue publishes details of incomes before and after tax. As we saw before, in theory taxes eat heavily into top incomes. So it may be that, although retaining much property, the rich lose heavily on the incomes they draw from this property. Figures for the financial year 1966/67 show that 6,300 persons[3] received £20,000 a year or more *before tax*. But tax reduces £20,000 to about £6,000. So the Inland Revenue supplies figures for those still receiving £6,000 or more a year *after* tax. In 1966/67 there were 25,400 of these. The 6,300 received £217·8 millions before tax, i.e. £34,600 each; but *after* tax they got a total of only £51·7 millions, or only £8,200 each.[4] Since many of these, perhaps most of them, were company directors or managers, they, unlike the landed aristocracy, are supposed to have little property-income, living entirely on their salaries or directors' fees.

Further, these are only money incomes. If the rise in the cost of living is taken into account, the picture is even worse (from top people's point of view, of course). Comparing pre- and post-war, Professor

[1] Meade, p. 33.

[2] This is confirmed by the latest Inland Revenue statistics, which show a steady rise in the proportion of estates over £5,000 out of all estates, from 17 per cent in 1961/62 to 27 per cent in 1967/68. Estates of £100,000 and over continued to rise from 942 in 1961/62 to 1,248 in 1967/68. See also Appendix I.

[3] Strictly, "income units". This distinction, as will be shown later, is important.

[4] B.I.R. Report for 1967/68, the latest issued at the time of writing.

Sir John Hicks obligingly calculated the fall in top incomes in 1957 pounds, as shown in the following table:

Personal Incomes above £3,000 p.a. in 1957 pounds.[1]

	No. in class			*Average income* (1957 £'s)		
	1938	*1949*	*1957*	*1938*	*1949*	*1957*
Before tax	288	230	180	8,030	6,200	5,620
After tax	288	230	180	5,490	3,105	2,870

The ordinary layman with a bit of "nous", confronted with this challenge, would very likely be sceptical. After all, he knew or at least guessed at the various fiddles conducted by employers to avoid tax, usually direct tax evasions through unregistered transactions, or legal operations such as inflated "business expenses". But the full extent of tax avoidance and evasion and, therefore, the complete unreliability of Inland Revenue income statistics, was not fully revealed to the interested student until the publication in 1962 of Professor Titmuss' *Income Distribution and Social Change*, undoubtedly one of the most important books published since the war.

Professor Titmuss declared that the claims about growing equality were based on the uncritical acceptance of official and academic statistics. By steady questioning of the Board's officials, he found a remarkable lack of information about how they collected their statistics and what they meant by their terms, especially their "units" of income, which could be either individuals or families.

Titmuss referred to the striking rise in the number of marriages, especially earlier marriages, compared with pre-war. The Board's failure to consider income consistently on a family basis was, he pointed out, "... one of the major factors in producing a statistical illusion of greater income equality".[2] For earlier working class marriages meant that, for a few years at any rate, the low rates of pay of these girls vanished from the statistics; while, at the other end, the official figures would not show the number of top people who were married couples each getting top incomes, nor other top incomes obscured through marriage arrangements. In fact, Titmuss revealed that the Board's statistics showed a gap of 1½ million earning wives. They were simply missing. The incomes of children and of dependent adults were also missing. Those of children were particularly important, since the greatest concentration of wealth by age was among young adults.

[1] Hicks: *The Social Framework* (3rd edition, 1960), pp. 217–220.
[2] Titmuss, p. 50.

The Board reported a quarter of a million children unaccounted for, mostly, he suggested, because parents did not include them in their tax returns, especially if they had incomes of their own.

Titmuss devoted a large part of his book to showing how British tax laws allowed wider "family settlements" than almost anywhere else in the "West", reflecting the importance of inheritance in the maintenance of top British fortunes. "The vast majority of taxpayers", writes Judith Todd, "who submit to weekly deductions under PAYE in a spirit of outraged incomprehension, have little opportunity of being 'astute'. They can fix the date of their wedding to the optimum tax advantage. They can notify promptly the birth of each child. If their income is large enough, they may gain some relief through building society or mortage interest. After that, their powers of 'tax arrangement' are pretty well exhausted."[1] Not so the really rich. Private arrangements, which the Royal Commission on the Taxation of Profits and Incomes in 1955 described as no better than frauds, operate widely, wrote Titmuss. Such "deeds of covenant" were then estimated to lose £12½ millions a year in tax which should have gone to the Government. Changes in the law on estate duties have left many loopholes, particularly in avoiding payment of any duty if the estate is handed over to children more than five (now 7) years before death. Of such arrangements no statistics have ever been published.[2] Then there were "marriage gifts", "separation payments" (the separation may not be a fact, but in 1959 these payments lost the Exchequer £10 million),[3] and benefits to children (including education covenants). Nor had the Inland Revenue any figures on those tricks. Companies also went in for a lot of school fee paying, which tax laws regarded as admissible business expenses. Gifts to "charities" were tax free, so that in effect the State subsidised bodies legally accepted as charities: the Royal Commission estimated the tax loss on these to be about £35 millions a year. Not much was known about the avoidance of taxes

[1] *The Conjurers*, p. 33.

[2] "So many judicious methods of mitigating the burden exist, that estate duty is often known as 'the voluntary tax', only paid on the estates of careless (rich) who make an unnecessary present to the Estate Duty Office." J. Todd, p. 48. Miss Todd adds that any valuables certified by the Treasury as of national, scientific or historical interest, escape duty even if sold to certain public institutions for cash!

[3] "The odd situation had now come on us, in which a man of large means who paid surtax was able to have several wives ... and to be very little worse off ... whereas a working man who paid neither surtax nor any considerable amount of income tax found it quite impossible to comply with the law which ... enabled divorced wives to obtain maintenance ..." (Lord Justice Hodson, quoted Titmuss, p. 77.)

through "discretionary trusts" increasingly widespread; but Lydall and Tipping estimated that in 1954 trust funds were of the order of £1,000 millions. Revell estimated that by 1961 they totalled as much as £6,500 millions, or about one-eighth of the total wealth of all persons in Great Britain!

As regards the channels through which business practised tax evasion and avoidance, these were legion. The Inland Revenue recorded unemployment pay, but not compensation for loss of office, N.I. sick benefit but not top executive benefits in kind.[1] In 1959 differences between Blue Book (National Income and Expenditure) and Inland Revenue figures, largely accounted for by untaxed capital gains, amounted to the colossal sum of £3,260 millions, or 17 per cent of the total national income. And it is important to repeat here that most stocks and shares are owned by only a small percentage of the population. Since Titmuss wrote there have been two capital gains taxes, a short-term introduced by the Tories in 1962, and a long-term introduced by Labour in 1965. The former was only a gesture, as was to be expected from the Tories, but the latter did mean more tax—but also ways of getting around paying it.[2] New legislation has from time to time been introduced to stop the tricks known as dividend stripping and bond-washing, which in past years accounted for an annual tax loss of £50 millions, but, as Titmuss points out, previous legislation has failed to stop them. One-man companies were in the past happy channels for tax avoidance, and the number of small companies proliferated until the 1965 Budget introduced certain restrictions on profit distribution within such companies. But the smart boys can avoid this by splitting their interests among several companies. The Inland Revenue could provide Titmuss with no information about such companies except their number. Free share distribution to executives (increasingly popular in today's boom conditions); buying property abroad (to avoid estate duty); hobby farming; owning agricultural and woodland; living in debt (on permanent overdraft); "golden handshakes" which were tax free; all these undermined the argument for growing income equality since the war.

One of the biggest post-war developments in tax avoidance and the acquisition of large sums of money has taken place through life assur-

[1] The 1965 Budget made certain alterations in these and other loopholes, but loopholes still remain. Miss Todd's book describes some of these. None could be said to alter the picture substantially. They mostly merely make the accountants think harder.

[2] See *The Conjurers*, p. 36 f. for details.

ance and superannuation schemes. Either the firm deducts a sum from the top executive's salary to pay the premium on the huge policy; or the rich man pays part of his income on smaller, separate policies which are tax-free under the law. Such premiums do not appear in the calculations of personal income. Further, as everyone with a life policy knows, they result in actual tax reduction, so enhancing the appearance of lower-than-actual incomes among the better-off. "Top hat" pension schemes, *The Economist* reported (12th March, 1960), had grown to great dimensions in recent years: as far back as 1951 they were estimated to be worth £75 millions. Titmuss gave instances from the Civil Service, showing, for example, that in 1961 a Permanent Secretary got, on retirement, a tax-free lump sum of more than £10,000 and the gap between lower and higher rank payments had widened compared with pre-war. But even this is small beer compared to the private sector, where some tax-free lump sums on retirement run into hundreds of thousands of pounds.

And last but not least, benefits in kind. "We feel bound to say in conclusion", stated the Royal Commission on Taxation, "that the provision of untaxable benefits in kind is capable of becoming an abuse of the tax system."[1] Benefits in kind are taxable, but Titmuss was of the opinion that most benefits were not included in full on tax returns and, in any case, where reported were taxed on what the employer said they cost, not necessarily on their market value. In 1961 the Institute of Directors welcomed the Inland Revenue's "more liberal attitude" towards extra allowances and expenses. By 1958/59 deductable, i.e. tax-free, expenses rose to £157 millions. To this sum should be added assistance towards housing (including prestige flats for top executives), cars and travel (in 1956 four out of five cars were owned by firms), education, meals and entertainment. *Reynolds News* once commented: "Only Exchequer largesse, paid directly via the tax-free expense account, keeps the night-club industry ticking at all."[2] But this was under the Tories. In his 1965 Budget Chancellor Callaghan introduced a tax on business entertainment, except for the benefit of overseas businessmen coming here. But, as far as meals and entertainment go, many have been transferred to the canteens within the firm's building, which are not therefore subject to tax. "Bizarre as it may seem, technically these establishments rank as industrial canteens. This is important, for ever since the war companies have been allowed to

[1] *Royal Commission Final Report*, p. 71.
[2] *Reynolds News*, 13th November, 1960.

write off the cost of the food and service, enabling meals to be subsidised. . . . In Unilever House there are eight such dining rooms, the Distillers Company in St. James' Square have three, and nearly every new office block houses one.

"Nor are the meals served exactly frugal. According to a recent survey of such establishments . . ., five courses are by no means exceptional. Of the 61 companies surveyed 44 per cent employed chefs and 18 per cent butlers; of the 9 types of service available, the full treatment with flowers and silver service was the most popular."[1]

At the height of the wage freeze introduced by the Wilson Government, a survey by Associated Industrial Consultants of "perks" enjoyed by middle-level business executives revealed an upward trend in bonuses, subsidised lunches, free life insurance, subsidised housing, cars, non-accountable expenses, pensions, as well as basic salaries. If this was the case for those with salaries £2,000–£5,000, imagine the style of life and hidden income of those at the top! The *Economist* recently estimated the worth of "fringe benefits" as a proportion of salary as follows:[2]

Salary p.a.	*Fringe benefits % of salary*
£1,000	11%
1,600	15
3,500	19
4,200	21
7,000+	31

i.e. the higher the income, the bigger the proportion of fringe benefits, most of which are untaxed, or tax is paid by the company.

"I remember a colleague telling me that he had just had a conference with a client and at the end of it he said to his client: 'I see that your income is almost exactly the same as mine, about £20,000 a year. By the time we have paid income tax and surtax of £15,000 we have £5,000 left. I have a Rover car and I am all right. But when I look at your expenses I see you have a Rolls-Royce, a Bentley, and a yacht. How on earth do you do this with that income?

"He replied, 'I have the best accountant in London and I do what he says. He has provided me with 12 exempt private companies and

[1] *Sunday Times*, 11th April, 1965.

[2] *The Economist*, 27th August, 1966. See also Merrett and Monk: *Inflation, Taxation and Executive Remuneration.*

the whole thing is frightfully involved. The yacht belongs to an exploration company and the accountant has made it so complicated that the Inland Revenue do not seem able to puzzle it out. I have not paid any tax for six years, but my accountant tells me that as long as there is a letter on the files the Inland Revenue seem to be quite happy'."[1]

Marx already saw the whole fiddle of directorships a hundred years ago, when he wrote:

"On the basis of capitalist production, a new swindle develops in stock enterprises with the wages of management. It consists in placing above the actual director a board of managers or directors, for whom superintendence and management serve in reality only as a pretext for plundering stockholders and amassing wealth . . . these wages of superintendence are as a rule inversely proportioned to the actual superintendence performed by these nominal directors." (*Capital* III, ch. 23).

Even in Marx's time there were gentlemen like our own Mr. Harvey (who created a modern sensation with over £200,000 remuneration) and Mr. Aisher (£91,000 in 1967).

The most drastic method of avoiding tax is to taste, as Miss Todd humorously puts it, "the bitter bread of exile". The late Lord and Lady Astor were "forced" by the 1962 Finance Act to move from their former home, Hever Castle, Kent, to the Riviera. The Premier Earl of England, Lord Shrewsbury, was "driven into exile" to Madeira. Everyone knows that Noel Coward lives in the Bahamas and Dennis Price in the Channel Islands. But, for the most part, the rich manage without this drastic final step.[2]

Finally, the work of the Inland Revenue is being increasingly hamstrung by the worsening staff situation. In his address to the 1969 annual conference of the Inland Revenue Staff Federation the president warned that the staff shortage, when the number and complexity of tax laws were rapidly-increasing, was making nonsense of the whole system.

[1] The Lord Chancellor in the House of Lords, *The Times*, 23rd November, 1966.

[2] Yet, according to the Inland Revenue, as shown by Professor Hicks' figures, the number of top incomes before tax between 1938 and 1958 actually fell. Assuming a three-fold rise in personal income 1938–58, Titmuss has calculated that, according to the B.I.R. the number of incomes of £6,000 and over fell from 19,000 in 1938 to only 4,000 in 1958! On the other hand, Professor Meade calculates that the Inland Revenue may have under-estimated incomes from property by as much as £1,500 millions.

Titmuss concluded that, because of the outcry by those deluded by the propaganda about greater equality as well as by those directly gaining from such propaganda, there had been a growing trend towards tax regressiveness, i.e. taxing the poor more and the rich less. And, he ended,

> "... there is more than a hint from a number of studies that income inequality has been increasing since 1949, whilst the ownership of wealth, which is far more highly concentrated in the United Kingdom than in the United States, has probably become still more unequal and, in terms of family ownership, possibly strikingly more unequal, in recent years."[1]

In a book published in the same year, Mr. Douglas Jay alleged, like Crosland, that most of this movement away from growing equality took place in the 1950s under the Tories. Yet he himself quotes Lydall's findings, which do not fully support his case. Lydall in fact argued that the trend towards equality occurred between 1938 and 1949 and began to move the opposite way in 1949. Now this was the year that Cripps, following his visit to Washington, devalued the pound, began a sharp rise in the cost of living and so lowered the standard of living of manual and non-manual workers, just as Wilson set about doing from July 1966. Mr. Jay, whose principles have lost him his ministerial position under Wilson, must surely in honesty not blame the Tories for what Attlee and Cripps did.

In fact, there is some dispute about when the trend towards equality stopped. R. J. Nicholson claims that the trend continued up to 1957, when it went into reverse.[2] If he is right, then the trend towards equality continued under the Tories, for a few years at any rate. There is not much in it either way.

Mr. Jay also supplements Lydall's interpretation of trends since 1938. Lydall argued[3] that the principal cause of the improvement up to 1949 was the rise in the share going to employees due to full employment (now being cut away by the Wilson Government, as it was by the Tory Government in 1963). Little, added Lydall, was due to taxation. Mr. Jay, however, adds a reservation: it was also due, he says, to

[1] Titmuss, p. 198. Incidentally, evasions and avoidance cause the rates of taxation to be much higher than they need be, even under capitalism. *The Observer* (2nd May, 1965) estimated that if all loopholes were stopped up and all allowances eliminated, the Government could bring the standard rate down to a mere 4/– in the £.

[2] *Lloyds Bank Review*, January, 1967.

[3] *Journal of Royal Statistical Society*, 1959.

the far greater proportion of profits being diverted to reserves and to taxation. But we know now how difficult it is to estimate correctly the effectiveness of taxing profits. Hence Mr. Jay should really acknowledge that any change has been due to full employment (not a specifically social-democratic policy) and to firms putting more into reserves, which they can draw out later on more favourable terms. The so-called "income-revolution" has become less and less tangible, until one wonders what redistribution has occurred at all. Because of full employment, technological change and a great production boom, a wholesale upward shift of money incomes has occurred. But whatever has happened in between—and this is another story, to be dealt with later—the gap between extremes has widened, and the claims about drastic reduction of top incomes are false. Neither Seers' nor Hicks' figures are worth the paper they are written on.

The latest statistics reveal a situation since the election of the Wilson Government which can truthfully be described as shattering that government's pretension to be "reforming" capitalism in the interest of greater equality. An analysis by John Hughes, Senior Tutor at Ruskin College, Oxford, shows the comparative increases in earned income (wages and salaries) and income from property.[1]

Amounts	*1955* (£m)	*1960* (£m)	*1965* (£m)
Personal property income	1,534	2,372	3,595
Earned income	12,905	17,168	23,736
Indices (1955=100)			
Personal property income	100	155	234
Earned income	100	133	184

The figures show clearly that income from property has been rising much faster than earned income and continues to do so.

Hughes concludes that, taking capital gains into account, the top 5 per cent took, in the mid-1960s, over one-quarter of all income in Britain. And, although the statistics show there was a slight fall in this proportion after Labour took over in 1964, the share of the wealthy has since then been steadily climbing back.

[1] *New Statesman*, 8th November 1968. The figures, Hughes stresses, do not include capital gains. The latest Blue Book figures give the following for 1968:

	Amount (£m)	*Indices* (1955=100)
Personal property income	4,265	278
Earned income	28,107	218

Again, in the tax year 1967/68, the total tax bill rose by 15 per cent over the previous year. Of the main direct taxes only the yield from surtax fell, by 2·2 per cent, while the yield from income tax was up by 18 per cent. It is true that the yields from corporation tax, capital gains tax and death duties also rose, but all less so than income tax, another indication of the widening gap and the relative increase at the top end of the scale of incomes, despite the Inland Revenue figures showing a decline in the numbers of top incomes. Evidently, the tax accountants for the wealthy have been very successfully hiding their clients' true incomes.

Right-wing theorists from Bernstein onwards have repeatedly claimed a new basic aim for what they called socialism. Not the abolition of private ownership, but equality, including equality of incomes. While admitting the persistence of gross inequalities in wealth, they claimed, at least since World War II, much greater levelling of incomes, a clear indication of the superiority of social-democracy as a working system. This reduction of inequality we have shown to be at least uncertain and probably untrue. Alternatively, they have claimed income equality as an *aim* of social-democracy.[1] But we have shown that in the final two years of the Attlee Government steps were taken reversing the 1938–49 trend towards equality. Nor is that all; under Wilson, wage-restraint plus profit-boom continue the trend away from equality, which began during 1949/50 or later. As R. J. Nicholson[2] cautiously remarks: "... the present deflationary policies, the incomes freeze and the slowing down of the growth of the national product, following the stability of the income distribution since 1957, must make it doubtful whether the trend in the distribution of incomes for the immediate future is set in the direction of greater equality". And Mr. Crosland, the prime spokesman of the right-wing case, is a leading member of the Wilson Government.

COMPANY TAXATION

However conclusive the evidence of personal inequality, the right-wing propagandists will still point to the crushing burden of taxation on companies. What with income tax, profits tax and excess profits tax,

[1] "This is indeed the heart of the matter. What socialists wish to avoid are the extravagant differences of income which divide people into classes unable to mix on equal terms." (*Twentieth Century Socialism*, Penguin 1956, p. 29).

[2] R. J. Nicholson, *Lloyds Bank Review*, January, 1967.

which are now all merged in the new corporations tax, British industrialists have for years argued that it was impossible for British industry to re-equip itself, to bring itself up-to-date, because it could never find enough money. In a sense British industry, unlike the individual person, has a greater burden; it faces the double problem of trying to make a profit and finding enough new capital to keep up with foreign competition and technological change. No wonder that the "entrepreneur" is given a unique importance in sociology and placed in Census Social Class I. Though primarily a question of political economy, it is desirable to see briefly how far the allegation is true.

Bearing in mind that the company profits have, according to the Blue Book of *National Income and Expenditure*, risen steadily in post-war years, the percentage of taxes paid by companies since 1938 are very illuminating

Year	*Taxes on companies as percentage of Gross National Product*
1938	1.8
1946	7.4
1950	6.6
1955	5.5
1960	3.1
1965	2.4
1966	2.4
1967	2.8
1968	3.0 [1]

No figures could be clearer or so damning an indictment of the special place given to "free enterprise" under the Tories or the Wilson Administration. In our capitalist society the private firm receives handsome subsidies in the shape of investment grants, loans at special rates, factories and machinery, aid in research and so on, not to mention plain graft especially on Government contracts. The clear picture is that ever since its exceptionally high level during and immediately after the war, the contribution made by company taxation to the total wealth of the country has steadily declined until, four years after the present very right-wing Social-Democratic Government took office, it is still less than the lowest figure under the post-war Tory Governments. Indeed Mr. Callaghan assured financiers, shortly after he

[1] Figures amalgamated from separate replies from the Chancellors of the Exchequer to two Labour MPs: from Mr. Callaghan to Mr. Driberg and from Mr. Jenkins to Mr. Hooley.

introduced the new Corporation Tax in 1965, that companies would pay no more in taxes under the new system than under the old.

Of course, capitalism cannot stand still in the face of conflicting pressures; and this is reflected in the tax system also. Inflation and increasing Government costs force taxation upwards. While a Tory Government keeps direct taxation as low as possible, Labour believes that proper government means more expenditure. And the capitalist class is snarling because, despite Callaghan's assurance, the new Corporation Tax took in 1968 £1¼ thousand million. Unfortunately, taxes on business are generally passed on in higher prices. Big business demands lower company taxation because higher prices make selling more difficult, and because rising taxation means that anyway their amount of contribution goes up.

SHARES FOR ALL?

Linked with the never-ending woe-woe about taxation of profits is the myth of the widespread ownership of stocks and shares. Central in this propaganda is the poor widow who keeps herself just above the poverty line through her handful of shares and the meagre dividend a grateful and generous company sends her. According to this myth the majority of company shares are held in small packets by tens of thousands of such widows up and down the country. That terrible character, the nineteenth-century capitalist, whom Marx rightly reviled, has, thank heaven, gone. In his place is the board of directors, who own only a very small proportion of the shares and whose job is to see that the company makes a profit, or at least survives. Below the board sit the managers, who do not own shares (or only very few) and who often do battle with the directors over the running of the business. The boss is really the little widow with her 100 or 200 shares; it is she who has to be satisfied.

This fantasy lies at the heart of the theory of "managerial revolution". Yet, over a century ago, Marx even then observed how the owner was being displaced by the functionary, the capitalist by the manager. "The capitalist mode of production itself has brought matters to such a point, that the labour of superintendence, entirely separated from the ownership of capital, walks the streets. It (ownership) is, therefore, no longer necessary, for the capitalist performs the labour of superintendence himself. A director of an orchestra need not be the owner of the instruments of its members, nor is it a part of his function as a director, that he should have anything to do with the *wages* of the other musicians. . . .

"Stock companies in general, developed with the credit system, have a tendency to separate this labour of management as a function more and more from the ownership of capital . . . (until) . . . only the functionary remains and the capitalist disappears from the process of production as a superfluous person."[1]

Criticising the American economists, Berle and Means, who first used this displacement to prove "managerialism", the Marxist economist Aaronovitch writes:

"Marx asserted that the capitalist was *superfluous* in the process of *production* (he can die tomorrow and it will all be carried on as usual), not that he had disappeared from society. . . .

"The division of labour which in the past created a separate class to perform the indivisible and necessary function of both owners and supervisors of production has now so developed that such a class is unnecessary—and in fact objectionable."[2]

In this, as in other spheres, the very subject of sociology, which was built up to counter Marx and Marxism, has paradoxically produced researchers whose work refutes the refuters. First, recent studies show that, although share-ownership has grown absolutely, relatively it remains concentrated. According to Lydall,[3] in 1952 only 5½ per cent of "income units" ("units" are, in this case, roughly the adult population over 18 years of age) owned any stocks and shares at all. And about half of this 5½ per cent owned only £500-worth or less. Clerical and manual workers very rarely owned any. Lydall added that he was unable to get adequate representation of the larger shareholder, which makes his figure of 5½ per cent an over-estimate.

In a further survey of incomes and savings two years later (1954), the Oxford Institute of Statistics concluded that seven per cent of the adult population now owned all stocks and shares.[4] Lest this should suggest a small but rapid expansion in share-ownership, it is necessary to add that by 1962, according to the Wider Share Ownership Council, the proportion was also seven per cent.[5] Of all these share-owners, only 18 per cent were manual workers, and their holdings were certainly small. The picture remains therefore roughly the same.

The average amounts in stocks and shares held by various social

[1] *Capital* III, ch. 23.
[2] *The Ruling Class* (1961), p. 19.
[3] *British Incomes and Savings*, p. 96.
[4] *Bull. Ox. Inst. Stats.*, May 1955.
[5] Quoted in *The Anatomy of Britain Today*, p. 400.

occupational groups was shown in the following table, drawn up by the *Oxford Institute of Statistics* in 1956:

Sample Group	*Gross Income* £	*Net Income* £	*Holdings* £
Debrett	4,285	2,421	13,620
Directors	6,883	3,159	28,087
Doctors	3,036	2,077	5,811
Dentists	2,513	1,886	2,091
Accountants	2,676	1,774	5,965
Recent heirs	1,974	1,394	10,349
Mean of total sample	3,364	2,076	9,128
Mean of units with incomes £2,000 and over	4,520	2,628	13,077

Even the greatest stretch of imagination is hardly likely to conceive the average manual worker owning over £9,000 of stocks and shares; and if the "widow" owns such a holding she is hardly likely to be poor. Also these figures must be much swollen now with the rise in share values, which have more than doubled over the last ten years.

In his important and much-quoted work, *Ownership, Control and Success of Large Companies* (1961), Professor Florence described the growing concentration in industry between 1936 and 1951. In 1951/52 less than one per cent of all companies received 55 per cent of all company income. Four years later, just over one per cent of all companies earned 61% of all income. This inequality, he remarked, was wider than that of personal incomes (he wrote before Titmuss's book was published) and perhaps the maximum inequality known. The top one per cent of companies also accounted for 40 per cent of the business of all concerns in private enterprise. This concentration towards bigger and bigger companies was increasing, he declared.

Crosland, the reader will recall, did not find this disturbing. The trend towards bigger and bigger units, he argued, was taking place in all advanced industrial countries and much more so in the communist than in the capitalist countries, because of the need for over-all planning. What Crosland casually dismissed as "irrelevant" was who owned the companies. We have already quoted the fact that about seven per cent of the adult population own all stocks and shares. In fact, there is wide variation within the seven per cent as to the amount owned. According to Inland Revenue statistics for 1965–66, all British ordinary (quoted) shares are held by about 1½ million persons. 57 per cent of all the shares are held by about 11 per cent of these 1½ million persons, or by one third of one per cent of the adult population (170,000 individuals). *80 per cent of all shares are held by the top one per cent of the adult population (just over 400,000 persons).* This, to cap Professor Florence's claim, is in fact the greatest inequality in Britain today. It means that property and the power that goes with it are largely concentrated in the hands of the top one per cent of the adult population, 400,000 persons. We may regard this number (which excludes dependants), as roughly the size of the British capitalist class.

But, goes the argument, the vast numbers of share-holders, each with their few votes, can dominate meetings of shareholders. After all, the typical big company has on average 12,000 share-holders. Florence exposed the worthlessness of this argument. In any committee composed of two sections, the "resolute" and the "indifferent", it has been proved statistically that a small, resolute group can exercise a surprisingly powerful influence over the whole. Three resolute votes in a committee of 23 can control 75 per cent of all decisions. In a company with 1,000 voting shares, 60 voteholders (say, three individuals each having 20 voting shares) can carry all decisions with 96 per cent chance of winning.

Florence therefore investigated voting-share ownerships; and found a remarkable situation. By various devices votes can be concentrated (vote-gearing). In 1936 the 20 largest voteholders—roughly one in 600 of all shareholders—held on average 30 per cent of all the company's votes. By 1951 the 20 largest voteholders still held on average nearly 20 per cent of all votes.[1] Statistically, this assured pretty complete control of all the company's doings by the 20 top shareholders. Added to this is the well-known fact that shareholders' meetings are usually attended by only a handful of people, who generally don't know one another.

But within this small group there is still more variation. Size of holding tapers downwards from the top. The single largest voteholder holds on average over 40 per cent of the total votes of the group. Certainly there has been a drop in vote-concentration compared with pre-war. On the other hand, many of these largest single vote-holders

[1] "This represents far greater inequality than that of incomes for the country as a whole, even before taxation, and is similar to the extreme types of inequality shown by the national distribution of wealth." (Florence, p. 67.)

are institutions (banks, insurance companies, investment trusts), concealing some counter-concentration. Also the bigger companies have more interlocking directorates, which have been increasing in number.[1] Statistical examination, added Florence, shows that high vote-concentration among shareholders is usually connected with control by directors, who themselves have large holdings of ordinary shares (even though these large holdings might be a small *percentage* of the total). Florence emphasised that decisions do not always rest with the board of directors, many of whom only attend the monthly board meeting, but most likely with the chairman or managing director. Top managers, or large shareholders who are not directors, can also exercise decisive influence. But, generally, *the individual who has a large holding and is a director* is most likely to be very influential. Other directors help in determining broad policy and keep a watching brief for other companies they may represent.[2]

Despite all this, Crosland wrote: "The idea of the managerial revolution is now widely accepted." His argument rested on Florence's figures, given above, showing the falling proportion of all shares held by the 20 largest shareholders in 1951 compared with 1936. But he carefully ignored Florence's whole thesis about the small proportion needed by a resolute group for total control. Crosland also argued in great detail about the description in M. Barratt Brown's *The Controllers*,[3] which he claimed was false. Briefly, Crosland based his argument on the fact, which we have shown to be unimportant, that in most big companies the directors on average hold only small *proportions* of shares. Also that most shareholders are passive which, again, merely concentrates power at the top. It doesn't prove at all that power rests with the "managers", whoever they may be. The "passivity" line is overdone: everybody knows that in most organisations the ordinary member doesn't interfere much, provided the organisation is roughly carrying out his wishes, or is at least not making a hash of things. The same applies to business. So long as the shareholder is getting what he regards as a fair profit on his investment, he will

[1] *The Conservative Enemy*, p. 68. Strangely, too, Florence himself failed to grasp the meaning of his own statistics, which he interpreted as supporting the thesis of control/ownership separation and "managerialism".

[2] Copeman found in 1955 that 70 per cent of company directors held directorships in more than one company. M. Barratt Brown, in "The Controllers" (*Universities and Left Review*, No. 5) found that the directors of leading merchant banks and commercial banks held over 560 other important directorships, chiefly in the largest British industrial enterprises. For further details, see also Aaronovitch, *The Ruling Class*, ch. 3.

[3] *Universities and Left Review*, No. 5.

remain non-active. The argument about "owner-control" is really the red herring, which Marx landed a hundred years ago. In addition to the passage quoted above, Marx remarked that the coming of the joint-stock company meant that the private individual could now control social capital, i.e. capital in a company. Protected by the laws of limited liability, the company director now had far greater power, over far greater resources. Naturally, he helped himself to a large slice of the profit. As Marx very trenchantly pointed out, "a new swindle develops in stock enterprises with the wages of management. It consists in placing above the actual director a board of managers or directors, for whom superintendence and management serve in reality only as a pretext for plundering stockholders and amassing wealth." The position of the modern capitalist was far more secure than the earlier capitalist relying only on his own, plus some borrowed, capital. "A command of social capital, not individual capital of his own, gives him command of social labour."[1] This struggle for power and wealth results in some directors being ousted and new ones taking over; but the overall system continues. Again, Crosland plays down the influence of interlocking directorates; but admits (quoting Florence) that over half the very large industrial and commercial companies have directors in common. He repeats the argument about the "common goals of management in all societies", but is then forced to admit that they are not so common after all.

> "At one extreme, in a capitalist society where entrepreneurial income derives from profit, the economic goal at least is clear-cut,—the maximisation of profit.
>
> "At the opposite extreme of Soviet Russia, the goals are more complicated."[2]

Like George Brown, Ray Gunter and all other right-wingers, Crosland is very much in favour of *private* profit (*The Future of Socialism*, ch. 20). A Soviet enterprise also takes profit, though not maximum profit, as some sort of guide. What is the *real* issue, then? After many pages, Crosland comes to the point.

> "The real question is one of power and wealth. The corporation inevitably wields economic and social power; and it aggravates, especially through the medium of capital gains, existing inequalities of wealth. The essential requirements are therefore that the demo-

[1] *Capital*, III, ch. 27. [2] *The Conservative Enemy*, p. 85.

cratic state, by legislation, controls and taxation, should . . . correct the inequalities of wealth."[1]

But this is just where the "democratic" state has failed. This is just where we came in.

One final point. How is the enormous concentration of wealth in private hands possible when the State has such a large share in the economy—over two-fifths of the country's real property? The answer is that the State is hopelessly mortgaged to private individuals in what is known as the National Debt. At present this stands at nearly £30,000 millions, which is considerably more than the State owns. And we have, further, an increasing debt to foreign bankers, as the people are being constantly reminded. So State property, objectively the property of the people, is not ours at all, but in pawn mostly to a small, tightly-knit group of domestic and foreign bond holders, who fight among themselves even as they unite to protect their class interests.

WHO ARE THE RICH?

While Marxists reject Mills' and Riesman's more extreme theory of the non-existence of a ruling class, they do recognise the divisions within it. Now, when we talk of capital, we generally appear to mean only industrial and financial wealth. But much of England's wealth still lies in land and land-ownership. And although we rightly emphasise the interweaving of aristocratic and business families, of relatively impoverished aristocrats with new, thrusting, aggressive, industrial and financial magnates, wealth in Britain has a long history. Let us look at the oldest branch of Britain's ruling class, the landed aristocracy.

The popular picture of the twentieth-century aristocrat is mostly of an impoverished owner of a decaying castle, forced to open it to a trampling public at half-a-crown or five bob a time to pay crippling death duties and the enormous expenses of upkeep. But, as Anthony Sampson—no Marxist but (at least when he wrote his book) an enthusiastic disciple of Harold Wilson—first revealed in detail, this is a misleading picture.[1] In the first place, the aristocracy are still deeply involved in politics, though less so than in, say, the eighteenth century. Who would have thought that an earl would become British

[1] *The Conservative Enemy*, p. 91.

[2] *Anatomy of Britain Today* (1965) I gladly acknowledge taking a fair amount of my information about the rich, and especially about the landed aristocracy, from this entertaining and informative book, as well as from Roy Perrot's *The Aristocracy* (1968).

prime minister in the middle of the twentieth century, or that Labour would not merely refuse to abolish the House of Lords but endeavour, by legislation and the creation of a large number of new peers, to turn it into a second chamber? Reference books on the British nobility continue to grow. There are still nearly 1,000 hereditary peers and peeresses and 116 "life" peers. Of the 700 peers qualified to attend the House of Lords, only about 100 are Labour but 300 Conservative. The main feature of the pattern of "occupations" among the Lords, as Perrott points out, is a close balance between land owner and business director. Out of his random sample of 100 members of the House of Lords, 43 got their income wholly or partly from land ownership and 46 wholly or partly from company directorships. So, as Perrott correctly concludes, "... the Labour Party's gesture against the aristocracy, after all the inflammatory talk of the early days, was in fact an extremely conservative one".[1] Secondly, the aristocracy are still very rich. True, there have been many changes. Most of the great town houses have been demolished and replaced by hotels and office blocks. But the aristocratic landowners collect the ground rents, which allow them to continue to live and entertain lavishly, though perhaps less obtrusively, in their country houses.

The most exclusive and among the richest men in Britain are the dukes. The Duke of Beaufort owns 52,000 acres in Gloucestershire. The Duke of Buccleuch has three big country houses stacked with art treasures; he is also chairman of the Royal Bank of Scotland. The Duke of Bedford, who turned his Bedfordshire estate into a public circus, allegedly to pay death duties, makes an estimated £1,000 a week from it; and he still owns a great deal of Bloomsbury. The Duke of Northumberland owns 80,000 acres in his home county. The most political duke is Devonshire, nephew of Harold Macmillan and related by marriage to the late President Kennedy. He owns 72,000 acres, has a house in Mayfair, a shooting lodge in Yorkshire, a house in Ireland, and Chatsworth, his Derbyshire palace with 111 bedrooms where, as Sampson puts it, "he entertains ducally while the public mill around the lawns: even after £2½ million death duties, much of the family estate is still intact".[2] Finally, the Duke of Westminster, probably the richest of all, owns a large slice of central London, including most of Belgravia, 18,000 acres in Cheshire and Shropshire, as well as estates in Canada, Australia and South Africa. And this in spite of the incredible fact that when the 2nd Duke died in 1953 (Westminster is the newest of the

[1] Perrott, p. 5. [2] *Anatomy of Britain Today*, p. 9.

dukedoms), a whole sub-department of the Inland Revenue was engaged in collecting death duties. Eventually, the family paid £11 million on estates worth £50 million.

Some idea of the fabulous incomes required to keep up the pluto-aristocratic way of life (which, readers will remember, Weber and his followers tried to separate from ownership of property) can be gathered from the cost of upkeep of a very large household. According to *The Times*, quoted by Sampson, the staff of a big house would include butler, footman, chauffeur, chef, housekeeper, cook(s), nannies, housemaids, lady's maid, parlour maid; and according to the agencies this would cost about £6,000 a year. Yet officially, an individual with an income of even £100,000 a year would, after tax, be left with "only" £14,000 a year. And there are still a quarter of a million men and women in "private domestic service", including a considerable number in very large households. At regular intervals the careful reader of *The Times* Personal Column will see advertisements like the following:

> "Wanted for highly intelligent six-year-old boy. Governess capable of full instruction up to Preparatory or Public School stage and standards. Large staff kept and some months of year spent on Family Estates in France and Scotland. Please reply to the Hon. Mrs. Norman Butler, Kilboy Castle, Kilboy, near Dolla, Co. Tipperary, or care of Barclays Bank, Monte Carlo."[1]

The political and social influence of the aristocracy should not be underestimated for being less obvious; it is still very strong. Perrott describes "aristocracy" as the spirit of the élite of our present society. "It is an element which has *unconsciously* been present in the widest range of social and political matters: in the regulation of social stability and movement; the shaping of foreign policy, the formation of English attitudes to certain professions, to the ideals of education, attitudes to the countryside; the social categorising of various sports and pastimes; the code of manners which comes to be regarded as 'good form'; the design of middle-class clothes, and much besides."[2]

A very special place is occupied by the British royalty. Although not the richest (the wealth of the Queen of Holland, who is richer than Queen Elizabeth, is estimated at £200 million), the British monarch

[1] *The Times*, 9th July, 1966. The advert was immediately followed by another: "If any old clothes etc. to spare we would be most grateful. Rev. L. R. Moore, St. Lukes Vicarage, Victoria Docks, E.16."

[2] *The Aristocrats*, p. 21.

is still one of the richest women in the world. It is sometimes argued that the State makes a profit out of our monarchy because, in exchange for taking over Crown lands, the Government gives royalty incomes less than the £2¾ million a year the State gets from all Crown property. "But", Sampson comments, "the Crown lands should be regarded as belonging to the State, and by any calculation the monarchy is an expensive affair."[1]

Here are the main annual payments, tax free, to our royals:

	£
The Queen	475,000
The Queen Mother	70,000
Duke of Edinburgh	40,000
Duke of Gloucester	35,000
Prince of Wales	30,000
Princess Margaret	15,000
Total:	865,000

The Prince of Wales's allowance was, in fact, doubled when he reached the age of eighteen: and this piece of generosity was suitably carried out and defended by the Wilson administration during the toughest attempt at holding back wages ever carried out by a Labour Government. In November 1969, the Prince took over the Duchy of Cornwall but generously decided to retain only half its revenues, a mere £100,000 a year. In addition, the State, through the Ministry of Public Building and Works, pays for the upkeep of the royal palaces, total estimated cost in 1968/9 nearly £1 million, made up as follows:

St. James' Palace	£114,000
Buckingham Palace	288,000
Windsor Castle	277,000
Kensington Palace	30,000
Holyrood House	63,000
Other palaces etc.	54,000[2]

The Queen's Flight of two helicopters and five aeroplanes, looked after by 80 individuals, is paid for by the R.A.F. The costs of the royal

[1] Sampson, p. 30.

[2] *Civil Estimates 1968–69*. Class IX. Some e.g. Windsor Castle and Kensington Palace are partly open to the public. Note the expense of Buckingham Palace, enough to keep about 200 families.

trains, royal postage and telegrams (which have precedence) are all borne by the state. The yacht *Britannia* is paid for by the Navy: it cost £2 million to build, has a crew of 250 and costs nearly £400,000 a year to run. In all, as mentioned before, the monarchy costs us nearly £3 million a year.

It might even be argued that this fantastic expense is necessary to maintain an otherwise propertyless Head of State. But a list of the Queen's private possessions makes nonsense even of this. For she personally owns what is regarded as the world's finest private collection of art, small selections of which she graciously allows the public to view at half-a-crown a time in a little gallery set just inside the wall of Buckingham Palace. (The Palace itself has 600 rooms and is the largest private house in the country. A revolutionary government could turn it into one of the world's greatest museums.) She still personally owns Balmoral Castle and Sandringham, the royal jewellery (value unknown), the royal stamp collection (valued at over a million pounds), the royal racehorses (the Queen is devoted above all to horses) and five tons of gold plate. There have been various estimates of the Queen's wealth, but in 1963 Kingsley Martin reckoned it was probably between £50 million and £60 million.[1] None of this is ever subject to tax, although some of her income is; but some income is not, for example, her £160,000 a year from the Duchy of Lancaster. Her private income is in fact a secret and to the right-wing royalty, its privileges and wealth are an undebatable subject. Indeed, Prince Phillip's recent much-publicised remark about the Royal Family being in the red got the suitable reply from Mr. Wilson that the problem would be attended to after the coming General Election. It is almost certain that the State (i.e. the community) will shoulder an even higher burden of Royal "household expenses".

There has been no large-scale survey of land-ownership in Britain since 1873, but Mervyn Jones recently tried it on a small scale.[2] It seems that *less than one-ninth* is under public ownership, leaving fifty million acres in private hands. Of the latter over a fifth belongs to companies and trusts, but most of these are private companies and merely a disguise for individual ownership. The biggest private landowner is the Queen, who owns 239,000 acres *in her own right;* that is to say, apart from the Crown lands, the revenue from which goes to the

[1] *The Crown and the Establishment*, p. 142.

[2] Articles in *The Observer*, 21st March, 1965 and 28th March, 1965. Perrott provides a selective list of large estates held by members of the nobility (*The Aristocrats*, pp. 150–56).

Government and in exchange for which she gets all the income listed above. Next come aristocrats like the Duke of Buccleuch (pronounced Buckley) with 220,000 acres (over 340 square miles), the Countess of Seafield (213,000 acres) and Lord Lovat (190,000 acres). Size isn't all, however. The Duke of Hamilton's estate of a mere 13,000 acres covers the industrial towns of Motherwell and Cambuslang, where factory rents are 4½ times pre-war and development land is worth £3,000 an acre. The Hamilton Estates Company includes eighteen businesses, from hotels to sawmills. The wisdom of holding on to land lies not only in the fact that it is one commodity which steadily increases in value, but that estate duty on it is at the rate of 45 per cent compared with 80 per cent on other types of wealth of £1 million and over. Tax rebates on maintenance and improvement grants can be collected over a ten-year period. Even the apparently useless, wild country of the big Scottish estates has its value. "Increasingly it is being planted with forest", writes Mervyn Jones, "at a subsidy of £22 an acre and at a cost which is tax deductible. The Countess of Seafield is having a million and a half trees planted every year." Grouse moors are let at handsome rentals to the slaughterers of those birds and fishing rivers bring in £2000 a mile. The Countess of Seafield has nine grouse moors and 20 miles of the River Spey. " 'Don't attribute this quote to me', said the owner of one fine property cheerfully as I admired the family portraits, 'but the truth is—the landowner has never had it so good.' "[1]

Perrott compares a sample of estates held in 1967 with their sizes in 1873. His list shows that, despite some reduction (in certain cases substantial), nearly every estate is still of the order of thousands of acres. True, many estates have been given up entirely; but the fact remains that peers and old-established gentry are still easily the biggest individual landowners in every county which is mainly agricultural. Moreover, the value of agricultural land has increased four-fold over the last twenty years, more than offsetting, in many cases, the decline in size. In terms of land value now, the owner of a 5000-acre estate can call himself a millionaire. And all this under a Labour Government.

Interwoven with land-ownership is, of course, big business, and big business has replenished and expanded the aristocracy. In 1966 the

[1] *The Observer*, 28th March, 1965. This recalls a similar remark made by a stockbroker, who declared that stockbrokers ought to go on their knees and thank God for Harold Wilson.

boards of Britain's top hundred companies included 91 peers and thirteen held chairmanships. Most of these peers were newly titled. Among them were Lord Blackford (13 directorships, 5 chairmanships, peerage created 1935), Lord Brocket (9 directorships, 5 chairmanships, peerage 1933), Lord Caldecote (12 directorships, peerage 1939), Lord Geddes (12 directorships 5 chairmanships, peerage 1942), the Earl of Inchcape (31 directorships, peerage created 1929) and Lord Nelson (11 directorships, in electricals, peerage 1960). But some belong to old titled families, for example Lord Hampden (merchant banking, peerage created 1321) and the Earl of Verulam (engineering, peerage created 1633). One little aspect of this interchange is the sale and purchase of big country mansions. For example, in February 1967 Lord Ednam sold Great Hundridge Manor in Buckinghamshire to Mr. R. Ingram, son of a leading stockbroker, for over £200,000. Besides formal gardens around the house, said the report, there is an estate of 790 acres. "Lord Ednam, heir to Lord Dudley, and Lady Ednam have decided to live in London."[1] More recently Mr. Harry Hyams, the property developer, paid Lord Rootes, the car manufacturer, about £650,000 for Ramsbury Manor in Wiltshire. The aristocracy's business interests range over most of Britain's major industries.

Industrial and merchant capitalists, by intermarrying and otherwise joining up with the landed aristocracy, created the present ruling class.[2] This class itself splits into small fish and big sharks, with some movement between and among them. There is an expanding American element, following on the rapid increase in U.S. capital penetration. Also the ruling class recruits from among its abler, more loyal and aspiring servants. Why does it go on fostering an aristocracy? For the well-known reason that a nobility helps powerfully to sustain the idea of the naturalness and rightness of a class society. Above all, there is Royalty, which sheds part of its charisma on the "nobility" and without which aristocracy would lose half its reason for existence.

However, the bulk of the rich are not aristocrats (although a large proportion has some minor honour or title). Does this mean they have all risen from the bottom? Clore, Wolfson, Kearton, Thomson and Weinstock, to mention only a few of the best known, as well as a few wealthy young pop stars, strengthen the view that somehow a totally new, brash set of individuals has climbed to the top of the tree and usurped the positions formerly held through family inheritance.

[1] *The Times*, 20th February, 1967.
[2] Aaronovitch, *The Ruling Class*.

Undoubtedly as the capitalist system changes economically and technologically new people rise and others fall. But the power of background and inheritance is still much greater than the capitalists' hack propagandists want people to know. The table of shareholdings given above is one indication of this.

Another was provided by G. H. Copeman, editor of *Business*, who studied the careers of over 1,000 company directors.[1] Nearly three-quarters of them began in business and those with commercial or non-technical experience outweighed those with technical experience 3 to 1. Nineteen per cent had fathers who had been directors of the same firm. Twenty-two per cent had fathers who had been in "administration" or the professions. Over half started their careers with the advantage of having business connections in the family. Twenty-eight per cent succeeded their fathers in the same firm. As regards educational background, 58 per cent went to public school, 36 per cent to university, 20 per cent to Oxford or Cambridge. The younger the directors the more pronounced were these tendencies, showing the strong pull of background and inheritance in top business positions. Comparing his results with those found for the U.S.A. by Taussig and Joslyn, Copeman concludes that "... on both sides of the Atlantic only a minority of the leaders of large-scale industry got to the top without the benefit of influence or financial aid or higher education beyond the secondary school stage".[2]

Managerial revolution? Rule by the technocrats, the engineers, the experts, according to Veblen or Burnham? Or by the unschooled Clores and Thomsons?

In 1955 D. P. Barritt found that on average only one-quarter of the directors of 500 big firms had "formal" qualifications for managing a large business (university degree, professional, financial or other "paper" qualifications).

In 1965 the Institute of Directors itself published a survey of the qualifications of 10,000 company directors, showing that

13% went to secondary modern schools
15% went to technical schools
31% went to grammar schools
13% went to private schools
48% went to public schools
23% went to universities.

[1] Copeman: *Leaders of British Industry* (1955).
[2] Copeman, p. 132.

An analysis in 1967 of the directors of the leading 102 companies revealed the following:

Attended State schools	29%
Attended public school	71%
Attended Oxford or Cambridge	32%
Attended other universities	19%
Family connections with the company	17%
Previously employed by other companies	48%
Professionally qualified (accountants, lawyers, scientists, technologists)	27%
Other directorships	33%

The proportion who had attended university was even higher in the top ten companies, being nearly two-thirds. It was less in the fastest growing companies, due to the rise of new entrepreneurs (the Blooms, Clores and Wolfsons) but even then it was not much less: 27 per cent of all directors were ex-Oxbridge and a further 20 per cent had attended other universities. The investigator added that some of these figures fell short of the truth, because many companies were shy of revealing the secrets of their Board members.[1]

My own investigation of the chairmen of the 110 largest companies in 1968 also reveals that 77 per cent of all have titles (inherited or "earned"); additionally many are sons of titled persons, though without titles themselves. Fourteen per cent are scientists or technologists (mostly engineers), showing the relative poverty of promotion of such advisers. Some of them get State recognition, for example, Kearton of Courtaulds and Alan Wilson, his predecessor. There can be no disagreement with Anthony Sampson's comment:

"With all the talk in the past 20 years about the 'managerial revolution' it is often assumed that the revolution is virtually complete—that most of industry is run by committees of managerial men, divorced from ownership or ineritance. This is far from the truth. Only in a few giant companies which have outgrown their families, such as Shell, Unilever, or I.C.I. has the revolution been achieved; at the top of most companies an individual or a family still wields large influence."[2]

The figures also put the other popular myths into perspective. Despite the rise of new tycoons, the ruling business class tends to perpetuate itself; and in doing so acquires State honours, thus slowly (or not so slowly) infiltrating into the aristocracy. Nearly three-quarters

[1] R. Heller: "Britain's Top Directors" (*Management Today*, March 1967).
[2] Sampson, p. 529.

of top company chairmen have a title; and indeed it is becoming rare for a chairman not to be at least Sir A- B-.

The mixture of new with old is illustrated by naming some of the top businessmen in Britain today (1969), although the selection is arbitrary, because wealth concealment is such a fine art that figures quoted by the financial press can mean a good deal or nothing at all. But according to *The Times*, the ten *most powerful* company chairmen in Britain in 1969 (as measured by the proportion of the company shares they personally own) were:

Sir Max Rayne (property), grammar school and London University, married to Marquess of Londonderry's daughter
Sir Isaac Wolfson, elementary education only
Lord Cole (Unilever), educated at Raffles School, Singapore, worked his way up through United Africa Co.
Lord Cowdray (press) Eton and Oxford, inherited title, related to Churchills. Said to be the richest man in Britain and worth £100 millions.
John Brooke (Brooke Bond), worked his way up through family business.
Sir Jules Thorn (Thorn Electrical), own business, probably elementary education only.
Lord Iveagh (Guinness), 3rd earl, Eton and Cambridge, inherited business.
W. H. Whitbread, Cambridge, inherited business
Lord Rootes, 2nd baron, Harrow and Oxford, inherited business
Lionel Jacobson (Montague Burton)

"The new acceptability of the businessman", wrote Sampson, "can be detected everywhere: in the cosy gossip paragraphs in newspapers; in photographs in *The Times* of boards of directors staring at their blotting paper; in the university 'Magnates Club' at Oxford; in advertisements showing lovable chairmen on winter cruises. The old aristocratic prejudice against trade—always hypocritical—has weakened. 'When I was a boy', said Sir Miles Thomas, chairman of Monsanto, 'I was always told that the gentry didn't want to soil their hands with trade; nowadays it's very different. I'm a member of White's, for instance, and people like Lord Dudley and his brother are very proud of their place in business."[1]

Within a few days of the Tories' defeat in the 1964 General Election, ex-ministers rushed off to, or were whisked on to, the boards of big companies. Reginald Maudling, ex-Chancellor of the Exchequer, scooped up directorships of Dunlop and Kleinwort Benson, the powerful merchant bank. Edward Heath joined the board of another

[1] Sampson, p. 562.

merchant bank, Brown Shipley. Ex-housing minister Sir Keith Joseph returned to Bovis, the family firm of building contractors. Geoffrey Rippon, former Works Minister, was rewarded with a directorship of another big building firm, Holland Hannen and Cubitts.[1]

Their incomes and the incomes of all top businessmen were, until recently, difficult to find out, unlike the U.S.A., where they have always been openly published, probably as an incentive in the country where a working man can supposedly rise easily to riches. In Britain, each company gave the total of its directors' "emoluments" and students could only work out an average per director. For example, a 1965 list of top emoluments gave the following:[2]

Company	*No. of full time directors*	*Average directors' emoluments*
Plessey	6	£35,500
B.M.C.	7	34,400
I.C.I.	15	32,633
British Petroleum	7	31,427
Boots	7	30,660
Leyland Motor	7	27,652
Unilever	22	27,500
Dunlop	10	27,461
Shell	8	27,333

These figures did not include "expenses" and other fringe benefits, which did not have to be revealed in the published accounts. Such average figures concealed wide variations; for example, it was well known that Paul Chambers, then chairman of I.C.I., got around £50,000 as against the average £32,633; Sir William Black, then Chairman of Leylands, was entitled to £89,000 a year and Sir Donald Stokes (as he then was) its managing director, to £45,000, although according to *The Times* full emoluments were not taken up in every case.

The 1967 Companies Act, requiring businesses to publish fuller details of their directors' "salaries", confirmed what previously might have been regarded as just "left-wing propaganda". But the latest company reports at the time of writing show the "top ten" to be

[1] The full details of all such connections is provided regularly by A. Roth: *The Business Background of M.P.s.*

[2] *Labour Research*, August, 1967. Part-time directors were left out, £2,000 being deducted for each from the total of emoluments.

Company	*Chairman*	*Salary*
Marley Tile	Owen Aisher	£77,460
Shell Transport	David Barran	72,818
I.C.I.	Sir P. Allen	45,750
British Leyland	Lord Stokes	45,000
Assoc. Portland Cement	Sir J. Reiss	42,401
Tube Investments	Lord Plowden	42,000
Turner and Newall	R. Bateman	41,336
E.M.I.	Sir J. Lockwood	41,000
G.K.N.	R. Brookes	35,000[1]

Even this list is incomplete; for example, Sir Paul Chambers in his new post of chairman of the Royal Insurance Group is missing and only a few days later Cope Allman International's accounts showed that Leonard Matcham received £40,472 as 1967/68 chairman. Also in 1968 David Hegland of Vauxhall got over £64,000, John Clark of Plessey over £50,000, Sir M. Bridgeman (B.P.) and John Davis (Rank) £50,000 each. Many company chairmen do not necessarily have large holdings, but some, like Aisher and his family (total including trusts over £7½ millions) do. The latter tend to be heads of family concerns. Other family concerns pay themselves (i.e. family owners and other partners) little in the way of "salaries"—the few big owners live on the dividends, for example, Sir J. Cohen, H. Kreitman and L. Porter of Tesco Stores, who each hold over £11 million worth of shares. Most chairmen of the biggest companies do not hold quite such large blocks of shares, relying for policy control, as was explained before, on their innermost circle of major shareholding directors.

"The whole subject of boardroom wealth in Britain", says the author of the article, *Sunday Times Business News* Editor, Peter Wilsher, "is wrapped in layers of myth and ignorance. On the one hand there is the Left-wing view that anyone described as a company director is at least second cousin to a Rockefeller; on the other, the Right-wing version, most trenchantly expressed some years back by Lord Robbins,[2] that the tax-structure is 'relentlessly, year by year, rushing us towards collectivism and propertyless uniformity' . . . the results (of Wilsher's survey) . . . show, if nothing else, that big money has not totally disappeared in the course of the twentieth century managerial revolution."

Open publication of company directors' incomes has started up

[1] Quoted from *Sunday Times*, 30th March, 1969.

[2] Who will be remembered as chairman of the governing body of the London School of Economic s.

controversy. Through their press the industrialists and financiers argue that (*a*) these "salaries" are necessary to attract and hold that scarce managerial and entrepreneurial talent[1] and (*b*) they are small beer compared to the incomes of American magnates. Recently the heads of our nationalised industries, led by National Coal Board chairman and former union official Lord Robens, agitated about their salaries which, though ranging from Sir Stanley Brown's £11,000 to Lord Melchett's £16,000, were, they said, too low; and naturally their cry was answered. Over three years their pay will be increased to up to £20,000. The chief executive of the C.W.S. was recently appointed also at a salary of £20,000 a year. Significantly, the C.W.S. is joining with big capitalist concerns in the exploitation of Co-op products.

The Times' list of the 300 biggest companies in 1966 reveals how private wealth accumulates—through the workers' labour. Net profit per employee in the five largest companies was as follows:

Company	*Net profit per annum per employee*
B.P.	£15,500
British-American Tobacco	1,370
I.C.I.	920
Unilever	790
Imperial Tobacco	1,190

Mr. Peter Shore, then the new Labour M.P. for Stepney and an avowed left-winger, now Mr. Wilson's right-hand man on economic affairs, moved a bill in February 1965, for the disclosure of pay and expenses of all directors earning £10,000 a year or more. The Government refused to support the bill and it died still-born. Thus we shall not know what, over and above the huge emoluments listed, directors gain by way of "expenses" and other perks. And on 28th November 1969, Labour M.P. Arthur Lewis asked the Secretary of State for Employment and Productivity (Mrs. Barbara Castle) if she would refer to the Prices and Incomes Board the evidence showing that company directors had had their salaries increased over the past three or four years by amounts ranging from 5 per cent to 50 per cent. The Minister's reply was: No.

As for their way of life and, especially, the way of life of their wives, mistresses and offspring, the high and low snob press are only too

[1] How did the socialist countries, in particular the U.S.S.R., achieve their industrial progress without the fantastic salaries?

anxious to reveal details. You may read "William Hickey's" snippets in the *Daily Express*, or *The Queen*, the *Illustrated London News* and the newer, smart magazines, plentifully peppered with photos of the smiling upper set. Just when the Wilson Government imposed the wage-freeze upon the working population, one of the Sunday papers devoted part of its colour supplement to the "debs", no longer presented to the Queen, alas, but still busy hunting for eligible bachelors. About one deb dance it wrote:

> "But it's not the catering that runs away with the biggest money, though nobody's going to see any change from well over £1,000; the transformation of a backyard into a garden runs away with several times that sum. No one mentions money; Anna's mother says she doesn't even ask for estimates; but there's no doubt the bills will be large enough to keep half a dozen families well above the poverty line for a year. 'They're not skimping', said one of the interior decorators. 'Ten thousand for the whole dance, I'd say.' It might be more: it won't be very much under."[1]

Nor is there evidence of any slackening in the round of jollities. While, for example, members of the National Union of Teachers were imposing sanctions partly in response to an inadequate pay award, the following advertisement appeared on *The Times*' front page:

> "'Andes' 78-day Winter Cruise. From Southampton, January 7th. The reshaped itinerary of this oustandingly attractive cruise now includes visits to Teneriffe, Luanda, Durban, Colombo, Singapore, Penang, Mauritius, Cape Town, St. Helena, Rio de Janeiro and Madeira. Accommodation (limited to less than 450 passengers, all first-class) is available from £1,055 per person (double-cabins only)."[2]

"Far from the Season wilting," wrote Roy Perrott in 1967, "the dynamic surge for social recognition was making it uncomfortably overcrowded. 'Try getting to the paddock at Royal Ascot', a columnist complained, 'and the chances are you turn up like a piece of driftwood at the Tote.' By 1967 there were at least six times more private events than there had been in the 1930s: about two hundred private dances in town and country, each with around four hundred guests, and a similar number of small ones; and five hundred cocktail parties.

[1] *Sunday Times*, 7th August, 1966.

[2] *The Times*, 9th September, 1967.

Though the number of 'official' debs had stayed about the same at four hundred, there were now reckoned to be at least 1,500 extra describing themselves as such. Competition for a mention in the gossip-columns had become fierce; public relations men were hired by some."[1] And so we could go on.[2] How empty do the vapourings of those sociological apologists sound now, who base their case on the alleged reduction of inequality of incomes. How worthless are those brave words about Labour's aim of reducing this inequality, in the face of mounting evidence to the contrary, not least Douglas Jay's own retort when dismissed by Prime Minister Wilson that there was still a great deal to be done by Labour in the sphere of social justice! Crosland denies there is a capitalist class? But such a class derives its way of life from its wealth and income, which in turn come directly from share or land ownership, or in the form of "fees" or "emoluments" derived from private profit or, usually, both. Either way they are members of the families comprising the capitalist class, the class which the statistics have shown own the bulk of the nation's capital.[3]

Let this argument be summarised in the words of a leading Tory publicist:

> "... when we come to examine the whole spectrum of our 'wealthy class', it becomes obvious that the diversity is very wide. Not only is the Marquess of Salisbury not at all the same sort of person as Jack Cotton, he is not even in the least the same sort of person as the Duke of Bedford. The importance of Charles Clore is quite different from that of the Duke of Norfolk. Whereas the importance of the Grosvenor family or Lord Cadogan can be said, without disrespect, to depend largely on what they own, that of Dr. Beeching depends primarily on what he does, that of Sir Hugh Fraser or Sir Isaac Wolfson on a combination of what he owns and does, and that

[1] *The Aristocrats*, p. 229. Of course, not all the rich go in for conspicuous consumption, in Veblen's famous phrase. Some, especially those whose power and influence do not need to be bolstered by public display, can even publicly do the opposite, as on the famous occasion when Macmillan was photographed wearing patched trousers. But this means they consider public display just bad taste.

[2] Judith Todd gives more examples. See *The Conjurors.*

[3] On Monday, 20th November 1967, James Callaghan, then Chancellor of the Exchequer, announced devaluation of the £ by 14·3 per cent. He admitted it would result in a rise in the cost of living of about 3 per cent. On that very day, *The Times* disclosed that the devaluation would also result in a rise in the value of private British capital overseas of about £450 millions! Such is a consequence of a right-wing programme for Labour solving the country's problems.

of Lord Poole on a combination of what he does and what Lord Cowdray owns.

"But there is a sense in which the wealthy do tend—and always have tended—towards becoming a more homogeneous social class. The homogeneity of the class is invariably slightly marred in each generation by the irruption of new men with their own idiosyncrasies, by the behaviour of the inevitable mavericks and even by an occasional throwback among the inheritors of wealth. But the influence of wealth upon the *families* of rich men—and perhaps even more the influence of the families on the rich men themselves—does tend to give these families certain common characteristics and something of a common way of life.

"This is of course truer of second and subsequent generations of wealth, but it is to some extent true even of the first. The wealthy do tend to send their children to the same sort of schools, to live in the same kind of country houses and the same areas of London, to go to the same sort of place for their holidays, to drive (or be driven) in the same kind of car and to frequent the same kind of hotel and restaurant. This often makes them appear to be much the same kind of people, not readily to be distinguished from one another at deb dances or in the Royal Enclosure at Ascot. They may be loud and arrogant, or quiet and detached, or sweetly gentle and polite. But in the end, they all look and sound like money.

"To this extent they are a social class and they exercise a social influence."[1]

WHO RUNS BRITAIN?

Some sociologists and right-wing apologists would agree that a wealthy class continues to exist in Britain and even defend it, as Pareto did. Where they otherwise part company with Marxists is whether this same small group exercises the real power in our society. Certainly, Crosland and Strachey argued, the capitalist class had economic power before the war and used it ruthlessly, but "Today the capitalist business class has lost this commanding position".[2] To whom? To public authorities, chiefly State bureaucracy, to the nationalised industries (run by the "largely autonomous class of public industrial managers") and to labour. Galbraith talks about the "counter-

[1] "Wealthy People", by Angus Maude (*Aspect*, April 1963).
[2] *The Future of Socialism*, p. 26.

vailing power" of workers' unions and of the consumer. Riesman and other American sociologists theorise about the dispersal of power; and Sampson follows them at first in confessing not to know who runs Britain. (In the second edition of his book, however, despite Wilson's premiership, he openly wrote that the influence of a "relatively tiny group from a few public schools" outweighed that of the Labour Government.)[1] Even C. Wright Mills demurred at the idea of a "ruling class", preferring the view that there were three separate "élites", the military, business and political, and that they combined only in times of crisis. Tory publicist Maude happily adopted this line, too.

But this line was dramatically exposed (if it wasn't already exposed by the whole post-war history of British governmental economic and foreign policy) when the Tory Government fell in 1964 and there was a scuttling of ex-ministers to the boardrooms of many of the biggest companies. The interlocking of company directorates and their actions as pressure groups[2] were reinforced by direct political interweaving. In some cases the ex-ministers were returning to boardrooms they had formally vacated on becoming ministers. In addition, it is well-known that of the 21 Tory ministers 18 went to public schools—10 to Eton, the rest to Harrow or one of five other top schools—14 were formerly company directors and almost all had considerable shareholdings or ownership of land. Out of 39 Cabinet and non-Cabinet ministers in 1962 there were eight barons and other peers. Among the old Etonians were Sir Alec Douglas-Home, Harold Macmillan, Quintin Hogg, Duncan Sandys, Sir Peter Thorneycroft, Sir Edward Boyle, Christopher Soames and Butler. Macmillan was a director of the family publishing company; Butler twice married a Courtauld; Home owns several thousand acres in Scotland and was a director of the Bank of Scotland; Duncan Sandys (understandably) was on the board of Ashanti Goldfields in Africa; Enoch Powell was a director of the A.E.G. Unit Trust and is now on the board of the National Discount Co.; Marples, ex-chairman of Marples Ridgeway, now a Lloyd's Broker; and Basil de Ferranti, one-time Minister of Aviation, has recently shown his firm's ability to extract excessive profit on arms contracts. Selwyn Lloyd went back to Alliance Assurance; Harold Watkinson scooped very lucrative directorships of Plessey's and Schweppes; Eccles went to Courtaulds,

[1] *Anatomy of Britain Today*, p. 680.

[2] See S. E. Finer, *Anonymous Empire*. Professor Finer sees nothing wrong in this.

as did Aubrey Jones until his appointment as chairman of the Prices and Incomes Board. Lord Hill of Luton, new B.B.C. chairman, moved into the board of the giant chemical combine, Laporte Industries. Macmillan is related by marriage to the Duke of Devonshire and to Lord Salisbury, the aged defender of the Smith regime in Rhodesia, as well as to Lord Dilhorne, ex-Tory Lord Chancellor. Lord Cowdray, owner of vast press interests and reckoned to be worth £100 million, is married to the late Sir Winston Churchill's cousin. Julian Amery, former Minister of Aviation, was of course Macmillan's son-in-law. The wealthy without political influence?

But these Tories are out of office. (For how long?) Instead we have a Labour Government. Who are these men who now (1969) lead this country? Much used to be made of the fact that Wilson and two of his top ex-lieutenants, Brown and Callaghan, come from modest backgrounds. Wilson's father was a works chemist, Brown's a lorry driver and Callaghan's a chief petty officer. Wilson, academically brilliant, went to Oxford and became a university lecturer before entering the upper ranks of the Civil Service. George Brown soon left manual labour in the background to become a T. & G.W.U. official in his twenties. Callaghan began working life in the Inland Revenue and became an official of the union before entering parliament. Thus we see the modest background as springboards for able and ambitious young men with Labour views formed by these backgrounds. And they were not unique; the backgrounds of the Labour renegades of 1931—MacDonald, Snowden, Thomas were even lower socially than those of Wilson and Callaghan (though similar to Brown's). It doesn't need middle or upper-class origins to be right-wing.

But Brown is today an exception.[1] An examination of the backgrounds of the chief Labour Government ministers in 1969 showed the following: of 24 Cabinet Ministers nine went to grammar school, nine to public school, 17 to university, 11 to Oxford. As Sampson wrote: "At the heart of this world (of the Labour leadership—H.F.) are the group of ex-Oxford politicians who now occupy top positions in the government."[2] And, he adds, ". . . most of them are 'revisionists', bored by old party dogma, rather ill-at-ease in trade union gatherings and looking torwards the kind of classless, half-American society outlined in Anthony Crosland's books . . ." Reshuffles and resignations have reduced the working-class element still further:

[1] Also he is now (1969) no longer a member of the Government.

[2] Sampson, p. 115.

Bowden, Bottomley, Griffiths, Lee, Fraser are out, not to mention Cousins. Apart from Callaghan, all the top ministers today are—ex-Oxford!

"It is not always easy", he continues, "to differentiate the Oxbridge Socialists, sipping whisky in Kensington, from the Bow Groupers, or to detect what mysterious force, if any, has pulled one group to the left, the other to the right. There are radicals and reactionaries on both sides, and the words left and right often seem to lose their meaning."[1] Furthermore, the movement between company boardroom, top civil service, nationalised industries and the Labour Government continues to grow. Both George Brown and Douglas Jay have joined Courtaulds in executive positions. Richard Marsh, ex-Transport Minister, is now a company director as well as an M.P. Conversely, more and more Tories and big businessmen have been drawn into the so-called "socialist" state apparatus, or have switched back to big business after occupying a high State post. The former Tory Minister, Aubrey Jones, is the retiring £16,000 a year head of that very influential body, the Prices and Incomes Board. Lord Melchett, banker and son of the founder of I.C.I., became chairman of the new nationalised Steel Board at £16,000, rising soon to £25,000 a year. Sir R. Edwards, former chairman of the Electricity Council, has taken over Beecham's. Sir Joseph Lockwood, boss of E.M.I. (the giant musical and gramophone record combine), is chairman of the Industrial Reorganisation Corporation, whose job is to speed mergers; its managing director, C. H. Villiers (Eton and Oxford), salary £20,000 a year, is also on the boards of the Standard Bank, Sun Life Assurance and Banque Belge. Last but not least the new director-general of the Confederation of British Industry (the employers' national organisation), Campbell Anderson (Rugby and Cambridge) a former director of Richard Thomas and Baldwins, the steel concern, was until recently the Labour Government's chief adviser on industrial affairs.

Peter Wilsher, editor of the *Sunday Times Business News*, in the article already referred to, writes:

> "Perhaps the most hopeful development, though, is the steadily increasing cross-flow of high-powered people between the sectors of independent entrepreneurship, established industry and the various ramifications of Government and quasi-Government enterprise."[2]

[1] Sampson, p. 119.

[2] Article, "Pay and Wealth", *Sunday Times*, 30th March, 1969.

Now this situation leads us back to the theory of élites. The reader will recall that, according to élite theory, people rise to the top of society because of inherent superiority (mental or physical or both). Important élitists like the right-wing Pareto, as well as the left-wing Wright Mills, stressed the connection between élites and wealth, but for opposite reasons, Pareto to defend it, Mills to attack it. But élite is not necessarily the same as ruling class. For example, Mills included "celebrities" (mostly entertainment idols) as part of the "power élite". Of course, a few may be capitalists, but only a few. In other words, within capitalist society there are always aspirants to, and willing servants of, the capitalist class and its inner, ruling group. Some élites, particularly the celebrities for whom Mills uses some of his most scathing remarks, are not at the centre of power; their contribution is, like that of the yellow Press, to dazzle and befuddle the people. Similarly, the right-wing Labour leaders are an élite who serve to confuse people. Raised to power by the votes of the electorate who want to see social progress, a few join the ruling class. Others strive but fail to join; and it is the particular historical skill of the British ruling class that it can absorb some of this Labour élite. It is the particular strength of British capitalism that there is always a section of non-capitalists willing and, in fact, eager to help perpetuate the system, some who have benefited from it, some hoping to benefit.[1]

Lord Balniel is one of those who can speak from the inside. Conservative M.P. for Hertford since 1955 and a member of the Shadow Cabinet since 1967, he is the elder son of the 28th Earl of Crawford and nephew of Lord Salisbury. He was educated, in traditional, aristocratic fashion, at Eton and Trinity College, Cambridge. In a recent essay he[2] stressed the curious situation of the British upper class that at one and the same time it, in the shape of the House of Lords, is despised yet still plays a significant role in the government of the country.

"Although the class has long ago shed the mantle of a ruling class,

[1] Among non-Labour men with humble backgrounds who do their bit for the ruling class they have joined the best-known today, apart from Edward Heath, is perhaps Aubrey Jones. Jones came of working-class parents, went on to the London School of Economics and rose rapidly in business to become, for a short time, director of the British Iron and Steel Federation (the employers' organisation), then director of G.K.N. and Courtaulds from 1950–65

[2] Lord Balniel, "The Upper Class", in Rose (ed.) *Studies in British Politics* (1966).

it has inherited a tradition of public service which gives it influence in the higher reaches of political and executive government. To demonstrate this one has only to look at the educational background of the (Tory) Cabinet (15 out of the 19 members having attended public school), or the diplomatic corps, or the colonial service, or the commissioned ranks of the army."

And later:

"They do not strive to maintain their position. Indeed a great merit of our upper class is that they do so little to remain 'upper'. . . . And just as Norman blood had to be enriched with American money, so the pulse of the Lords has had to be quickened, not by their own efforts but by the efforts of new arrivals. Indeed, the entire Establishment is preserved not so much by the conscious efforts of the well-established, but by the zeal of those who have just won entry, and by the hopes of those who still aspire."[1]

Yet it would be flying in the face of facts to deny that the representation of the people has altered. Decades of struggle, peaceful and violent, had to be fought to gain universal franchise. At first, the aristocracy allowed the vote to go only to the rising middle class, then slowly, piecemeal, to the working class. Women didn't fully get the vote until 1928. But by the last quarter of the nineteenth-century, working men were getting into Parliament, even if on the Liberal ticket. By 1906 the new Labour organisation got 30 members and since then there has always been a substantial number of Labour members in the House. Working men have also gone "up" into the Lords and apparently in increasing numbers. But when, from a broad picture, we come down to statistical details, something, again, rather different from the popular conception, emerges.

The ruling group in the politics of the British State is, of course, the Cabinet. Manual workers did not enter the Cabinet until 1906, but the proportion of aristocrats began an uneven decline before that, while the proportion of the new middle class rose to a peak in Lloyd George's post-World War I Cabinet.[2] The trend is shown in the table below:

[1] Same. Notice how he uses the terms "upper class" and "Establishment" interchangeably.

[2] W. L. Guttsman—*The British Political Elite*.

Class Structure of Cabinet Personnel 1868–1955

	1868–86	*1886–1916*	*1916–35*	*1935–55*
Aristocracy	27	49	25	21
Middle Class	22	49	62	57
Working Class	—	3	21	21
	49	101	108	99

Guttsman's breakdown must be treated carefully, however. His "working class" includes not only those whose fathers were manual workers, but those whose fathers were clerks, tradesmen, or members of the armed forces. Thus, it is not clear how many had fathers who were actually *manual* workers. The indications are that very few were. Equally the "middle class" includes, in the current academic fashion, many whose fathers were business men, professional workers, administrators and the like, some possibly belonging to the ruling class, many on its fringe, few on the fringe of the working class. In this breakdown therefore, both "working" and "middle" classes tend to be weighted on the upper side. Nevertheless, the table indicates only a slight increase in "working-class" membership of the Cabinet since 1916, with only a slight decline in the proportions of aristocrats and "middle class". Hardly a revolution! In fact, Guttsman goes on to show that the overwhelming majority (85 per cent) of middle-class members of the Cabinet belonged to the Conservative and Liberal parties. The class composition of the Cabinet remained heavily weighted towards the upper strata of British society and, of course, towards the Conservatives.

But, critics will say, this is all past; concentrate on the advance of the Labour Party since 1945. Out of the twenty-three years since, Labour has been in power ten; and the Labour Government is the government of labour, of the working class. But Wilson's Cabinets have been almost entirely non-working class, sons and daughters of professional and administrative people of the middle and upper-middle strata, marking the furthest step so far in eliminating industrial working-class influence (Attlee's Cabinet included such prominent ex-members, or sons, of the industrial working class as Bevin, Morrison and Bevan). This is not necessarily a deliberate move, but one dictated by the need for a common ideology, more easily shared by middle-strata intellectuals with a common background. An increasing number of Labour parliamentary candidates come from this class also.

Another way of looking at this trend is via educational background.

Education is very formative of an individual's ideology. Here we are simply concerned with type of school attended, showing parents' economic situation. Guttsman shows that between 1868 and 1955 only 41 out of 294 Cabinet members (less than a seventh) had elementary education only, but over one-quarter went to Eton and something like two-thirds either attended other public schools or were privately educated, leaving only 52 (about a sixth) with grammar school education. The relative decline of land-ownership among the aristocracy and their intermarriage with the rising bourgeoisie means that the Cabinet has remained dominated by the combined bourgeois-aristocratic élite. Career diplomats (often of aristocratic descent), barristers, bankers and "entrepreneurs" supplement the old landowning artistocracy and marry into it. A minority of ambitious trade union and Labour Party officials, coming into Balniel's category of "those who aspire", gives the false impression that in the last 50 years we have been increasingly getting "rule by the manual workers". Nothing could be further from the truth. The few ex-Labour Party and union officials climbing on their members' backs are often even fiercer in defence of the system than others—witness George Brown's and Ray Gunter's defence of private profit! A growing share of top positions has been going to a handful of ex-university teachers, specially skilled in switching from Left to Right. Labour Cabinets have always drawn most of their members from these aspirant groups and hardly any at all direct from factory, mine or mill. Increasingly the "uncommitted professionals" have taken over, aiming to run the system better (they hope!) than the Conservative capitalist-aristocrats—the "managerial revolution" is in business. Each time, as Labour fails, some of its leaders join the ruling class openly, usually via a peerage, or company directorships.

"The British upper class . . . comprises less than one per cent of all households. In the late 1940s the topmost one per cent measured in terms of wealth . . . and the boys who are currently educated at one of the 'top 20' most exclusive Public boarding schools comprise about 0·5 per cent of their generation. While these three groups are, of course, not completely identical, they do overlap to a considerable extent. The membership of élite groups is largely recruited from men who belong in any case to the upper layers of society."[1] Of these élites—parliamentary government, civil service, the law, the Anglican church, the military, Big Business, top professionals—the Government stands at the head. But, contrary to Wright Mills, the conclusion must be

[1] Guttsman, p. 321.

that, when it comes down to the issue of keeping the capitalist system going, they all hang together.

In fact, Britain is moving rapidly towards what the American writer, Eells, calls "metro-corporation feudalism". During the nineteenth-century, when companies were individually owned, governments assisted but did not generally interlock with them. Businessmen were frank about their aim—to make money. In contrast, the present giant combine (metro-corporation) is owned or controlled (or both) by a small group, who hide their real intentions by shouting about the "good of the country" and who are increasingly linked with the State, so becoming a quasi-public corporation with all the benefits of that linkage but without public responsibility. (There is a counter-movement of public (nationalised) corporations towards less and less public accountability also.) Untouched by "progressive" taxation the big privately-owned combines increasingly dominate State policy. It was towards this corporate feudalism that Mr. Peter Shore (then a rebellious university teacher) warned ten years ago that Britain was moving. The process is going on faster than ever; and Mr. Shore has become one of its willing, and well-rewarded, serfs.

Is there then a ruling class? Guttsman's answer is quite clear.

"There exists today in Britain a 'ruling class'," he writes, "if we mean by it a group which provides the majority of those who occupy positions of power and who, in their turn, can materially assist *their* sons to reach similar positions."[1] While its character and composition have changed, and there are fewer aristocrats, the rest are, he adds, almost exclusively drawn from the "upper middle class", a confusing term referring to all people in higher occupations, except the aristocracy. Its members have little in common with the lower middle class. As for those Labour politicians who have moved up, Guttsman's observation is the same as ours; they have . . . ". . . tended to become absorbed in the wider political ruling class". In doing so they have accepted its outlook, although they quarrel over method.[2] As the economic and political difficulties of capitalism worsen, the quarrels become noisier and internal squabbles over political position (who is to rule) increase, while Big Business re-asserts its claim to rule directly as the Labour "managers" fail. It is worth noting, in closing this section, that Guttsman reckoned the political élite, the directing core of the ruling class, to number only about 12,500.

Perrott reduces the very wealthy core of this ruling political élite

[1] Guttsman, p. 356. [2] See Aaronovitch, ch. 5.

still further. This innermost group he calls The Rich ("meaning very rich"). "The group comes together in an area of the plateau where the worlds of the influential business plutocracy, of inner Tory politics and the wealthier members of the old aristocracy, meet and find that they have something in common."[1] The Rich, in Perrott's estimation, numbers only one or two thousand. "Ye are many, they are few", wrote Shelley.

THE OLD SCHOOL

Does the "old school tie" still count as it used to? It certainly does. A study of the social background of higher civil servants found that there had been a lot of improvement since 1945 in recruitment for higher posts among the lower ranks of civil servants: but still only 50 per cent were recruited this way. Of the 1950 group of recruits (while the first post-war Labour Government was still in power), 23 per cent had been public school boarders and a further 42 per cent had been educated in private day schools. So that, in all, nearly two-thirds of all higher civil servants had come from the independent schools. Twenty-six per cent, i.e. over one-quarter, had gone to the top nine "public" schools. Roughly the same percentage had come from Oxford and over one-fifth from Cambridge, 16 per cent from other universities and just under 37 per cent from none. Although the Oxbridge figures were down compared with pre-war, in fact these top two universities had between them provided nearly half the top civil servants of that (typical) year.[2]

Their social class background was similar. Thirty-one per cent came from Social Class I (higher managerial professional and administrative, three per cent of the population), but less than two per cent from Classes IV and V (semi-skilled and unskilled workers, 28 per cent of the population); and these figures had hardly changed from pre-war. The only significant change occurred among recruits from the homes of skilled manual workers; their representation had doubled compared with 1929.

Using the finer stratification of the population in the 1951 Census into 13 "socio-economic groups", Kelsall found an even sharper class division among top civil servants. Over three-fifths had come from the higher and intermediate professional, managerial and administrative

[1] Perrott: *The Aristocrats*, p. 250.
[2] Kelsall: *Higher Civil Servants in Britain* (1955).

groups, but only 13·5 per cent from skilled and semi-skilled workers (together comprising nearly 60 per cent of the population). The rise of the sons of skilled workers was, nevertheless, evident from the fact that, of the 6 key posts (permanent secretaries of the chief offices and ministries), two had fathers who were manual workers and had come up through the Civil Service and grammar school. "Well done, thou good and faithful servant" obviously applied in those cases. Of course, of the other four, three came from Oxford and one from Cambridge. In sum, 90 per cent of higher civil servants came from the middle or what Kelsall, unfortunately in common with most other sociologists, confusingly calls the upper-middle classes. Among them were few scientific specialists. Also those civil servants who had risen through the ranks had got to the top at a late age.

The situation, despite all radical proposals, hardly changes. One recent survey shows that three-quarters of the teachers in the public schools are themselves graduates of Oxford and Cambridge, although this is an improvement on pre-war, when the proportion was over 80 per cent.[1] Evidence to the Public Schools Commission reveals that all independent schools, which educate only six per cent of the population, provide 40 per cent of the applicants *and 70 per cent of successes.* "In effect", says the report, "this means that in 20 years' time the majority of top-flight civil servants would be from exactly the same educational background as at present."[2] Among the "revolutionary" proposals now before the Public Schools Commission is one that 50 per cent of places should be allocated to State-aided pupils. But, the report goes on, already one-quarter of all places have to be set aside for such pupils and the "public" schools haven't changed.

The rewards of a public school education have been startlingly shown in a very recent investigation.[3]

Period 1950–56	*9 top public schools* %	*Other public schools* %	*Total public schools* %
Conservative M.P.s	41	42	83
Labour M.P.s	5	18	23
Top civil servants	14	45	59
Top managers		34	34
Top professions		69	69

[1] R. Szreter, in *British Journal of Sociology*, quoted in *The Times*, 14th August, 1967.
[2] *Sunday Times*, 23rd July, 1967.
[3] Bishop & Wilkinson: *Winchester and the Public School Elite.*

As compared with before the last war, the proportions have risen considerably. Thus in the 1930's, 78 per cent of Conservative M.P.s went to public schools, but by 1950–56, 83 per cent. Only nine per cent of Labour M.P.s between the wars came from public schools, but 23 per cent in 1950–56. Two-thirds of Winchester boys go on to University, but only 16 per cent on average from grammar schools, although their rating according to I.Q. doesn't warrant this enormous difference. Ex-Wykehamists (meaning ex-Winchester) include Crossman, Cecil King and the late Hugh Gaitskell.

The two authors, both ex-Winchester, are forthright in their conclusions. For the last century, they declare, the public schools have been a self-perpetuating élite out of reach of 95 per cent of the population. Their influence has been overwhelmingly class-biased and on the whole reactionary. And, far from declining, the only top group in which their influence has not been *increasing* is the Civil Service. Their characteristic, say the authors (like the ruling class they help to perpetuate) is their resilience: however much they are "diluted" with State-aided pupils, they remain the same.

But when all has been said, the question is still asked, is it really necessary to be "educated" to get to the top—is it *essential* to go to a private school to become a member of the capitalist class? Obviously, if we look at the Thomsons, Clores, Wolfsons and politicians like Bevin and George Brown, the answer must be, No. There are other routes than through a top public school and Oxbridge, or even a good grammar school and Oxbridge. It depends to some extent on what the aspiring youth wants to do. If he is the heir of a wealthy peer, then Eton or Harrow and Oxford become part of the grooming for eventual succession. If, like a large number of Tory and right-wing Labour politicians, he wants to climb the political ladder from relatively modest beginnings, public school and top University are undeniable assets.But, if the son of a manual worker leaving school early, a full-time trade union position is a favourite springboard for a political career (Bevin, Brown, Richard Marsh, Bottomley, Robens). Finally, if he merely wants to become a capitalist pure and simple, academic qualifications have relatively little direct value. The unity of the capitalist class is, after all, a unity in opposites.

There is, especially among middle-class, professional people, a tendency to overstress the value of education in getting to the top. They either despise, or aggressively defend, with a mixture of envy and admiration, the uneducated Bevins and Wolfsons. An eminent U.S.

sociologist investigated this problem, which is described in sociological jargon as whether or not vertical mobility is closely dependent on formal education.[1] Anderson referred to the fact that some previous investigations had found that, if sons had higher occupations than their fathers, they tended also to have higher schooling. But this, he argued, had not much significance. What would be more conclusive would be an investigation into the careers of those who had actually got to the top. One such investigation, by Carlsson in Sweden, published in 1958 concluded that schooling was, "hardly the decisive factor in the majority of cases where people have moved upwards on the social ladder". Carlsson's data of a national sample of men in Sweden showed that about four-fifths of the upwardly mobile, as well as of the downwardly mobile, had only had an elementary schooling.

Anderson went on to examine certain British figures produced in the 1950's by Professor D. V. Glass of the London School of Economics. Of 257 sons then at the top, 124, or nearly one-half, had inherited their positions. Of the remaining 133, 35 per cent came from the social stratum immediately below and only seven per cent from the lowest stratum of society. Half the sons who had gone up into the top layer had had the two poorest types of schooling. All in all, two-fifths of the top social layer originated in the two lowest strata of society and three-fifths of these (about one-quarter of the total) had less than a grammar school education. Like Carlsson's, Prof. Glass' figures showed that the distribution of the types of schooling among the upwardly mobile was not very much different from that among the downwardly mobile.

"While education certainly influences a man's chances to move upward or downward", Anderson concluded, "only a relatively modest part of all mobility is linked to education."[2] He found, of course, that education was least important for those who had risen from the lowest stratum to the highest (like Bevin and Wolfson).

In an earlier article, on the other hand, Anderson had demonstrated a correspondence between mobility and I.Q. He claimed that as much as two-thirds to three-quarters of all mobility correlated with I.Q. differentials. To put it crudely, this is the same as saying that the more intelligent tend to go up the social scale, the less intelligent to go down. But this, we ought to add, depends on the meaning of I.Q. and how far the whole concept of I.Q. is geared to a specifically bourgeois-academic

[1] C. A. Anderson, in Halsey, Floud and Anderson (eds). *Education Economy and Society*.

[2] Anderson, same.

idea of "intelligence" within a capitalist society. This is not the place to discuss that question. Nevertheless, it is true that, among those who have reached the top since the last war are many "managerial" types, whether financial experts like Chambers and Weinstock, technologists like Kearton and Beeching, or economist-politicians like Wilson and Crosland. But, like the property speculators, their promotion occurs in times of great technological and economic change. In order of ease of entry into the ruling class, it is of course the privileged inheritors first, then the experts and "managers" and, hardest of all, the new business tycoons and speculators. Having hoisted themselves up, the climbers pay for their sons' entry via the public schools and Oxbridge. It is, of course, true that *who*, among the aspirers, gets to the top depends to a considerable extent upon the individuals' characteristics (quick-wittedness and ruthless self-interest above all). But *who*, individually, gets there is related to the pattern much as the selection of officers affects a battle. Whether the battle is lost or won, which officers survive or are killed, does away neither with the fact of the battle nor the existence of a corps of officers. And, in a capitalist society, education is one means of rising. But, in the end, it is family or individual wealth that finally determines the power to rule, or to employ those trained (educated) to carry out the policies required by the owners of wealth.

THE SPECULATORS

Of all sections of the British capitalist class, one of the richest and most indifferent to the public good is the handful of successful property speculators. The post-war boom and an immense shortage of office space in city centres due to Nazi bombing gave these men the chance to exploit the demand (or speculate over demand) by the big firms for prestige head offices. This boom in office space provided for the speculators and their financial backers one of the biggest profit bonanzas of all time, brought the danger of an increase in traffic congestion such as London and other major centres have never seen and gave those centres the huge blocks of offices which were often still empty years after completion.

"The starting gun for the most intense phase of the property boom", Oliver Marriott, Financial Editor of *The Times*, tells us, "was fired on the afternoon of November 2nd 1954. Mr. Nigel Birch, Minister of Works in the first post-war Conservative administration, announced to the House of Commons that building licences were to be dropped entirely."[1] Two years before that, Macmillan, then Minister of Housing and Local Government, had abolished development charges, by which some of the improved worth of building sites went to the local authorities, with the memorable words, ". . . the people whom the Government must help are those who do things: the developers, the people who create wealth whether they are humble or exalted . . ."

And the developers were only too ready to be helped. Planning permission for offices by the Labour-controlled L.C.C. went up from 2·4 million square feet in 1952 to 3 million in 1953 to 4·7 million in 1954 and to nearly 6 million in 1955. By this time everyone going about in central London was aware of these concrete-and-glass, or steel-and-glass egg-boxes, being erected mostly for what purposes few people knew. The ruthlessness of the men behind it all came to public attention when, in 1957, Felix Fenston bought the St. James' Theatre and, in spite of a brave attempt by theatre-lovers led by the late Vivien Leigh to prevent that act of vandalism, demolished it for an office block. The names of Jack Cotton, Charles Clore and others began to be widely known and quoted with the sort of infantile enthusiasm that prompted Macmillan's description.

What exactly did they do? Here is an early example. A week before Mr. Birch ended building licences, 26-year old estate agent Harry Hyams bought the lease on a bomb-damaged site in Grafton Street, Piccadilly, for £59,000. Immediately after Mr. Birch's announcement, planning permission was granted for 40,000 square feet of office space on the site. Costs of construction came to about £250,000, bringing total costs up to about £310,000. The offices were let to Union Carbide, a giant American corporation, at £55,000 a year, after allowing £5,000 a year to the freeholders, the City of London. The building was then worth £840,000. Profit to Hyams and his solicitor, Spiro, £530,000.

The speculators "went to the market", that is to say, made their businesses into public companies, for two reasons. First, company taxation being much lower, they avoided very high tax rates on personal incomes. Secondly, since they themselves hadn't the enormous sums of money needed for huge building projects, they could, as companies, more easily persuade the banks and insurance companies

[1] Oliver Marriott: *The Property Boom*, ch. 1. I gratefully acknowledge drawing on this very readable book, the first detailed account of the whole fantastic business.

to lend. It did not, in fact, take much to induce the latter to back the speculators in view of the likely profits. Among those which benefited were Barclays, Lloyds and Midland Banks and the Commercial Union, Eagle Star, Legal and General, Norwich Union and Pearl insurance companies. In this way property development had the backing of some of Britain's most powerful financial institutions. This undoubtedly helped when local authorities had to be pressurised.

Were they men of particular genius? Not in Marriott's opinion.

> "Property developers", he writes, "have often been portrayed as wizards with land and money, and men with an uncanny foresight. This is nonsense. They deserved this reputation no more and no less than any other group of proprietorial businessmen. Some operated intelligently; others crudely. But they were men who happened to be in the right business at the right time and, given the profit margins in the business, could hardly fail to make money."[1]

What business? Estate agency. Forty per cent of them started as estate agents and another 10 per cent as solicitors. They were, of course, concerned above all with the highest possible profit; and that meant lowest possible cost. That meant that aesthetic design, even if the speculators were capable of appreciating it (and some were), counted for nothing. Nor were they always sure of a tenant or tenants. Some waited years and some are still waiting.

Who were the best tenants? The best *customers* were the big industrial firms; but the biggest single *tenant* was the Government who, Marriott tells us, were often referred to as the "developer's friend". Government offices occupied (at December 1965) over 41 million sq. ft., of which over half was on lease from private developers. These cost the Government an annual rent of nearly £11½ millions. For New Scotland Yard in Victoria Street alone, the police in 1966 paid a developer £6 million down plus an annual rent of well over £½ million. No wonder that over this particular item the parliamentary Committee of Public Accounts observed: "Your Committee take the view that the . . . Department showed scant regards for the interests of the Exchequer."[2] In all, the Government could have saved themselves nearly half the

[1] *The Property Boom*, Ch. 1. Marriott's view of their abilities may not be entirely correct. After all, even if in the right business at the right time, to seize the opportunity requires a certain audacity. Give the devils their due!

[2] Quoted in Marriott.

£11½ millions rent had they acquired the land and built the offices themselves. No wonder the biggest of them all, Sir Harold Samuel's Land Securities Investment Trust, value in 1944 when Sir Harold bought it perhaps £30–£40,000 was worth £11 million in 1952 and a gigantic £204 million by March 1968.

There were, of course, snags, chiefly the law; but the special ability of advisers (architects and solicitors) to find loopholes in the law enabled the developers to squeeze far more office space on to a site than the regulations intended. It was the specialist ability of architect Richard Seifert that enabled Hyams to erect Centre Point opposite Tottenham Court Road tube station.

Everybody who travels by underground knows how jammed this station is, even during off-peak hours: yet why was Hyams given the go-ahead? As Marriott tells the story, Hyams literally got the London County Council officials to turn a blind eye to his project. The L.C.C. wanted the land to make a traffic roundabout, but could not pay the exorbitant prices demanded by some of the owners, who were only too ready to fleece the Council. Hyams offered to buy up all the land in the area and hand over free the space the Council needed, provided the Council shut their eyes to his plan for a 385-feet-high skyscraper with exactly double the permitted building density.[1] Neither the Royal Fine Art Commission nor any other public body was consulted, nor did any firm or Government department request the building, which stands empty to this day (end of 1969). But it went up just the same, to the amazement of nearly everyone except Hyams, his associates Seifert and Wimpeys and perhaps a handful of L.C.C. officials. Did the Ministers of Local Government and of Transport know? We are not told. But we do know by how much Mr. Hyams benefited. Marriott calculates that the land Hyams handed over to the L.C.C. cost him £1½ millions; construction and interest charges £3½ million, making a total of about £5 million. The annual rental when the whole is let will be well over £1 million, giving a total value to the building around £16¾ million and a *profit on a single building of £11¾ million.* (or over twice the amount saved by the Government when it stopped school milk).

When, in 1965, Hyams decided to buy himself a country house, it was Ramsbury Manor in Wiltshire, the most perfect example of

[1] Hyams was introduced to County Hall by Lord Goodman, solicitor, friend of Harold Wilson, chairman of the Arts Council, director of British Lion Holdings. Lord Goodman, however, played no further part in the business.

Restoration architecture not open to the public. Once the home of the earls of Pembroke and Wilton, Hyams acquired it from Lord Rootes, the car magnate, for around £650,000. Hyams' personal fortune has recently been estimated at between £30 and £40 millions, making him one of the richest men in England today.

The profit on Centre Point is not, however, the biggest. The enormous development known as Euston Centre includes a colossal 34-storey glass tower (now, December 1969, nearing completion) opposite Warren Street tube station, in addition to a long shop-and-office stretch along the Euston Road. Owned jointly by Joe Levy of D. E. and J. Levy (the D. E. is now deceased) and Robert Clark, who is also boss of the Associated British Picture Corporation (presently under a takeover bid by E.M.I. for £43 million), it is the subject of a whole chapter in Marriott's book. In 1952, faced by a threat to use the law which would have awarded the developers £1 million from the Council for loss of development rights, the Labour-controlled L.C.C. gave planning permission for this enterprise. If, however, Levy (or his clients) were prepared to give the L.C.C. free that slice of the site needed for a new road, the Council would in return grant planning permission on the rest of the site to the same density as though the entire site was being built over. This arrangement was concluded. To raise the money for such an enormous development (nearly an acre), Levy and Clark joined forces with two giant building firms, Wimpey and Wates, and secured the financial backing of the Clydesdale Bank and its parent, the Midland. Within two years the share value of Levy's and Clark's company, Stock Conversion, leaped from £1 (1959) to £25 10s. (1961). When it is finished in 1970 the Euston Centre will be worth around £38 million. It will have cost £16 million, giving *a profit of £22 millions*. Of this, half will go to Wimpeys (Wates dropped out) and half to Stock Conversion. Levy and Clark will get about £5 million each.

In November 1964, shortly after Labour's return to power, although with a tiny parliamentary majority, George Brown performed, on the new Government's behalf, what was probably the most praiseworthy act of his political career. Alarmed by the way the speculators drove a coach-and-horses through the building regulations and the nightmarish effects all these so-called developments would have on transport within central London, Brown imposed a ban on all further office building in London and certain other cities. Unfortunately, those developers who got wind of it rushed through their contracts before the ban came into force, which explains why building is still going on. Unfortunately, too, in a capitalist society the ban has the effect of raising rents still further. No wonder that Hyams, the coolest customer of all, is prepared to keep his office blocks empty for years until he gets the rent he is demanding.

How much wealth these enterprising citizens of the "post-capitalist" epoch amassed can be reckoned by the rise in value of all property company shares. On 31st March 1958 the total value of all ordinary shares in these companies was £103 million. *Exactly four years later, the total value was £800 million, a rise of nearly £700 million.* "Since the majority of the companies were controlled by single individuals or within a family, and since there was no capital gains tax until 1962, this extra £700 million represented an astonishing increase in personal wealth in an age which has complained as never before of the crippling effects of tax on the individual," comments Marriott. By 1967 the total share value had dropped a little to around £600 million, but in the "bull" market period of 1967/68, under the Wilson administration, it rose to a new peak of £833 million. And, most recently (*The Times Business News*, 17th February 1969), Mr. Marriott has estimated that property company shares are now worth £1,350 millions. *So, in five years the wealth of the speculators has increased by about £1,250 million*, a sum so vast as to stagger the imagination. It is equal, for example, to over half the total national expenditure on the whole of education throughout Britain.

Now that the big rush is over, property speculation has entered on its next phase; combination on a truly big scale based on rapidly rising site values. Land Securities Investment Trust has already swallowed Cotton's and Clore's City Centre Properties and recently acquired the City of London Real Property Co., for which Hyams bid unsuccessfully, making Sir Harold Samuel master of a £400 million colossus, by far the biggest of all, and one of the richest men in Britain today. It seems likely that, having become part of the business Establishment, these top men will seek more joint enterprises with the Government. If the Tories return to power in 1970/1 a relaxation of the office ban is probable and we may see further monsters of development rising on yet more sites. In the meantime the speculators enjoy their enormous wealth and power, while an article in *The Times* of 14th February 1969 could be headed "Solution to the housing famine is no nearer" and Harry Hyams' empty skyscrapers soar above congested streets and overcrowded homes and workplaces.

NATIONALISED INDUSTRIES

A residual argument concerns the nationalised industries. Now covering a fifth of all British industry, they are mercilessly attacked day after day by the more virulent sections of the capitalist press. This must surely mean that they comprise a socialist pocket within the capitalist system as a whole and that their managements (boards) consist of socialists dedicated to putting people before profit. In this sense they would be an important breach into the system, proving Attlee's Government acted socialistically. Is that so?

Why did the post-war Labour Government nationalise several major industries so quickly after the end of the war? First, nationalisation of all the basic industries had long been a plank in every socialist and social-democratic organisation, from Marxist to Fabian. Nationalisation of the basic industries was essential to put an end to capitalist ownership, which had grossly exploited the workers for private ends and prevented the full use of natural resources and human capabilities. Sidney and Beatrice Webb, outstanding social-democratic investigators, proposed that the industries should be run by boards composed of administrators and workers within each industry, plus consumers' representatives.

But nationalisation was not unique to the 1945–51 Labour government. Between the two world wars, Tory governments set up the Central Electricity Board, the B.B.C. and B.O.A.C. Post Office nationalisation goes back to 1912. The 1929–31 Labour Government, with Herbert Morrison as Minister of Transport, nationalised London Transport, appointing Lord Ashfield, chairman of the old private company, chairman of the new board at a salary of £12,000 a year (which, reckoning the value of the pound then, must be regarded as way above the salaries of chairmen today, dwarfing even Beeching's £24,000). It was about this time, too, that Morrison refused worker representation on the board, arguing that appointments should be made only "on grounds of ability".

This principle was accepted by the Labour Party and T.U.C. in 1931, but continued to arouse opposition within the Labour movement. *Let Us Face the Future*, Labour's 1945 General Election programme, went a little way towards worker representation by declaring: "... The members of the Boards will be selected purely on the basis of their competence to manage the various industries, and should include representatives of labour." Since then there have been a number of such appointments, generally of ex-trade union officials of decidedly right-wing views, who have merely become part of the management, rarely dissenting from its viewpoint, at least publicly. And even Aneurin Bevan, as Minister of Health, refused worker representation on the highest level of the N.H.S., on the ground that he knew of no workers capable of rising to the job.[1]

The second reason for rapid nationalisation after 1945 was that, when taken over, all the industries were in serious difficulties and some in a very bad state indeed. Yet all, to varying degrees, have been re-equipped, modernised and expanded and all have improved in efficiency. Again, at least for the first 10–15 years, they provided security of employment and better pay than was usual under private ownership.

But they were bogged down by three serious defects. In the first place they were burdened with very heavy compensation, as the following figures show:

Transport	£1,132 millions
Electricity	508 millions
Coal	388 millions
Iron and Steel	244 millions
Gas	229 millions
— a grand total of	£2,500 millions

Not only were these enormous sums a first charge on the industries; huge sums had in addition to be borrowed from the State to bring the industries into a fit condition, just at a time when demand for the services they provided (heating, transport etc.) was expanding at an explosive rate. No government calling itself socialist could ever justify such enormous compensation to people who had, for the most part, allowed those industries to rot. Yet the Wilson Government coolly fixed a second round of compensation to the steel barons to the tune of £480 millions. Of course, the price of steel must rise; of course, there will be talk of "cutting costs" by "rationalisation", as in the railways and coal.

Secondly, the prices charged to industry and to the domestic consumer have been heavily favourable to the former. Indeed, in coal-mining the public can only guess what big business pays for its fuel, because the N.C.B. doesn't tell. On British Railways it costs a firm only 3·44 pence per ton mile as against 2·36 pence per *passenger* mile; and passenger fares have gone up while freight charges have

[1] In this respect Britain is behind many West European countries, especially West Germany. The newest (re)nationalised industry in Britain, steel, has however come forward with a worker-representation scheme.

gone down. Similarly, industry buys electricity at 1·48 pence per unit, but the domestic user at 1·95 pence per unit; while gas costs 2/1½d per therm to the domestic consumer, but only 1/4d. per therm to industry.[1]

Thirdly, they were from the start run as capitalist institutions by capitalists and their trusted lieutenants. Conservative governments, Clive Jenkins tells us,[2] tried to remodel the nationalised industries into carbon copies of big capitalist institutions with the task of supplying cheap goods and services to the private sector. But the Tory governments were only carrying out more openly and fully the policy implicit in the actions of the Labour government of 1945–51. For it was Attlee's Government which appointed big businessmen and their experts to the boards (plus the odd ex-union official, primarily to deal with "labour relations"); and it was under Attlee's Government that the nationalised industries started by selling their products more cheaply to private industry than to the domestic consumer. The nationalised industries, in Clive Jenkins' words, "... gave a shot in the arm to an ailing capitalist economy". The basic aims of the Social-Democratic pioneers were overturned.

Take, for example, the price of electricity, as shown in the table below:

Electricity supply: average price per unit sold (in pence)

	1948/49	*1952/53*	*1956/57*	*1966/67*
Domestic	1·34	1·47	1·58	1·95
Industrial	0·95	1·08	1·27	1·48
Domestic as % of Industrial	140%	136%	125%	132%

Under Attlee's Government, therefore, the domestic consumer paid more relatively to industry than under the Tories. Under Wilson's administration, the gap has rewidened.

The top boys running the industries reflect the policy Clive Jenkins describes so well. Writing in 1959 Jenkins analysed the boards and found the following:

Industry	*No. of board members*	*Former Company Directors*	*Professional or technical Reps.*	*Labour representatives*
Transport	13	7	4	1
Electricity	5	0	2	1
B.O.A.C.	10	4	3	2
B.E.A.	8	4	0	2
Coal	11	1	5	3

[1] Figures for 1967.

[2] *Power at the Top*, p. 21.

The pattern had been set, however, by the Labour Government of 1945–51. Jenkins tells us that by December 1949, of 131 names listed by Attlee on central nationalised boards 61 had other, private directorships, 23 were knights, nine were lords and three generals. In the nationalised airways, some board members had interests in private shipping companies, now joining with the private airways in competition with B.E.A. and B.O.A.C. The airways were thus used to profit private firms, even to the extent of joining with them to do so, for example, in B.O.A.C.–Cunard. Competition was forced on them: the Tories deliberately gave routes to private airlines and even compelled B.E.A. and B.O.A.C. to supply them with planes and lend them money. The first N.C.B. chairman, Lord Hyndley, was formerly chairman of Powell Duffryn, one of the giant mining firms. British Railways repeatedly placed contracts with private firms like Westinghouse, English Electric, British Thomson-Houston and Vickers, often without even asking for tenders. As a result the B.R. workshops were steadily reduced. Indeed, Jenkins shows that most capitalists on the board of the British Transport Commission never had any connection with railways. Finally, both the chairman and deputy chairman of the Gas Council in 1959 were ex-directors of National Benzole. The invasion of the oil companies into exploitation of off-shore natural gas was just part of the merging of private and nationalised industry, to the greater benefit of the former.

The composition of the nationalised boards has since steadily changed. In 1967/68 they were:

Board/ Industry	*No. of board members*	*Former company directors*	*Technical experts*[1]	*Labour representatives*
B.R.	8	2	5	1
N.C.B.	9	1	2	2
C.E.G.B.	6	0	4	0
Gas	(nearly all technical experts)			0
B.E.A.	10	3	5	0
B.O.A.C.	9	3	4	1

The former Iron and Steel Board, set up by the Tories when they returned the industry to private ownership, was, naturally, exceptional in its composition. Three prominent ex-trade union leaders, Lincoln Evans and Harry Douglass of the Iron and Steel Trades Confederation and Lord Williamson, ex-general secretary of the N.U.G.M.W.,

[1] There is some duplication here, as some technical experts are also ex-company directors.

demonstrated by joining the board how right-wing ex-union leaders identify themselves with Toryism as much as their predecessors Jimmy Thomas and Clynes did. The remaining seven members of the board consisted of top business men, mostly in iron and steel, an accountant (always handy) and a professor of economics.

The backgrounds of the present (1969) chairmen reinforce the picture given in the table.

Board	*Chairman*
British Railways	Sir Harry Johnson, secondary school, started as railway apprentice.
National Coal Board	Lord Robens, secondary school, ex-union official, director of Bank of England.
Electricity Council	Sir Norman Elliott, privately educated and Cambridge, engineer.
C.E.G.B.	Sir Stanley Brown, grammar school, Birmingham University, engineer.
Gas Council	Sir Henry Jones, Harrow and Cambridge, director of former gas companies.
B.E.A.	Sir A. Milward, Rugby and Cambridge, with BEA since 1946.
B.O.A.C.	Part-time chairman C. E. M. Hardie, chartered accountant, chairman of Metropolitan Estate & Property Corporation and director of many other companies.
National Steel Corporation	Lord Melchett, Eton, director Guardian Assurance. Grandson of founder of I.C.I.

We see, among the chairmen and via the table of the board membership above,[1] that the industries are run now more by elevated managerial staff. The boards still consist of a mixture of former directors of the nationalised companies, imported financiers and upgraded experts. As Kelf-Cohen points out,[2] initially the great capitalists from the industries themselves made sure they dominated the new boards. Once the policies were settled however, the post-war governments were content (as part of the "managerial revolution") to promote willing servants to take their places, knowing that these men would pliantly carry out orders, while big business men returned to their first interest, making profit in private industry. But capitalist policies applied to

[1] Salaries of all chairmen (except the recently constituted Steel Corporation) were raised by substantial amounts in 1964; and now (March 1969) by 20 per cent as the first stage towards £20,000 a year each. Lord Melchett does better still. In April 1969 his salary was raised to £22,500 as a step towards a final £26,000. (There have since been some changes in personnel.)

[2] R. Kelf-Cohen: *Nationalisation in Britain* (1958).

basic services bring the industries sharply up against the fundamental contradiction—that these services cannot be profitable, weighted as they are with the burdens of compensation, and at the same time cheap and satisfying public need. Hence the periodic crises and the need from time to time to draft in financiers like Melchett and Guthrie, and occasionally plain butchers like Beeching, to trim the sails of the industries to the prevailing wind. Crises appear less in younger growing industries, but even airways are meeting severe international competition and experiencing violent ups and downs. The crisis in transport particularly shows how public need is put second to the capitalist principles of reducing a money-losing service and forcing the rest to make a profit. In this case Britain's rulers are much more ruthless than their West European counterparts.

Thus the nationalised industries particularly demonstrate the contradictions one might expect from publicly-owned industry within a capitalist society. These industries were nationalised either because they had been run down under private ownership, or because they were considered important to the economy as a whole. In either case they were basic to the nation and had to be maintained. In most cases, the workers regarded national ownership as vital and Labour reacted to this demand with pledges of nationalisation. But they were never a socialist sector within the capitalist economy. Directed by former owners or other company-directors, and later jointly with "managerial" representatives of the capitalist class, burdened with heavy compensation and the requirement to provide their services cheaply to the private sector, they must be considered as State-owned industries subordinated to capitalism as a whole. As Clive Jenkins puts it, the nationalised industries became ". . . an instrument in maintaining the frozen class structure of British society".

Of course, to be State-owned is better than being privately owned; the Tories regard any extension of State-ownership as a threat. Hence, succumbing to Tory propaganda, right-wing Labour leaders have abandoned further nationalisation, except of steel. And in the notion of cutting losses and making the industries "pay their way", right-wing Labour policy converges to Tory. To allege, as Crosland does, that the industries are ". . . of greater significance than the economic power to control production and distribution. . . .", would seem to indicate one of two things: either Crosland has shut his mind to the facts, or he is trying deliberately to deceive his readers. Maybe he was doing both.[1]

[1] See Appendix 2.

IS THIS NECESSARY?

A lot of people still reply, when faced with the facts of great personal wealth, "Good luck to them if they can get it". The answer to this is threefold.

First it is, truly, a matter mostly of luck, of being born into the right family; and there, merit or ability hardly comes into it, except to make sure that one doesn't squander one's inheritance.

Secondly, while ability should, undoubtedly, receive its reward, the accumulation of great wealth is not necessarily its just or proper reward. Argument on this took place in the United States in 1953 between followers and opponents of Parsons' functionalist theory, Parsonians arguing that certain functions important to a society get due prestige and reward. The critics pointed out that basically the "functional importance" of any occupation or skill itself arises out of the type of society. So a company director will enjoy special prestige and wealth only in a society which recognizes his functional importance; in societies, whether pre-capitalist or socialist, which have no company directors, they will obviously have no functional importance and hence neither prestige nor wealth. Furthermore, there are other ways of rewarding special skills or important occupations than great wealth; in certain simple societies, for example, the idea of accumulating private possessions is viewed with abhorrence; and even in capitalist societies other reasons than purely monetary ones motivate people to do certain jobs, particularly pride in one's skill. The "functional importance" argument is obviously an attempt to defend the *status quo* in the capitalist United States. Logically it is a tautology.[1]

Thirdly, great accumulations of personal wealth perform several "dysfunctions". The wealth of a society consists of a private and a public sector; the more is accumulated in a few private hands the less the overwhelming majority have. It has often been argued, however, that if the wealthy were expropriated and their riches distributed among the population, each person would receive only a few pounds or less. Now gross company profits and rents in 1968 totalled about £7,500 millions: redistribution among the 19 million British households would mean an average increase in each household's income of nearly £8 per week. But, of course, it is unfair to take *gross* profits and rents, since they are taxed. (Of course, it should be evident to any reader that

[1] The argument appears in articles by Davis and Moore and by Tumin (*American Sociological Review*, 1953).

these figures are an understatement of *true* profits and rents; but let that pass.) Taking *net* profits and rents would in theory reduce that £8 a week considerably. But, again, arguing along these lines means falling into the trap laid for us by the capitalist propagandists. First, as Titmuss and others have pointed out, we have to consider not only income but wealth. In 1966, for example, the Inland Revenue Commissioners estimated as follows:

Estimated wealth of individuals in Great Britain 1966

	£ millions
Gross personal wealth (other than landed property)	62,446
Total deductions	4,392
Net personal wealth (other than landed property)	58,054
Gross landed property	22,809
Total deductions (mortgages etc.)	4,056
Net landed property	18,753
Total gross wealth	82,255
Total net wealth	76,807

As Dr. Revell estimated, the top five per cent of the adult population owns approximately three-quarters of the country's wealth, or, taking the figures above, about £57,605 millions. If redistributed among the other 95 per cent this would mean a net gain to every man, woman and child in the population (roughly 52,300,000) of about £1,160, no mean sum. But again we would be playing the hack propagandists' game, for much, indeed most, of this huge sum of £57,605 millions is fixed capital, land, factories, buildings, machinery. Socialists have no intention of redistributing fixed capital. This would be not merely absurd, it would be impossible. What we intend to do is to take it all into public ownership, to be managed by the working people. The figures supplied by the Inland Revenue Commissioners merely show Britain's immense wealth and how the people would benefit from public ownership. More than that, as Tumin pointed out in his argument against the functionalists (see note on page 137), extreme inequality tends to be highly dysfunctional because it limits the rise of talent and creative potential and of new discoveries and their application and it encourages envy and conflict. Socialists and communists have always believed that common ownership of the means of production, distribution and exchange acts in the long term to encourage people to develop themselves and to give their best for their own good and the good of all.

5

BULGING IN THE MIDDLE?

INTRODUCTION

The second powerful argument advanced by right-wing apologists of capitalism is that, particularly since the Second World War, the working class has so altered that it would be ridiculous to call it the proletariat, as Marx did. The proletariat of a hundred or so years ago was truly property-less, its standard of living was abominably low, employment was miserably paid and insecure, living conditions were shocking, the average expectation of life might be thirty years and infant mortality was high. Today the standard of living of the working class has risen very substantially, mass unemployment (as in the 1930s) has disappeared and the family enjoys a whole range of consumer goods which, even if they existed, were previously enjoyed only by the well-to-do. The structure of employment moreover has radically changed. Work itself is becoming increasingly mechanised, so that traditionally dirty manual labour is being rapidly replaced by technical operations performed by workers in white coats. The manufacturing industries are a shrinking sector of the economy, while secondary and tertiary occupations, particularly clerical and professional work, have expanded enormously. Workers have moved into middle-class areas and old social barriers broken down. The old working-class ideology is fast disappearing and the old working-class culture has been superseded, so Professor Hoggart tells us, by a new class-less culture. Workers are becoming less class-conscious and less militant. Distinctions of education, appearance and behaviour have vanished. In terms of earnings, hours and conditions of work and in all attitudes and manifestations of behaviour both on and off the job, the working-class is rapidly becoming part of a bigger and bigger middle-class.

Now there is little new in this. We described earlier how Eduard Bernstein demonstrated statistically the existence and growth of a large sector of self-employed in the latter part of the nineteenth century. Of the period between the two world wars M. Abrams wrote:

> "Between 1911 and 1938 the lot of the adult man in full employment improved more than the average 20 per cent. . . . His working week declined by at least 10 per cent, and his real earnings . . .

increased by about 40 per cent. The number of his dependants declined, and the improvement in his and his family's standard of living was of the order of 50 per cent."[1]

Since 1938, when, Abrams admitted, this improved standard was still well below that of the average lower-middle-class family, the working-class standard of living has risen still more and faster, while that of the lower middle class has failed to keep pace. It would, therefore, be very foolish, to say the least, to deny this relative improvement in working-class standards, particularly as it is so obvious to the eye. But, granted all this improvement, it still does not answer such important questions as, has the class structure changed radically? Is Britain really becoming a *middle-class* society?

THE CLASSES IN BRITAIN

The most authoritative surveys of the population of Great Britain are, of course, the decennial Censuses, now supplemented by sample censuses every five years, despite the fact that comparisons over the years are, as the Census authorities have readily admitted, very difficult because of the changes made by the Registrar-General (who is responsible for the Censuses), due partly to the changing structure of British society.

The Censuses divide the population in two ways. First they group the occupied population according to occupation; and this is done in detail. Secondly, the occupational groups are assembled into a smaller number of "Social Classes", in which other factors like income are taken into account. In the 1951 Census classification, the Registrar-General felt that each of the five Social Classes was too broad; so he introduced a further division into what he called Socio-Economic Groups, determined by "employment status" as well as occupation, although, he admitted, ideally such groups ought to have taken into account people's social, cultural and recreational standards and behaviour. In 1951 there were 13 such Socio-Economic Groups. For the 1961 Census, however, the Registrar-General adopted a U.N.-recommended list of 17 Socio-Economic Groups. The reader will now understand why comparisons of the Socio-Economic Groups is difficult. Fortunately, however, the division into the five Social Classes

[1] M. Abrams: *Condition of the British People 1911–1945*, p. 114. Notice that the adult working man he wrote about enjoyed full employment: the number of unemployed in the 'thirties never fell below a million.

has continued. The following table gives the proportions of the five Social Classes in 1951 and 1961:

Class	*Description*	*Percentage of total occupied population*	
		1951	*1961*
I	Higher administrative, professional and managerial	3·3	2·7
II	Farmers, intermediate professional and small business	18·8	14·8
III	Clerical, shop assistants, foremen and supervisors, personal service and skilled manual	51·0	47·7
IV	Semi-skilled and agricultural workers	15·4	22·1
V	Unskilled workers and armed forces other ranks	11·6	8·1
Not classified		—	4·6

The table shows two significant features. Even though the figures are not really comparable, it is certainly not the middle class that has grown, but the class of semi-skilled manual workers. Classes I and II have shrunk. Secondly, the Registrar-General lumps routine clerical workers and shop assistants with skilled manual workers in the same Social Class. This means that, whatever else might differentiate them, their occupations have roughly the same status in present-day society. According to Lockwood, Marxists make the mistake of regarding clerical workers as proletarians, whereas clerical workers generally consider themselves a cut above manual workers.[1] Lockwood's understanding of the Marxist view is incorrect; and it is interesting to see that, from one point of view, the Registrar disagrees with Lockwood. This question is discussed later.

In the London School of Economics' study of social mobility, Glass and Hall took the age-group 45–54 years, because they felt that at this age-range men had achieved their final occupational status. The investigators found that both the Census figures and the data obtained from their own sample enquiry showed that, over the crucial years 1911 to 1941, the percentage in manual occupations *actually increased*. Even taking all ages between 1911 and 1941 they found little change in the manual/non-manual ratio as far as *men* were concerned. The big increase in non-manual employment was taken up by *women*, doing mostly semi-skilled work.[2]

[1] D. Lockwood: *The Black-coated Worker* (1958).
[2] *Social Mobility in Britain* (ed. Glass), Ch. 8, pp. 192–3.

The Hulton Readership Surveys since the last war produced a picture similar to the Censuses. These surveys, undertaken to help the Press slant their publications to particular sections of the population, divided people into five groups based on personal appearance, occupation, type of dwelling and district lived in and similar, easily obtainable information. The classes were:

A well-to-do
B middle-class
C lower middle-class
D working-class
E poor

Even though there are wide differences between this classification and the five Census Social Classes, the Hulton figures below are interesting in themselves. For they show that changes which took place mostly during the war, resulting in the proportions given for the year 1947, were largely reversed during the 'fifties.

Percentage of population over 16 years

Year	*Class*				
	A	B	C	D	E
1947	5	10	20	55	10
1950	3½	7½	17	63	9
1955	4	8	17	64	7

The upper classes (upper and middle) became smaller and the working class bigger. Only among the "poor" did the reduction continue. The working class in 1955 comprised nearly two-thirds of the population, the middle classes together one-quarter.

Again, in the 1950s, G. D. H. Cole, who wavered uncertainly between support for a Marxist approach and the view that both the upper class and the proletariat were disappearing, accepted the picture given by the 1951 Census. These, he said, showed that 14·5 per cent of occupied heads of households were administrative, managerial and professional workers, 7·6 per cent farmers, small employers and shopkeepers and 73·6 per cent workers, manual and non-manual, excluding foremen. Of this last group, however, Cole pointed out that 12·2 per cent were non-manual, 38·7 per cent skilled manual, together making up the 51 per cent of Social Class III and 27 per cent semi-skilled and unskilled. Nevertheless, he admitted that the Marxist definition of class based on ownership of the means of production was largely true and concluded:

"Six years of Labour Government did not materially alter the social structure, except at the two extreme ends."[1]

This broad picture of the working class comprising nearly three-quarters of the population (or three-fifths if non-manuals are omitted) is supported by the Hulton Readership Survey. For, bringing the Hulton percentages for 1955 together, we get an upper class of 4 per cent, a middle class of 25 per cent and, assuming the poor (E) to be working class, D and E together—the working class—adds up to 71 per cent.[2]

Finally, if we take the Census Social Classes III, IV and V as working class, we get the following table:

Social Classes		*1951*	*1961*
I	Upper Class	3·3	2·7
II	Middle Class	18·8	14·8
III, IV, V	Working class	78·0	77·9

showing that according to the Registrar-General, between three-quarters and four-fifths of the population are working class.

A century ago, in 1867, Dudley Baxter tried to classify the population of England and Wales according to income. His figures were:[3]

Class	*Income P.A.*	*Number*		*% of total*	
Upper	£1,000 & over	49,500		0·5	
Middle	£300–1,000	150,000		1·5	
Lower Middle	Less than £300	1,853,500		18·8	
Skilled Labour	—	1,123,000	7,785,000	11·4	79·1
Less skilled	—	3,819,000		38·8	
Unskilled and Agricultural	—	2,843,000		28·9	

All non-manual workers were included in the lower middle class, irrespective of income; and in view of the economic and social position of non-manual workers a hundred years ago, it may well be argued that they could be regarded more truly as *middle* then than as a mixture of middle and lower-middle, as they are today. Hence it may be said that the two upper classes (Baxter's "upper" and "middle") are more comparable to our present top 2–3 per cent and that the proportions of

[1] Cole: *Studies in Class Structure* (1956), p. 77.

[2] Even excluding "the poor", the "pure" working class (D) comprises nearly two-thirds of the population.

[3] Condensed from those given by Cole and Postgate: *The Common People 1746–1938*, p. 347.

real middle and working classes are roughly the same as they were a century later. The closeness of the proportions is almost uncanny.

OCCUPATIONAL GROUPING

But, following the Census authorities, it may be argued that "Social Classes" are too broad. So let us see how the population is broken down into the new Socio-Economic Groups, even though those of 1951 differ from 1961.

Now, since the main criteria of these groups are "employment status" and occupation, we need to see how the occupational structure of the population has altered over time. As every text-book tells its readers, there have been drastic changes this century in the type of occupations. The numbers employed in agriculture and mining have declined steadily. So, surprisingly, have manufacture and building. So has domestic service, replaced by those providing personal services or working in one or other form of entertainment. Employment in banking, insurance and commerce has, on the other hand, gone up (despite mechanisation of office work). So have those providing professional and technical services and employment in local and national government, including "defence". Today, roughly 10 per cent of all "occupied persons" are clerks or typists. As the population has grown, so roughly has the *number* of "occupied persons", although as a proportion they haven't altered much over the last 50 years or so, fluctuating around 45 per cent of total population (except during the Great Slump). The figures therefore reflect the fall in the proportion employed in the primary industries (extraction, like mining, and industrial production) and the growth of secondary (transport and communications) and tertiary industries (particulary clerical and professional work).

Between 1951 and 1961 the same process continued, but with a couple of additions. Many more married women went out to work, mostly part-time. The biggest proportionate increases in employment occurred in the newer industries of the "technological age"—electronics and plastics. With these increases came further expansion in the newer professional and technical jobs and in the numbers of clerical workers. This is the well-known shift to "white collar" employment.

But does this shift signify a movement away from the picture given by Social Class measurement? Has there, in particular, been a shift away from employee status to employer/managerial status?

In 1945 M. Abrams, writing for the Fabian Society, observed that in 1931, 94 per cent of all occupied persons were "operatives", only 3 per cent employers and managers and only 3 per cent working on their own account. But Abrams excluded those working in agriculture, commerce and finance which, had they been included, would have reduced the percentage of "operatives" slightly and increased the others a trifle. Nevertheless, he concluded:

"The figures of the most recent Censuses of Production make it clear", he wrote, "not only that the status of practically every occupied person in the industries covered is that of an employee, but also that he is often employed as one of thousands on the pay-roll of a great concern where there can be no question of a personal employer-employee relationship. For a great many workers the employer is the board of a firm employing several thousand 'hands'; and at best this board, in an attempt to restore and imitate the old human relationship, might provide a welfare department."[1]

How have the proportions altered since then? Professor D. C. Marsh, of Nottingham University, summarising Census statistics 1921–61, gives us the following comparative table:

Status group as percentage of occupied population

Status	*1921*	*1931*	*1951*	*1961*
Employers	3·7	—	2·1 } 5·9	5·8
Managers	—	6·4	3·8 }	
"Operatives"	90	86·7	88·7	87
On own account	6·3	7·0	5·4	7·4
Totals	100·0	100·0	100·0	100·0

Difficulty in comparing the size of the employer class is due to the fact that the census authorities sometimes separated employers from managers and sometimes merged them. But if there was an expansion of this class between 1921 and 1931, it has shrunk slightly since then. Similarly, the proportion of self-employed has fluctuated, but has never risen above about 7½ per cent, Bernstein's forecast notwithstanding. Employees ("operatives") still account for nearly nine-tenths of the population, the decline being relatively negligible. Even by 1961, employers, managers and the self-employed totalled only about 13 per cent of the occupied population. As Marsh remarks: "Ordinary

[1] Abrams: *Condition of the British People 1911–1945*, p. 65.

observation would lead us to believe that most of us were, and are, employees . . ."[1]

Abram's comment in 1945 applies equally, if not more, today after more than 20 years of Dahrendorf's "post-capitalism". The welfare departments may have increased in size and number, but only because of increases in the size and concentration of firms and because of employees' rising expectations. So much for the big three-fold divisions of (i) employers, people working on their own account and the employed and (ii) higher, middle and working classes.

WHAT IS "CLASS"?

But, say Crosland and company, you Marxists persist in putting most employees into one class. Marx may have been justified in talking of a single proletariat a century ago; but today, as the seventeen Socio-Economic Groups of the 1961 Census show, the situation is quite different. Certainly nearly 90 per cent of the occupied population are employees, but what a world of difference there is between the road-sweeper and the skilled engineering worker, and even more between them and the bank accountant or the modern professional scientist! There is enormous inequality among employees, not only in income but in status, education and way of life. Of course, the "relations of production" are still, as in Marx's day, a big influence: a miner can hardly have the same attitude as a member of the Coal Board or a process worker at Billingham the same attitude as the chairman of I.C.I.; and industrial struggles haven't disappeared (although it is claimed that strikes in the "West" are going down).[2] But Marxist sociology isn't enough now: capital or lack of it isn't all. Weber's theory is much more appropriate.

The history of sociology is, as we saw in Chapter III, spattered with various attempts to by-pass Marxism, especially in the field of social stratification. But all the alternative theories in this field boil down to diminishing the role of class in the Marxist sense in the world of the twentieth century. The reader will recall that Weber set the argument going by claiming that status, defined by "way of life", was assuming a greater and greater role in modern times. Thorstein Veblen popularised this theory with his description of "status symbols" and his idea of "conspicuous consumption".[3] According to Veblen, people's

[1] D. C. Marsh: *The Changing Social Structure of England and Wales 1871–1961*, p. 152.

[2] But see later, Ch. 7.

[3] T. Veblen: *Theory of the Leisure Class* (1899).

positions in society, at least in the U.S.A., were shown by the sort of houses they lived in, the clothes they wore, their hobbies and recreations and the unnecessary luxuries with which they surrounded themselves.

Between the world wars the American investigators Mr. and Mrs. Lynd, studying a typical mid-West industrial township with the fictitious name of "Middletown", first divided the town's population into (*a*) the "working class", defined as those who, to get their living, were primarily concerned with things and used tools and (*b*) the "Business Class", including professional people, defined as those who, in their work, dealt predominantly with people and were concerned with selling. Within the Business Class they distinguished an "Upper Business Class" centred on one powerful and very wealthy family. This family had considerable industrial holdings, had lived in the town a long time and dominated town life. The "Upper Business Class" circling around this family consisted of a wealthy élite with a characteristic pattern of leisure, including horse-riding and flying in aeroplanes.

The coming of big business (i.e. the giant U.S. corporations) complicated the old structure. In particular, a new middle class of salaried employees of the big corporations grew up beside the old middle class of small manufacturers and merchants. Middletown society could now be divided into six classes: upper, middle, lower middle, upper working, middle working (skilled and semi-skilled) and lower working (unskilled, the "poor whites"). But—and this is notable—these divisions were, the Lynds emphasised, less important than the two main classes.

After reading Crosland, Dahrendorf and others, one might suppose absence of class-consciousness to be a purely post-World War II phenomenon. The Lynds found an absence of class-consciousness in Middletown before the war and even during the Slump, mainly, they concluded, because of the widespread American idea that, provided a man worked hard and saved, he could get ahead. But reality contradicted the idea, even when economic life began to pick up again. The shop-floor worker could rise to be foreman, but the move from foreman to the Business Class was pretty well non-existent. The "American dream", as it was later to be called, or the "rags to riches" myth, persisted as the gap between the two classes in respect of "ways of life" got wider. Yet underneath it all the Lynds found a *class awareness* which, despite the enormous power and influence of the Upper Business Class and the fact that both local papers were right-wing Republican, got Roosevelt a decisive majority in the town vote.

Another and more controversial theory of social class was elaborated in the 1930s by W. Lloyd Warner. Warner, a defender of U.S. "free enterprise", argued that social inequality was necessary, because only the promise of personal reward could force people to strive upwards, a point of view which, readers may recall, structural-functionalists repeated in the 'fifties.[1] Warner's method of determining the class to which a man belonged was to ask the people who knew him to rank him in some position on a social ladder. This was an example of the method known as "subjective determination", that is to say, the man's rank is determined not by objective, scientific criteria but by subjective ideas in other people's minds. This method led Warner to distinguish six classes in "Yankee City", the name he gave to the U.S. town he studied: Upper-Upper, Lower-Upper, Upper-Middle, Lower-Middle, Upper-Lower, and Lower-Lower. Sometimes the top two merged and conversely, sometimes he had to sub-divide these classes further, reflecting the shifting nature of subjective criteria. Just the same, the resemblance to the Lynds' six classes is striking.

Where did property (capital) fit in Warner's picture? Strictly speaking, not at all. The nearest he got to it was income and, significantly, he admitted that income was the most important factor in social class determination.

> "Economic factors are significant and important in determining the class position of any family or person, influencing the kind of behaviour we find in any class, and contributing their share to the present form of our status system. But, while significant and necessary, the economic factors are not sufficient to predict where a particular family or individual will be or to explain completely the phenomena of social class. Something more than a large income is necessary for high social position. Money must be translated into intimate participation with, and acceptance by, members of a superior class."[2]

Despite criticisms, however, Warner's subjectively-determined classes matched remarkably well with status divisions of "Yankee City" population based on objective criteria like type of dwelling, residential area and level of education. This was to be expected, since people tend to rank others by such criteria. Among his more valuable discoveries,

[1] See Ch. 4.

[2] W. L. Warner: *Social Class in America*, p. 21. Taking income alone is, of course, open to the criticism of the minority of the Royal Commission on Taxation that "economic power" must take wealth into account.

however (no discovery for any class-conscious person), was the connection between social class and political power. Power belonged to and was exercised by the Upper and Upper-Middle classes. Even though a strike for unionisation and higher wages in a local shoe factory was successful, this in no way altered the top classes' sway in the political, economic and educational set-up of the community. In short, in honest defence of U.S. capitalism, Warner produced a class study of "Yankee City" in which society was fundamentally economically based.

Warner's further investigations showed the connections between social class, occupation and power. Power was exercised jointly by the old "aristocracy" and the new plutocracy together, even though socially the former ranked higher than the latter. There was also a close connection between social class position and occupation (as in the British Censuses): 83 per cent of the Upper-Upper and 86 per cent of the Lower-Upper were in "professional and proprietory" occupations; 82 per cent of the Upper-Lower and 93 per cent of the Lower-Lower were workers, skilled, semi-skilled and unskilled. These figures support a basically simple, fundamental division of population into bourgeoisie and workers, except for professional people, who could constitute a third class. It is particularly interesting that Warner found his six-fold division to be fluid in the middle range. This very fluidity led him on to a slippery slope of more and more sub-classes, until he produced 54 possible "positions" plus a further 73 "clique positions" ending in 89 "behavioural situations" based on 34 "class types". The doubtful value of such a complicated *static* classification, covering only a small American town, is shown by the fact that it was not taken up to any extent by later sociologists. It demonstrates the acute problems arising from the use of narrower criteria. Like Weber's, Warner's analysis begins to break down under test.

The social-psychological approach is perhaps best known from the work of the American, R. Centers.

> "Classes", wrote Centers, "are psycho-social groupings, something that is essentially subjective in character, dependent on class consciousness (i.e. a feeling of group membership), and class lines of cleavage may or may not conform to what seem to social scientists to be logical lines of cleavage in the objective or stratification sense.... Class, as distinguished from stratum, can well be regarded as a *psychological* phenomenon in the fullest sense of the term. That is,

a man's class is part of his ego, *a feeling on his part of belongingness to something*; an *identification* with something larger than himself."[1]

Now class consciousness, i.e. consciousness by individuals and groups of belonging to a class, is an essential factor in class formation. There can be no class action unless there is, at least, some awareness, even at the subconscious level, of class membership sufficient to cause the individual to associate with his class fellows in some action, be it only "murmuring", to use Weber's expression. Both Marx and Weber understood this, but Weber tried to use this fact to play down the significance of class consciousness, i.e. consciousness of class interests, in the modern world by arguing that since capitalism did not necessarily produce it, or produced it at a low level, the concept itself was vague. No one, least of all Marx, would deny that class consciousness could be at a low level. Counter-posing *status* consciousness, Weber suggested it was becoming more important than class consciousness, especially in the United States. Weber thereby took a step towards transforming the issue into a psychological one, because status, he said, was based on social estimation of the subjective concept of *honour*.[2] His contemporary, F. Tönnies, carried this psychological trend further by declaring that the different types of society derived from the types of "social will". Capitalism, the modern example of *Gesellschaft*, or society in which people were essentially separate individuals, inevitably fed upon the working class, which struggled against it. Thus did class consciousness lead to class struggle. Centers continued this trend to its logical conclusion. He turned the Marxist theory upside down, making class consciousness the *cause*, the *creator*, of classes. This had some queer results. For example, among Centers' respondents, 18 per cent of the unskilled workers said they belonged to the middle class; while 7 per cent of big businessmen and 10 per cent of professional people put themselves in the working class! This was partly due to Centers' own poor definitions, one of which stated that membership of the working class included anyone who "worked for a living"! Secondly, definitions of "class" depended purely on what any group of individuals felt.

But recording people's personal opinions has its value. In the years just after the last war, Centers and his co-workers interviewed a representative cross-section of male, adult, white Americans, asking

[1] R. Centers: *The Psychology of Social Classes* (1949), p. 27.

[2] "Class, Status and Party", in *Essays in Sociology*, by M. Weber (ed. Gerth and Mills).

their opinions on various political, economic and social issues of the time. At the same time he obtained background information about the respondents, such as occupation, religion and nationality. He found, as any class-conscious individual would expect, a close connection between people's socio-economic position and their opinions. Less than 2 per cent of big business people held radical opinions. Labour groups (i.e. manual workers) were conspicuously non-conservative and most radical in their opinions, although there was, as in Britain, a big section of "don't knows". Assessing their own class position, 3 per cent said they were upper-class, 43 per cent middle-class and 51 per cent working class. For obvious reasons these figures must be taken with a fairly big pinch of salt. Also, Centers' "middle class" included all white-collar workers. Yet the size of the upper class is roughly that of the capitalist class and corresponds closely to it. And, as he himself wrote, it was surprising that, with the means of propaganda overwhelmingly in the hands of his top 3 per cent, putting over the ideology of that class and seeking to obscure class differences, over one-half of the population still looked upon themselves as working class.[1]

On the other hand, M. Halbwachs, writing on class psychology, adopted an objective approach. Human beings are physically not much different today from their ancestors, but the psychological make-up is far different. Although each individual is different from the next, group characteristics exist over and above the individual; and these group or collective characteristics depend on economic and social situations. We are not born laywers or politicians or religious enthusiasts, wrote Halbwachs; we are born with certain tendencies which may or may not develop.

> "Each of these categories determines the conduct of its members and imposes definite motivations on them; it stamps each category with such a peculiar and distinctive mark, and so sharply, that men of different classes, even though they live amid the same surroundings and are contemporaries, sometimes strike us as belonging to different species of humanity."[2]

The data obtained by the foregoing representatives of the older school of social stratification investigators emphasise the underlying primacy of economic factors in the determination of social class. Even

[1] R. Centers: *The Psychology of Social Classes.* For a summary see Centers' article, "The American Class Structure", in *Readings in Social Psychology*, ed. Swanson, Newcomb and Hartley (2nd edition 1952).

[2] M. Halbwachs: *The Psychology of Social Class* (written 1938, first published 1955).

Centers' method of self-rating has some scientific value, despite the justifiable criticisms made of it. An individual's class self-rating and his political opinions are strongly correlated.

In spite of their authors' intentions, which were, in many cases, to counter the Marxist view, the data they produced strongly confirm it. For Marx and Engels themselves, while asserting the *primacy* of the economic factor, warned against turning their theory into one which claimed the economic to be the *only* factor. In that now well-known letter to Bloch in 1890 Engels wrote:

> "Marx and I are ourselves partly to blame for the fact that younger writers sometimes lay more stress on the economic side than is due to it. We had to emphasise this main principle in opposition to our adversaries, who denied it, and we had not always the time, the place or the opportunity to allow the other elements involved in the interaction to come into their rights. But when it was a case of presenting a section of history, that is, of a practical application, the thing was different and there no error was possible."[1]

Marx made a practical application when writing about the victory of Louis Bonaparte and the bourgeoisie over the proletariat in 1848. He made clear the roles of the different sections of French society—the caste of Bonapartist officials, the lumpenproletariat, the army and the clergy. In some ways he anticipated Weber, particularly as regards the status of these groups in the society and their relation to the main (property) classes, but also indicating how the society retained some relics of pre-revolutionary feudalism, for example, when he talked of the *caste* of Bonapartist officials. The rest are what Weber meant when he talked of strata, except the lumpenproletariat, who are at one and the same time a (low) status group and a stratum. In France, a land with an old civilisation, Marx wrote, classes were fixed, whereas in a new country like the U.S.A. classes "... continually change and interchange their elements in a constant state of flux ..." However (whether fixed or in flux), Marx went on, all those sections mentioned above helped the bourgeois republic to triumph in June 1848 against the Paris proletariat; and the bourgeois republic "... signifies the unlimited despotism of one class over other classes". He later repeated that, during the June days, "... all classes and parties had united in the Party of Order against the proletarian class ...".[2]

[1] Engels to J. Bloch: *Selected Correspondence of Marx and Engels*, 21st September, 1890.
[2] Marx: *The Eighteenth Brumaire of Louis Bonaparte* (Selected Works, Vol. II, pp. 324–5).

As one of the founders of modern revolutionary socialism and an active participant in the movement, Marx was only too aware of the fact that a class did not exist without class consciousness. In 1851 when the heightened class consciousness of the 1848 uprisings had declined after defeat, he wrote:

> "In so far as millions of families live under economic conditions of existence that divide their mode of life, their interests and their culture from those of the other classes, and put them in hostile contrast to the latter, they form a class. In so far as there is merely a local interconnection . . . and the identity of their interests begets no unity, no national union and no political organisation, they do not form a class."[1]

Note here how Marx refused to separate mode of life, interests and culture from the economic basis of class.

When Lenin defined class he stressed its basis in the system of production; yet, as the following paragraph shows, in no narrow way.

> "Classes", he wrote, "are large groups of people which differ from each other by the place they occupy in a historically definite system of social production, by their relation (in most cases fixed and formulated in laws) to the means of production, by their role in the social organisation of labour, and, consequently, by the dimensions of the social wealth they obtain and their method of acquiring their share of it. Classes are groups of people one of which may appropriate the labour of another, owing to the different places they occupy in the definite system of social economy."[2]

Such a comprehensive, yet precise, definition allows the variations which bourgeois sociologists preferred to investigate and analyse and to counterpose against class, arguing between themselves as to which was primary.

But a word of warning is necessary. Just as it is impossible to deduce from the notion, "man", all the qualities that men can display, so there is an infinite number of possible qualities arising from men's relation-

[1] Marx: *The Eighteenth Brumaire* (Selected Works, Vol. II, p. 415). Compare the following from a more intelligent critic of Marxism: ". . . of course Marx was not unaware of the texture of social life: as an inhabitant of Victorian England he could hardly fail to notice the complex interplay of class and caste relationships, and in fact his writings supply ample evidence that—like any other observer of the social scene—he was alive to their significance." (G. Lichtheim: *Marxism.*)

[2] Lenin: *A Great Beginning* (1919).

ships to the means of production. This is the age-old differentiation between deduction and induction, between going from the general concept to every possible particular and reasoning from a large number of particular facts to the general concept. Therefore, it is right to point out the particular characteristics of groups within the broad division of society according to Marxian class. Some of these group divisions come close to class: social class (defined mostly by occupation), socio-economic group (occupation and income), status (defined by "way of life"). The farther we go from the fundamental defining characteristic, however, the less fundamental is the mode of differentiation, although the particular definition may be analytically useful and politically important. That is why Warner, for example, found categorisation so difficult as he moved farther and farther from people's relationship to the system of production.

Leading schools of bourgeois sociology in the U.S.A. were further in error when they tried to put these subsidiary defining criteria on the same level as Marx's and even above it. To refute Marx, all the criteria anyone could think of—type of house, dwelling area, birth, length of residence in a community, education, political and social opinions, voting behaviour, dress, speech, type of education, leisure pattern, friendship cliques—all important for particular purposes, were blown up beyond their real importance and each one in turn put forward as a more fundamental criterion of social stratification than relationship to property.

Yet, surveying the history of the controversy and all the evidence so far, one American sociologist concluded:

> "In the dynamic interplay of all the stratification variables, the economic and occupational factors undoubtedly play the most significant role."[1]

And explaining the interrelation between the economic and other factors, he said what any Marxist would accept regarding the interweaving of "superstructural" elements with basic class divisions.

> "Social-class analysis represents", he wrote, "an attempt to come to grips with the cumulative effect of basic economic factors in stratifying a modern industrial society. Economic factors, however, do not operate in a vacuum. They function within a particular political

[1] M. M. Gordon: *Social Class in American Sociology* (1958), p. 251. It is true that Gordon included within the concept of economic power income, control of employment, power over wages and prices, as well as wealth; but observation today shows the close connection these have with wealth, although they are not identical with it.

and community power context which they, in turn, condition. They are associated with particular occupational specialisations. They have the effect through time of producing a status order, and this status order in turn plays a role in determining economic rewards in the current society. These economic factors, furthermore, make for different levels of consumption and correspondingly different 'ways of life', or cultural attributes. The cumulation of these phenomena produces restrictions on intimate social contacts which lead to 'group life' divisions in the society. All of these phenomena, set in motion basically by the operation of the economic system, in turn work back to some extent on the economic mechanism itself and affect its operation. The complex and innumerable interweavings of economic factors with politico-community power, with the status structure, with occupational pre-emption, with cultural attributes, and with group life divisions constitute what may be called the social class system."[1]

Focusing on one dimension of social class only, not seeing that the separate dimensions (variables, factors or criteria) were merely "conceptual distinctions", constituted, Gordon concluded, one of the major defects of American research into class. "The variables are", another American wrote, "inseparable aspects of a functional social whole."[2]

Finally, it must follow from Marxist theory that different classes in the same system will view the class structure differently. Many investigations into social-class order employed teachers or students either as subjects or judges and the order compiled usually placed employers and highly-paid professional and administrative people at the top and essential manual workers, even skilled manual operatives, below routine clerical workers. But, in 1956, as a follow-up of the London School of Economics' project, Young and Willmott investigated social-class grading by manual workers, who had been under-represented in the main enquiry.[3] The enquiry, conducted by personal interview, took place in East London, mainly among manual workers. As in the main L.S.E. investigation (by Hall and Jones), medical officer of health topped both lists and professional and administrative

[1] Gordon, p. 234.

[2] A. L. Kornhauser, quoted in Gordon p. 235. The use of the word "functional" here does not mean that Gordon accepts the functionalist point of view, which takes the "value-system" as primary. Gordon emphasises again and again that the one factor which is more basic than others is economic power.

[3] Young and Willmott: Social grading by manual workers (*B.J.S.*, 1956).

jobs (including company director) followed in roughly the same order; but the manual workers placed civil servants a good deal lower, as they did with such occupations as commercial traveller, insurance agent, routine clerical worker and shop assistant. Conversely, they generally rated skilled manual occupations, like miner, fitter and carpenter, much higher. In general, they placed skilled manual occupations well above routine non-manual, in contrast to the general run of social orders, including the Censuses, in which the opposite occurs. The discrepancies were even greater among the so-called "deviants" among manual workers, i.e. those whose opinions differed from the general (22 out of a total of 60). "Deviants" put agricultural workers at the top, followed by medical officer of health, farmer and coal-miner; and shop assistant, chef, commercial traveller and barman at the bottom. Half of all the manual workers taking part in the enquiry regarded ability as the most, and social standing as the least, important criterion of social class. For the "deviants", *social contribution* was the most important criterion; and they referred repeatedly to the "dignity of labour" and similar strongly class and socialistic political ideas.

A comparison of "occupational prestige" in the U.S. over the years showed some *shifting*, even though the studies were based on ratings by students and teachers. The results showed a slight upward shift between 1947 and 1963 of manual work ("blue collar"), a considerable upward shift of scientific, technical, educational and artistic occupations and a slight downward shift of other, lower white-collar occupations.[1]

Finally, social class ranking must differ *between* systems. As other American commentators have pointed out, international comparisons can only be made over those occupations which are *comparable*. The similarities found (as in the widely quoted American National Opinion Research Centre 1947 investigation) reflect the similarity of certain basic structures in different societies. But there are many occupations which cannot be compared, e.g. company director (non-existent in socialist countries), or which have substantially different ranking, e.g. priest and even manual and non-manual workers.[2]

Many sociologists have pointed out the dilemmas and contradictions in social class assignment in "Western" countries today. This is not to say that social class, status and other social distinctions have no meaning

[1] Hodge, Siegel and Rossi: "Occupational prestige in the U.S. 1925–63", in Bendix and Lipset (eds.): *Class, Status and Power* (2nd edition).

[2] Hodge, Treiman and Rossi: "A comparative study of occupational prestige", in Bendix and Lipset (eds.) same vol.

and investigating them serves no useful purpose. It does confirm that social class and similar distinctions are (*a*) secondary and (*b*) more temporary than (Marxian) class position and (*c*) they arise from class position, though reacting upon it; and that the emphasis laid on them has confused students and workers as to the basic divisions of capitalist society.

PAY

In all the best investigations income is, after occupation, the most important criterion of social position in Britain today. Many bourgeois commentators have written grandly about the "income revolution", by which they mean the high incomes enjoyed by the working class. But how high are these incomes?

Take, for example, the pay of a skilled engineering worker. In April 1969 the basic rate of a skilled engineering craftsman was £15 a week. If income tax and social security contributions were deducted from this incredibly low wage, the worker would indeed be at, or below, the poverty line. But, as critics emphasise, basic rates often mean nothing: most workers get above basic rates through overtime, piecework bonuses and rates which start above the basic. So, side by side with basic rates, we should show average *earnings*. This we do, in the table below, for a few major industries:[1]

Industry	*Basic weekly rate*			*Average weekly earnings (all workers)*			
	£	s	d	£	s	d	
Agriculture	12	8	0	16	12	1	
Engineering (skilled)	15	0	0				
(labourers)	12	0	0	23	1	6	
General printing (London compositors)	17	13	6	23	18	2	
Vehicle building (London craftsmen)	15	11	8	26	8	11	
(London labourers)	13	11	8				
Footwear manufacture	13	2	6	20	5	5	(clothing & footwear)
Tailoring (London top rate)	11	18	4				
Local authorities (London top rate)	14	0	0	17	11	0	

[1] Compiled from *Time Rates of Wages and Hours of Work*, April 1969 and *Statistics on Incomes, Prices etc.*

The rise in earnings since the war, we have been told often enough, has been phenomenal. Taking 1955 as the base year, the Ministry calculated that by October 1968, average *weekly* wage rates (basic) rose by over 76 per cent, basic *hourly* rates almost doubled (due to the reduction in hours worked), but *earnings* rose 111 per cent. In pounds, shillings and pence, average weekly earnings in October 1968 of all men over 21 (except in agriculture) were nearly £23.

Of course, the cost of living has risen, too. Taking 1955 as the base year, the Index of Retail Prices went up in the same period by 53 per cent. This is much less than the rise in earnings, but if we adjust the latter for the rise in retail prices, average earnings over the period 1955–68 rose by 52 per cent, or 4 per cent a year.

Still, an average of £23 a week in 1968 seems pretty good. But we've ignored a couple of facts. First and rarely stated in the press, this figure is *gross*, before all deductions. After average deductions, it would be fair to say that actual take-home pay is a good bit less—in the region of three or four pounds.[1] Secondly, it is of men aged 21 and over only. Women (18 years and over) average only £11 5s. 11d. gross and juveniles much less. However, just as Titmuss argued that among the wealthy the "income unit" is usually the family, so it is true to say that in most working-class families all members at work contribute to the family income. So we should look at average *family* incomes.

But, before doing so, we should note that the figures given above were for wage-earners, i.e. those who were paid hourly or weekly. What about the salaried worker? First, we should point out that not all salaried workers are paid monthly. Quite a lot, especially routine clerical workers, are paid weekly. Also investigations into salaries by the Ministry of Labour started only recently: in national and local government, the nationalised industries, education, banking and insurance in 1955 and in the administrative, technical and clerical occupations of private industry only in 1959. At October 1968, *gross* earnings of all salaried workers were (male) £29 8s. 11d., female £17 11s. 11d.

These last averages, like all averages, conceal important variations between upper and lower sections. The lower sections are, of course, overwhelmingly general clerical workers. For them average earnings were only £18 12s. 5d. for males and £14 8s. 0d. females. These averages, of course, hide more variations. The "aristocrat" of clerical

[1] See the figures of the Central Statistical Office and Family Expenditure Survey later on in this section.

workers, the bank clerk, enjoys a scale rising from about £360 (£5 a week) at age 16 to about £1100 a year at 31. At age 31, however, he stops there unless promoted. He gets certain concessions, chiefly a low interest rate for house purchase and a London allowance, as well as, in most cases, a non-contributory pension scheme. But unless he rises to managerial level, no bank clerk is likely to call himself "affluent". Still, the average bank clerk has, according to the *Economist*, maintained his pre-war level and even slightly exceeded it, whereas the local government employee has fallen behind. Some civil service grades have done better than others. A good secretary can start at £17 or £18; but, as everyone now knows, a non-graduate teacher received (December 1969), after a three-year training course, £17 a week gross (£13 net). Generally, it can be said that, where there are career possibilities, starting pay is lower. Over the thirteen years 1955–68, however, the average earnings of *all* salaried workers went up 107 per cent, or about 4 per cent less than those of wage-earners. From this we can say quite categorically that salaried workers have progressed at about the same rate as wage-earners and that the earnings of male *clerical* workers today compare unfavourably with those of male manual (wage) workers, both in amount and rate of increase. Or, in other words, *not only do they get less than manual workers, but the gap between them and manual workers has been increasing*. Unquestionably, a powerful, if not the most powerful, factor has been the low trade union membership among clerical workers in private industry and commerce. On the other hand, earnings of *administrative and technical* employees are as much above those of manual workers as clerical workers' earnings are below. So, when all earnings are sorted out, we get the following interesting overall pattern. From lowest to highest paid the order is: female manual workers, female clerical, male clerical, female administrative and technical, male manual, male administrative and technical. On this basis of earnings, therefore, the division between manual and non-manual is not the same as between lower and higher paid. Other factors play their part, including market situation, trade union organisation and traditional attitudes. It would be better to regard all from the standpoint of pay as workers, differentiated according to type of work, rather than the commonly-accepted distinction between manual and non-manual.

However, we must return to the point that so far we have been dealing with basic rates and earnings of *individuals*; and one of Titmuss' criticisms of official statistics was that a truer picture of income distribution would be obtained if the family rather than the individual were considered the basic unit. The Government does issue details of family income via the *Family Expenditure Surveys*, which began in 1953/54 with a large-scale survey of Household Expenditure. These figures are based on details provided by a cross-section of about 5,000 families, except that those at both ends—the very rich and the very poor—tend to be under-represented. In 1968, average income per household (roughly 3 persons) was about £30. Not only did this include all types of income, but it was *gross* income, i.e. before all deductions, especially income tax and National Insurance. Moreover, only about three-quarters of this average came from wages and salaries (inclusive of overtime and bonuses); the other one-quarter included pensions, income from self-employment and from investments. Average gross wages and salaries alone amounted to only £22 8s. per household, hardly princely and best described as subsistence income in the Marxist sense that it might just pay for the necessities and minor luxuries which the average Briton expects as minima for life.

However, much is made nowadays of what this money is spent on. Thus in 1968 average weekly expenditure per household on alcoholic drink was 20/6, on tobacco 25/8 and on buying, maintaining and running a motor vehicle 44/–. On the other hand, little was said in the capitalist press about the average 63/– a week on housing which did not include mortgages, or the 21/– on National Insurance (now renamed Social Security). But the largest outlay of this type was the 64/8 income tax. These three together reduced average income per household from £30 gross to only £22 11s. For those buying their houses, average mortgage cost an extra 24/8, reducing household income to less than £21 6s. net. Finally, if income from wages and salaries only is taken, the net figure after these unavoidable deductions (but not mortgage) could have been as low as £15 8s. There is not likely to be much dispute over the statement that, for the average wage or salary earning household, net income was about subsistence level. Marx argued at first that the proletariat were forced below subsistence level. He and Marxists qualified this later with the statement that trade unions could to some extent counter this downward pressure. The situation in Britain in the late 1960s shows that the Marxist view is correct; that the employed population (wage and salary earners) is kept for the overwhelming majority, at subsistence level, bearing in mind, of course, that ideas as to what this level is change through time.

Lastly, averages again conceal wide discrepancies. In particular, average *gross* income in clerical workers' households was £32 16s., but in manual working-class households £30 13s. Deducting expenditure on housing (rent and rates), national insurance and income tax left for manual worker households about £23 12s., for clerical worker households slightly more. The average household of retired and unoccupied people (2 persons) had, after deductions, only about £11 18s. This average included, however, those retired on private incomes. How much real poverty do these averages conceal? Since a minority unquestionably enjoys a higher income, it follows that there must be a minority well below the averages, which we have seen to be fairly low. But more about that later.[1]

Trends in wages and salaries during the twentieth century show a distinct pattern.[2] As between men and women the movements took place in opposite directions: for men, there was a narrowing of differentials, for women, surprisingly, a widening. But as regards *all* employees, there was an overall narrowing of differentials in the upper half, a widening in the lower half. To make this a little clearer, let us suppose that the average for all employees in 1910 was, say, £2 a week, and in 1960 £16 a week. Then there were more people earning above £2 in 1910 than above £16 in 1960. Conversely, there were more below £16 in 1960 than below £2 in 1910. In other words, over the past 50 years, the positions of both the better-paid and the worst-paid steadily worsened. And, after adjusting the figures for the rise in retail prices, Routh found that both those end groups were affected still more in the same directions.

Within this general trend the different occupational groups were affected differently. In 1960, higher professional earnings were three times the average of all earnings, compared with four times the average in 1913. Lower-grade professional and male clerical workers fell behind. On the whole, manual workers just about held their own. Managers, especially women, on the other hand, did well.[3]

How important are these relative changes? The answer is, really not very important. In the first place, none of the main groups changed places or significantly altered its relative earnings. For example, skilled manual workers have not only remained below higher professionals, but their differentials have only narrowed a little. On the other hand,

[1] Ch. 7.
[2] G. Routh: *Occupation and Pay in Great Britain, 1906–60.*
[3] The "groups" are the seven "classes" drawn up by Hall and Jones for the L.S.E. study of social mobility. For detailed figures, see Appendix 3.

although the average earnings of male higher professionals were over £2,000 in 1960 and therefore nearly four times the average for an unskilled male manual worker, this gap is very much less than the gap between the higher professional worker and the average top director's income, which was £14,000 in 1960, a ratio of 7 to 1. Moreover, all these figures are *gross* earnings; and taxation, which takes a great deal from the middle strata (professional and managerial employees), may further widen the gap between these and the top directors. Thus we find that, taking the criterion of pay, *the range between all employees has generally narrowed over the last 50 years, while the gap between the average and top capitalist incomes remains very large.*

The narrowing gap between manual and non-manual earnings is a fact of great importance. Contrary to a widely-held belief, it did not start during the last war. Routh and others have shown that narrowing of differentials took place even before the First World War. Between the two wars, however, due to mass unemployment, the manual workers suffered much more than the non-manual, with the result that differentials between them widened. But just before 1939 the manual workers began to catch up again and this movement accelerated during and after the war. Finally, by the middle 'fifties, Tory policies got to work and differentials began to widen again. Nevertheless, these fluctuations taken together are surprisingly small, as was stressed above. In contrast, the gap between the best paid employees and top company directors remains very wide, *far wider even than the gap between unskilled manual workers and the top 10 per cent of professional people like doctors and solicitors.*

The reason for this relative rigidity despite constant change is, as Routh points out, chiefly that, in an individualistic, competitive society like ours, everybody struggles to maintain his or her (or their) position, whether by moving up the occupational ladder, or by unorganised expressions of discontent, or through their professional association or trade union. Another factor affecting the manual/non-manual differential is the general economic situation. Under inflation, fixed salaries fall steadily in value while wages tend to rise, so that differentials are narrowed: the opposite happens under deflation. But the overall picture remains one of an "... occupational distribution and occupational pay structure supported by class stratification, not completely rigid and yet set enough to limit severely competition for higher-paid jobs."[1] This is much the same as when the economist,

[1] Routh, p. 141.

J. E. Cairnes, declared almost a century ago:

"What we find, in effect, is, not a whole population competing indiscriminately for all occupations, but a series of industrial layers, superposed on one another, within each of which the various candidates for employment possess a real and effective power of selection, while those occupying the several strata are, for all purposes of effective competition, practically isolated from each other . . . so that the average workman, from whatever rank he be taken, finds his power of competition limited for practical purposes to a certain range of occupations, so that, however high the rates of remuneration in those which lie beyond may rise, he is excluded from sharing them. We are thus compelled to recognise the existence of non-competing industrial groups as a feature of our social economy; and this is the fact which I desire here to insist upon."[1]

AID FROM THE WELFARE STATE

But pay is not all, say the popular propagandists. The Welfare State subsidises the lower income groups, and others as well, by the lavish benefits it bestows on all and sundry. From the cradle to the grave millions benefit by way of social security payments (including family allowances), State education (including student grants, subsidized dinners), national health service, not to mention lower rates of taxation for the poor and those with large families.

Let us take the last point first: does the tax structure really benefit the lower against the higher income groups, the working classes against the capitalists? Yes, say the Tories and all those basing themselves on Inland Revenue income statistics. Not as much as we are supposed to believe, say the Left-wing, but it's difficult to get at the true facts.[2] Titmuss says, probably not at all. The essential point often deliberately ignored is that income-tax and surtax comprise only one part of the tax system. These two taxes are distinguished from other forms of taxation by being *direct*, i.e. directly paid by each person. Another form is the *indirect*, paid indirectly when people buy goods and services. Finally there are the other forms of direct taxation outside the national tax system—mainly social security contributions and rates. Now the

[1] J. E. Cairnes, *Some Leading Principles of Political Economy Newly Expounded*, pp .64–8, quoted in Routh, p. 139.

[2] Within the last few years, however, left-wing writers have come up with much more information.

income tax/surtax system is designed to be progressive, meaning that the richer one is, the more one pays; and this is what the wealthy complain about. They do not complain about the rest; and the reason for their silence is clear when we look at the following table.

Tax payments as percentage of income 1962/3[1]

	£240	£440	£660	£910	£1,280	£2,330
Income tax, surtax & N.I.	0·9	3·5	8·3	9·6	10·8	16·1
Rates	8·1	6·0	3·8	2·9	2·4	1·8
Purchase tax	3·6	2·7	1·6	1·8	2·1	1·2
	12·6	12·2	13·7	14·3	15·3	19·1

The table shows that, while personal taxes are progressive, purchase tax falls more heavily on the lowest incomes *and rates do so even more* (a fact brought out by the Allen Committee). It is true, as Dr. Peston also shows, that the greatest increases in *purchase tax* were made in the years of Tory rule; for example, oil and petrol duty more than trebled between 1951 and 1963, while surtax was raised by less than 40 per cent. But, apart from adding a temporary surtax charge, the Wilson Government continued the process of increasing indirect taxes and *social security contributions* in order to "lower consumer demand", i.e. fleece the mass of people more, while at the same time raising subsidies to private industry still further. Indeed, compared with before the war, taxes on income in 1966 as a proportion of all taxation stayed at about the same level, taxes on capital fell sharply, taxes on spending (purchase tax) declined a little, but national insurance contributions rose sharply. The amounts collected in income tax, purchase tax and health and social security contributions take on average nearly a quarter of every family's income. No *household* paid, in 1967, less than a third of its original income in total taxes—except the very poorest and even then never less than a quarter.[2] On the other hand, in 1967 the total National Debt amounted to over £32,000 millions, of which the overwhelming part was in marketable securities. Even with as low an average interest as 4 per cent, this gave back to the coupon-clippers £1,280 millions a year, or almost as much as all surtax, corporation tax, capital gains tax and death duties combined.

[1] M. H. Peston, "Equality and the fiscal system", *New Society*, 1st April 1965. Remember, too, that on very high incomes tax evasion is enormous.

[2] "The incidence of taxes and social service benefits in 1965 and 1966." *Economic Trends* (C.S.O., Feb. 1968).

If we now turn to the question of direct welfare State benefits, we should remember that back in 1956 even Crosland admitted that the working-class pay fully for those benefits (State pensions, unemployment and sickness pay etc). The latest Government statistical analysis shows that, still, only the poor (households with income less than about £14 a week) received more in benefits than they paid in taxes. While benefits received by the poor have got bigger—and this is to be welcomed—the burden of taxation grows heavier (from average 29 per cent of income in 1961 to 35 per cent in 1967) on almost all incomes, *the biggest percentage increase being on household incomes between £16 and £24 a week.*[1]

In short, examination of taxation and State benefits undermine the hack progagandists' and Tory politicians' line. Certainly the Welfare State is a fact and it spends enormous sums on benefits of various kinds. But the burden falls more and more heavily on the mass of wage and salary earners. Tory/Big Business propaganda, feeding on the discontent produced by this burden, aims to lighten the burden by reducing public and social services and forcing people to pay into private schemes. Right-wing Labour policy only assists the Tories. Committed to maintaining the Welfare State, it only increases the tax burden. Capitalism can never resolve this dilemma, only change the form the burden takes.

MORE ABOUT MOBILITY

Although the facts about pay show a fairly rigid structure, popular propaganda continually puts it about that there is always room for the bright, aspiring young person to move up the ladder—providing, of course, he is prepared to work. Now we saw before that this was untrue as regards getting to the top. But it might still be true as regards moving up from manual working-class to the professional class (upper white-collar). As we pointed out in the section entitled "Occupational Grouping" in the present chapter, there has been a definite shift over the last fifty years away from manual to non-manual work, due to technological and economic change. But how much of this has been an upward movement within manual workers' families?

One of the pioneering works in this field, carried out shortly after the last war by a team of researchers from the London School of

[1] *Economic Trends*, February 1969.

Economics under Professor D. V. Glass, compared positions on the occupational ladder between fathers and sons.[1] It appears that this movement up the ladder was greatest among what they called the Higher Non-Manual Supervisory Grade (e.g. schoolteacher, commercial traveller), least among the Skilled Manual and Routine Non-Manual Grade (engineering fitter, shop assistant). But even the greatest change was still relatively modest. Whence, then, came the vast numbers of additional non-manual workers? As we pointed out before, women were taking these jobs over: Glass and his colleague found, examining both their sample and Census figures, that among *men* there had actually been little change in the relative proportions in manual and non-manual occupations since before the First World War. ". . . in general the picture of rather high stability over time is confirmed".[2]

Unfortunately, different methods used by Glass and his colleagues gave different results. The measurement of Indexes of Association (proportions of fathers and sons occupying the *same* occupational status) showed highest mobility not among the Higher Non-Manual Supervisory but among the Skilled Manual and Routine Non-Manual grades, least among the top grade, i.e. Higher Professional and Administrative. This latter grade displayed what is otherwise described as considerable self-recruitment; doctors' and lawyers' sons increasingly went in for their fathers' professions. However, whatever method was used, the conclusion was that, since about 1890, there had been no significant change in mobility and, indeed, what change had taken place was towards a lessening of mobility, bearing in mind the increase in non-manual occupations.

A rough comparison between certain Western capitalist countries found differences in social mobility between them; but this claim was rejected by two leading American sociologists in a book which, for a number of years, was taken as a standard reference on the subject.[3] The authors aimed to show, by means of certain published data, that total, i.e. up and down mobility, was roughly the same for all industrialised countries. This was due to a number of reasons connected with the processes of industrialisation. But their main conclusion was that where society was stratified, as modern societies were, there was bound to be a general drive to move upwards. This, they claimed, refuted the (Marxist?) assertion that class barriers were insurmountable. Even in

[1] *Social Mobility in Britain*, ed. D. V. Glass (1954).
[2] Same, p. 188. [3] Lipset and Bendix: *Social Mobility in Industrial Society* (1959).

the allegedly rigid caste society of India there was some movement. No society, they declared, was "closed".

This conclusion, that in all industrialised countries total social movement is roughly the same, depends, however, on a common system of social grading. Such a system was developed in the U.S.A. by the National Opinion Research Centre. On the basis of this system of social ranking, many occupations were found to be very close to one another as regards prestige between countries including Britain, the U.S.A. and the U.S.S.R. But Lipset and Bendix's own work uncovered some significant facts in this supposed uniformity between capitalist and socialist countries and between different capitalist countries. First, when total mobility is separated into its constituent parts, upward and downward rates differ quite significantly, even between capitalist countries. Secondly, even in the U.S.A., with its supposedly high upward mobility, there is much movement among small business men and workers (so many hoping to start up on their own) and between coloured and white workers as the former take over the less skilled jobs; but study of a San Francisco suburb with a higher-than-average rate of mobility showed that ". . . all those who work with their hands have spent 80 per cent of their working lives in manual occupations; all in non-manual employment have spent 75 per cent of their careers in such positions".[1] On the other hand, the authors found that since 1801, two-thirds of all the business élite came from families already economically established and only about 10 per cent from manual worker families. What all this amounted to was that, in the U.S.A., with its myth of "rags to riches", there is a lot of short-term shifting about, both within the manual and non-manual grades and across them, but that in the end, between three-quarters and four-fifths stay roughly where they start. So much for Lipset's and Bendix's "refutation", presumably of Marx who, they implied, claimed that class barriers were absolutely insurmountable. It would be interesting to hear from them where Marx actually said this. On the contrary, in often-quoted passages in *The Communist Manifesto*, Marx and Engels talked of members of the middle strata falling into the proletariat, as well as the constant replenishment of the middle strata. Nevertheless the data about U.S. manual workers and the middle strata show that the *insurmountability of barriers between them is largely the case*, at least within the individual's life-time. As between generations (fathers and sons), Lipset and Bendix agreed with Glass and his colleagues; i.e.

[1] Same, p. 165.

in the U.S.A., as in Britain, there is a high correlation between the occupational statuses of father and son. In other words, the son of a professional man is likely to become a professional man, the son of a manual worker a manual worker.[1] Other weaknesses in the book were that the data about the U.S.S.R. did not in fact come from the U.S.S.R. but from émigrés abroad in 1940; such data have to be used with care; and, finally, only occupations occurring in all the countries were compared; but this, as we indicated in the section "What is class?" of this present chapter, leaves out masses of people and lowers the value of the comparisons.

So it is not surprising that Lipset's and Bendix's conclusion was soon challenged. In a detailed rejoinder,[2] Miller pointed out that certain occupations enjoy considerably different status in different countries; for example, the civil servant's high status in Britain is rather exceptional. Again, job status often varies over time (the clerk today and 100 years ago, say). Status rises differ; for example, the rise from middle to upper class is much greater than from working class to middle. These, as well as other complications, make international comparisons very difficult. Miller did draw up, however, an elaborate set of international comparisons, from which he deduced that the countries considered could be placed in one of three bands. In the highest band lay the U.S.A., the U.S.S.R. (again the émigrés in 1940) and Brazil (the rich city of São Paulo only), with much upward and little downward mobility. In the lowest band came countries like Italy, the Netherlands and Japan, with movement mostly downwards. And intermediately came Britain and some other countries, with a high rate of movement, but limited upward and more pronounced down. Miller concluded that there was much less upward mobility in Britain than in the U.S.A.; and in the U.S.A., as we have seen, the real class situation is far more rigid than the "rags to riches" myth would have us believe. We do not live in a society so transformed that it offers much upward movement.

THE EDUCATIONAL LADDER

Reformers of capitalist society who are themselves highly educated, especially those who are or were teachers, always place great emphasis on the importance of the educational system as a means of reform.

[1] "Occupational and social status are to an important extent self-perpetuating." Lipset and Bendix, same, p. 198.

[2] Miller: Comparative Social Mobility (*Current Sociology, 1960*).

They argue that the working class can best break through the class barriers, not by social revolution, which is utopian pie-in-the-sky, but by educating their children. If only one tailor's son can become Arnold Weinstock, at least education can give every other tailor's son a chance to go to university and thence to a profession. So, as an instrument of social equality, social-democratic theorists tend to give educational reform first place. "The ideal of social equality requires the first priority to be given to educational reform", declared Crosland.[1] How much educational reform has therefore been achieved and has it produced equality of opportunity in the "post-capitalist" society?

The Act of 1944, product of the war-time Coalition Government, introduced for the first time universal, compulsory, secondary education. Before the war most children left at the end of "elementary school", usually at the age of 14: less than 15 per cent went on to secondary education, which generally meant grammar school. The 1944 Act decreed that secondary education began at age 11 and ended at 15; and it was hoped that the school-leaving age would soon be raised to 16. It made no division in types of State secondary education, except that schools be "... sufficient in number, character and equipment to afford for all pupils opportunities for education offering such variety of instruction and training as may be desirable in view of their different ages, abilities and aptitudes ..." What happened, however, was that the Government simply adapted what already existed; the grammar and technical schools just carried on and the remaining 70–80 per cent of pupils found themselves in the old elementary schools, extended and re-named "secondary modern". In this respect the ideology of post-war secondary education was the ideology of the 1926 Hadow Report, which divided schoolchildren into three types, the "grammar" (academic), "technical" (suitable for becoming technicians) and the rest (the hewers of wood and drawers of water).

The Act had something of importance to lay down about education after the age of 15 which, for the majority before the war, had been minimal. Local Education Authorities were to provide full- and part-time education for all young persons over the compulsory school-leaving age. County colleges were to be set up—within three years of the passing of the Act—where young people not in full-time education could develop their aptitudes and be prepared for citizenship. Attendance at such County Colleges was to be *compulsory*. To date, no County Colleges have been set up; nor is release of young workers wanting

[1] *The Future of Socialism*, p. 518.

part-time further education compulsory for employers. Both measures *may* come, but they are very slow in coming.

How, then, has State secondary education fared? Within the last few years the value of higher education and of educational qualifications has increased enormously. Acquiring these qualifications, especially a university degree or its equivalent, is generally accepted as a major means (second only to wealth) of rising to managerial or professional status. Has universal, compulsory secondary education given the working-class child greater opportunity of rising to these levels, the levels of the middle- and upper-middle classes?

Researches in the late 1940s and the 1950s produced startling disclosures, which have since become much more widely known. One of the earliest was Hilde Himmelweit's study in 1951 of the connection between social class and type of secondary school attended by a sample 700 schoolchildren aged 13–14 in Greater London.[1] Her results showed that, while children of the upper working-class (foremen, supervisors and skilled manual workers) were properly represented in the grammar schools, the middle class were over-represented and the lower working class (semi-skilled and unskilled) under-represented. This lopsidedness could not be justified by differences in I.Q.s, because I.Q.s varied more *within* each group than *between* groups. But it was the case that working-class children did less well at the 11+ than middle-class children; that, once in grammar school, working-class children (irrespective of I.Q.) did consistently less well than did middle-class children; and that there was a high wastage rate among working-class children. In the grammar schools teachers consistently rated working-class boys lower than middle-class, the working-class boy was less interested in school than his middle-class counterpart and tended to leave earlier, despite the fact that the working-class child realised just as well as the middle-class child that education was the key to advancement. In short, there was strong evidence that differences in performance were due not only to the economic pressures being greater on the working-class than on the middle class child, but to the parents' attitude, which was better among the middle than among the working class. Obviously, parents' attitude is, basically, economically conditioned: not only the sheer difference in present financial circumstances but, where this doesn't apply, to the almost ingrained disposition to fear or despise education, which is associated with membership of another "class". (A case of the "superstructure" reinforcing the "material base".)

[1] Article in Glass (ed). *Social Mobility in Britain.*

These disclosures were reinforced by a number of local studies. In one of these, two contrasting areas, Watford (S.W. Hertfordshire) and Middlesbrough, were selected; the former a more middle-class, the latter a predominantly working-class area based on the steel industry, with a record of pre-war depression and present affluence. In both, the number of grammar-school places after 1944 rose steadily. So did the proportion going to working-class boys—*but more slowly than the total.* Thus the extraordinary fact emerged that, by 1953, working-class representation in the grammar schools had actually fallen. Whose children were taking a bigger and bigger proportion of the increasing grammar-school places? The children of the Registrar-General's Social Class I—managerial, professional and administrative workers. In Watford these children took over twice, and in Middlesbrough nearly three times, the number of places gained by (manual) working-class children.[1]

Now this unequal distribution of places was widely regarded by the local authorities as due almost entirely to differences in mental ability as measured by the "11-plus". (This is not the place to argue about intelligence testing, which is in any case becoming an issue for history.) But, like Himmelweit, the investigators found that the child's *environment* exerted a powerful influence on the child's chances and progress. They found that poor homes and poor schools, what they called the "material" environment, naturally hindered the chances of success; but the greatest influence was "cultural"—parental attitude. (This produced the apparently contradictory situations that, in Watford, the more successful boys did *not* come from the more prosperous homes, while in Middlesbrough they did.) Greater success among children went with parents' higher educational background and ambitions, especially of the mother. When, however, it came to staying on at school till 17 or 18, social class became the most important factor. Although many working-class parents wanted their children to stay on, this wish was much greater among the middle class. The chances of a middle-class boy going to university were, therefore, at least twice as great as for a working-class boy of the same measured ability (I.Q.). This combination of economic and cultural factors, which had operated blatantly in the past, the authors observed, acted more subtly today. ". . . the number of working-class boys entering the grammar schools each year has been increasing fast, and . . . there are more in the schools today than ever before. Nevertheless, the probability that a working-

[1] Floud, Halsey and Martin: *Social Class and Educational Opportunity* (1956).

class boy will get to a grammar school *is not strikingly different from what it was before 1945 . . .*"[1]

Floud and her co-workers were pursuing their investigations when some local education authorities began to drop intelligence tests in secondary school selection; and they decided to extend their investigations to find out how this new, progressive step improved the working-class child's chances. In fact the very opposite was found. Whereas in 1952 (before testing was abandoned) 51 per cent of grammar school boys came from the (manual) working class, in the following year the proportion dropped to under 48 per cent and by 1954 (testing completely abolished) to only 39 per cent. But these figures don't tell the full story. For, since the proportion of *all* boys of secondary school entry age coming from the manual workers actually rose in that period, it meant that manual-worker representation in the grammar schools *fell more* than the above percentages and the chances for sons of the higher professional and managerial employees had grown even more.[2] It was the middle strata, not the manual workers, who were seizing with both hands the opportunities provided by the tripartite system of universal, secondary education.

Closely related to this situation was the problem of early leaving. Investigations showed that early leaving, with its massive waste of ability, stemmed directly from the tripartite system. Children who "failed the 11-plus" and were sent to a secondary modern school almost always regarded themselves as failures and schooling a waste of time, to be borne till the age of 15 when one could get away and begin to earn money. In effect, the selection at 11-plus very largely determined future occupation.[3] Those who stayed on at school became the managerial, professional and technical employees; those who left at 15 became the manual workers. Even by 1967, less than 20 per cent of children were in grammar schools, but nearly 60 per cent in secondary moderns. And it has been calculated that two-fifths of the top 10 per cent of children (ability wise) leave at 15.[4]

That this situation is basically a class situation was confirmed by an official committee, set up under the Tories, which produced the

[1] Floud, Halsey and Martin, same, p. 142 (my italics).

[2] Article: "Social class, intelligence tests and selection for secondary schools", in Floud, Halsey and Anderson (eds), *Education, Economy and Society*.

[3] Floud and Halsey: "English secondary schools and the supply of labour", in Floud, Halsey and Anderson (eds).

[4] Vaizey: *Education for Tomorrow*, p. 18.

following startling figures.[1] One-third of all grammar school boys who could get at least two A-levels left before doing so, mainly due to "home background". The managerial and professional groups or classes accounted for 15 per cent of all schoolchildren but 44 per cent of all Sixth-Formers, while the 12 per cent from unskilled manual workers accounted for only 1½ per cent of Sixth-Formers. Grammar schools started with two-thirds of their incoming pupils having working-class parents, but by the time their pupils reached the Sixth Form, only one-third were children of manual workers. A working-class boy had only one-third of the chance of a middle-class boy of going to university. Wastage, the Report declared, was a social class problem. Despite this wastage, the Tories are determined to maintain the system as it was and to oppose Labour's plan for comprehensive education.

The most important report on the adolescent in (post-capitalist?) Britain today added a lot more information reinforcing the picture already given.[2] Far from there having been an explosion in education, the Crowther Report revealed that by 1959 State expenditure on education had done little more than keep pace with national income. Less than half of all boys and girls aged 15–18 had any education at all, including part-time education. Most of those still in full-time education at the age of 17 were in grammar or independent schools; practically none were in secondary moderns. The Report also performed the valuable job of directly relating staying on at school to parental income, as the following table shows:

1955/56

Father's weekly income	*Proportion of boys and girls still at grammar or technical school at age 17–18*	
	Boys	*Girls*
£7. 10s. or less	29%	32%
Over £16	54%	64%

The figures given in the Crowther Report have changed, but not so much that one can speak of an educational revolution. It is true that more and more young people are getting part-time education (mainly day-release) under the Industrial Training Act; but about half of all still get no further education at all. It is true that more boys and girls are

[1] *Early Leaving:* the Gurney–Dixon Report, 1954. (Central Advisory Council for Education)

[2] *15 to 18:* (the Crowther Report).

staying on at school, but these are still only a tiny fraction of the total.[1] Social class advantages have hardly altered and the children of the middle strata still benefit more than those of the manual workers.

A recent survey confirms that these advantages continue.[2] Tracing the educational histories of over 5,000 children, Dr. Douglas shows the effects of social class, parents' attitudes, type of neighbourhood and similar factors related to socio-economic position. The children's own attitudes also connect with parents' class position: 26 per cent of upper middle-class children are "hard workers", but only 7 per cent of lower working-class. He calculates that, to give children of manual workers the same opportunities as those enjoyed by children of the upper middle-class, grammar school places would have to be increased by 25 per cent. Douglas' book is, in short, a massive exposure of the class discrimination of our schools system in the 1960s, after 20 years of supposed "post-capitalism". "Equality of opportunity" in State schools is still largely a slogan.[3]

What about the universities and places of higher education? The *Robbins Report* showed that, in 1961/62, of all university students 59 per cent had fathers in the professional and managerial classes, 12 per cent in clerical and only 25 per cent in manual occupations. Only 1 per cent of all students had fathers who were unskilled manual workers. The fact that the State grammar schools provided 65 per cent of all undergraduates tends to obscure the class basis. It only confirms, as was shown above, that the State grammar schools provided the middle classes with a new avenue to university education.[4]

This is not unique to Britain. An international comparison among capitalist countries shows a general picture of great inequality in opportunities for higher education. The "non-farm, non-Labour" sectors of society supply (according to country) from three-fifths to over nine-tenths of the students, although in all countries this group is only a small fraction of the total population.[5]

[1] Only just over 6 per cent of all young people over 15 in 1965 stayed on at school. Less than 4 per cent stayed on to 18, i.e. aiming to go on to some form of higher education. (Statistics of Education 1965.)

[2] J. W. B. Douglas: *The Home and the School* (1964).

[3] The former Chief Education Officer for Manchester and later Professor of the Sociology of Education makes the crucial comment: "We cannot hope to get near to equality of educational opportunity until we achieve something like a basic minimum in standards of home life and housing." (W. O. Lester Smith: *Education* (Penguin Books), p. 115.)

[4] *Report of the Committee on Higher Education* (1963), Appendix I.

[5] C. A. Anderson: "Social status of university students", in *Trans. IIIrd World Congress of Sociology* 1956.

And in 1964 no other than Dahrendorf himself, attacking West Germany's class-ridden system, quoted the following percentages of students of working-class origin:

United States	30%
Britain	25%
Sweden	20%
France	7%
West Germany	5%

and compared them with East Germany's 50 per cent.[1]

Comprehensive schools, desirable though they are, are also affected by the social set-up. Labour spokesmen believe that they will end class division in the long run. But a recent study of a London comprehensive school[2] found that while children of non-manual and of manual workers were in 40:60 proportion in the A-streams, the B-streams and lower were 85–90 per cent manual workers' children.

Pressure of the technological race is forcing an expansion of technological higher education. Such education takes place in Britain in technological universities, colleges of advanced technology and polytechnics. But a rearguard action is being fought to prevent equality between these institutions and the "pure" universities. The aim is the same as it has always been: to keep the universities as a training-ground for the future owners and "managers" of our capitalist society, to imbue them with the ideology of the ruling class, the future inheritors as well as the Wilsons, Heaths, Jenkinses and Croslands, while the technological institutions provide the advisers and technologists who, as we shall see later, are of key importance to *production*.[3]

[1] *The Observer*, 5th July 1964.

[2] Julienne Ford: "Comprehensive schools as social dividers", *New Society*, 10th October 1968.

[3] The projected economy cuts for 1969/70 and succeeding years, ordered by the Wilson administration, will slow down the rate of educational expansion considerably. According to W. Easton, principal of Southgate Technical College and president (1968/9) of the Association of Teachers in Technical Institutions, the cuts threaten to produce a situation in education worse than any since 1931, the worst year of the Great Slump.

APPENDIX 1

(to Chapter 4, "Wealth")

Stimulated by the criticisms, the Inland Revenue have recently made estimates of distribution of wealth; and it is interesting to compare these with those quoted in the main chapter.

According to the 111th Report of the Board, in 1967 only 17·3 million persons had any wealth worth speaking of, i.e. just over one-third of the population. Of these 13·6 million had less than £5,000 each. So 3·7 million shared £59·4 thousand million out of a total net wealth of £83·6 thousand million. In percentages, this works out that about 7 per cent of the population owned 71 per cent of the wealth. This estimate is therefore not very different from Revell's, which reckoned that in 1960 5 per cent of the population owned 75 per cent of the wealth. Also 1,486,000 persons (3 per cent of the population) owned £44·1 thousand million or 53 per cent of the wealth, compared with 2 per cent owning 55 per cent in 1960 according to *The Economist.*

But Revell's and *The Economist's* figures are themselves derived from Inland Revenue statistics which, as we have seen, can't take fully into account the "discretionary trusts" by which property is handed over more than 5 years before the owner's death. Hence their figures, as well as those of the Inland Revenue, understate the inequality. It is very probable, therefore, that the reduction in inequality of ownership and the fall in degree of wealth of the top 1 per cent—from 56 per cent (1936/38) to 42 per cent (1960) to 34 per cent (1967)—is much less than the estimates suggest.

APPENDIX 2

(to Chapter 4, "The Old School")

The directors of the Bank of England illustrate perfectly the interweaving of private and State banking, industrial capital, upgraded managerial representatives, the odd couple of trade union leaders and, most recently, international banking and finance. In 1969 the directors were:—

Sir L. K. O'Brien (Governor)	Grammar school, joined Bank 1927, keen on unemployment—for others.

Sir M. Parsons (Deputy Governor)	Private school, joined Bank 1928.
W. M. Allen (executive)	Dulwich School and London School of Economics
Lord Carron (deceased)	Secondary school, ex-president A.E.U.
J. Q. Hollom (executive)	Private school, joined Bank 1936
W. J. Keswick	Winchester and Cambridge, director Matheson & Co. (shipping and insurance), deputy chairman Alliance Assurance, vice-chairman Sun Insurance, director British Petroleum.
Sir M. Laing	Private school, chairman Laings
C. J. Morse (executive)	Winchester and Oxford, former director Glyn Mills, and Legal and General Assurance.
Lord Nelson	Oundle and Cambridge, chairman English Electric, joint deputy chairman British Aircraft Corporation, director Marconi Co., and International Nickel Co. of Canada, chancellor Aston (Technological) University of Birmingham.
Lord Pilkington	Rugby and Cambridge, chairman Pilkington Bros. and other glass companies, chancellor Loughborough Technological University.
Lord Robens	Chairman N.C.B., ex-union official.
Sir H. W. Smith	Grammar school and Cambridge, former senior Civil Servant, chairman Powell Duffryn, deputy chairman Guest, Keen and Nettlefold.
Sir R. Thornton	Private school, director Barclays Bank and United Dominions Trust.
J. G. W. Davies	Tonbridge School and Cambridge, occupational psychologist.
Sir Val Duncan	Harrow and Oxford, chairman Rio-Tinto Zinc Corporation.
G. H. W. Richardson	Cambridge, chairman Schroders (merchant bank)
Sir Eric Roll	Ex-professor of economics, economic adviser to Tory and Labour Governments, director Times Newspapers and S. G. Warburg (merchant bank)
Sir J. M. Stevens	Winchester. Managing director, Morgan Grenfell and Suez Finance Co. United Kingdom executive International Monetary Fund and International Bank.

The interweaving of industry with finance and the continuity of wealth are also illustrated by the chairmen of the biggest insurance companies, now among the most powerful business institutions in the country.

Company	*Chairman*
Royal Group	F. L. Orme (Charterhouse and Cambridge) director Midland Bank

Commercial Union Group	R. C. Brooks (Haileybury and Cambridge) director United Planters (Holdings) Ltd.
General Accident	Sir S. Norrie-Miller (Rugby and Oxford)
Northern & Employers	Lord Knollys (Harrow and Oxford) director Barclays Bank chairman B.O.A.C. 1943–47 chairman Vickers 1956–62 chairman English Steel 1959–65 Minister, Washington 1951–52
Royal Exchange	Lord Kindersley (Eton and Scots Guards) manging director, Lazards 1927–64 chairman Rolls Royce director Bank of England
Guardian	Lord Blackford (Eton and Sandhurst) deputy chairman Midland Bank Tory M.P., N. Croydon 1922–40
Sun Alliance Group	T. D. Barclay (Harrow and Cambridge) described in *Who's Who* as "banker and landed proprietor" director Barclays Bank
Phoenix	Sir E. Ferguson
London	Harald Peake (Eton, Cambridge and Coldstream Guards) chairman Lloyds Bank director Rolls Royce director Steel Co. of Wales
Norwich Union	D. E. Longe chairman East Coast Grain Silos Ltd.
Eagle Star	Sir B. Mountain, Bt. (Charterhouse and Sandhurst) chairman Phillip Hill Investment Trust Ltd.
Prudential	Sir F. Morgan (grammar school) director Midland Bank
Legal & General	Viscount Harcourt, (Eton and Oxford) director Morgan Grenfell chairman of several other insurance companies married first to a Grosvenor on I.M.F. 1954–7
Standard	Sir I. Campbell
Sun Life	C. G. Randolph (Christs Hospital) director, Glyn Mills (bankers)
Pearl	Sir G. Kitchen, Bart (Bradford Grammar and Oxford) chairman of several companies including connections with Portugal
Scottish Widows (oh, those widows!)	Sir A. Porritt (New Zealand and Oxford), a surgeon to the Queen, ex-athlete and member of International Olympic Committee. Son of a New Zealand surgeon.

APPENDIX 3

Average earnings 1913/14 and 1960 by occupational class

MEN

Class		*1913/14* £	*1960* £	*1960 as % of 1913/14*
1A	Higher professional	328	2,034	620
1B	Lower professional	155	847	546
2B	Managers	200	1,850	925
3	Clerks	99	682	689
4	Foremen	113	1,015	898
5	Skilled manual	99	796	804
6	Semi-skilled manual	69	581	842
7	Unskilled manual	63	535	849
	Averages	92	808	874

WOMEN

Class		*1913/14* £	*1960* £	*1960 as % of 1913/14*
1A		—	1,425	—
1B		89	606	680
2B		80	1,000	1,250
3		45	427	949
4		57	602	1,056
5		44	395	898
6		50	339	678
7		28	283	1,000
	Averages	50	436	866
Men and women	weighted averages	80	683	

(from G. Routh: *Occupation and Pay in Great Britain 1906–60*).

6

THE "MIDDLE CLASS": WHAT IS IT AND WHERE IS IT GOING?

DEFINITIONS

The picture given so far is rather mixed. It shows a distinct upper class, removed by wealth, income and way of life from the rest of the population, except for a section of "aspirants", mainly of Census Social Class I. This upper, or capitalist, class is divisible into smaller groups, including the most important, ruling group. Although the composition of this class, as of all classes, has changed over time and continues to change, there is considerable rigidity also. The rest of the population is, however, less clear-cut. Although, especially in educational opportunity, the middle class has distinct advantages over the working class, education is not the only, or even the most important, criterion of class; while as regards incomes, the middle strata are nearer to the manual workers than to the capitalists, and in part overlap the wage-earners. The distinction between middle class and working class is not yet clear. We must first find some satisfactory definition of "middle class".

What about the amount of capital held? To start with, there's the problem of how much. According to *The Economist* estimate for 1959/60, owners of fortunes between £3,000 and £25,000 comprised 10 per cent of all taxpayers (about 30 per cent of the population). If the upper limit is thought to be too low and is raised to £50,000, it only brings in another 1·2 per cent of taxpayers. On the other hand, many individuals who would be rated middle class own much less than £3,000. But there we enter the region of 88 per cent of tax-payers who own less than £100, where it would be impossible to distinguish "middle class" from "working class".

Perhaps a better criterion would be incomes. But what incomes? £2,000–£5,000 a year say? Then, according to the Inland Revenue, there were in 1966/67 1,339,000 such persons, or only 6·2 per cent of "income units", a reasonable proportion fairly near the Census 1961 figure—excluding clerical workers. But, then, there are many workers getting £2,000 a year gross. And are all over £5,000 a year capitalists? If we stretch the upper limit to £10,000 a year, only 138,000 more "income units" are drawn in, raising the proportion to just under 7 per cent.

For statistical purposes the Ministry of Labour distinguishes between manual and non-manual workers. This seems to be a distinction with some point. Nevertheless, it is being increasingly complicated by the pace of technological change. A shorthand-typist may be non-manual, but is she any more so than a skilled industrial process worker of today? On the contrary, with increasing automation the process worker may use his hands less, but has to know and may be paid more, than the typist; but he is classed as a "manual" worker. And there are large numbers of people like shop assistants and service workers (waiters, hairdressers) who can't easily be put into one compartment or the other, except that they are often poorly paid.

A sharp distinction between manual and non-manual labour was certainly possible in the early days of industrial capitalism. Then the manual workers, who created the goods, and those who did the clerical work, supervised or managed, were quite separate strata. Today the distinction is less meaningful and in certain respects irrelevant. Nevertheless, it can be neither ignored nor dismissed, as some Marxists were prone to do in the past. It has to be put in perspective (as we will try to do later).

Finally, there are differences in attitudes and ways of life. These, it has been said, tend to disappear where the working class moves into traditionally middle-class areas. But many habits still distinguish middle class from working class: speech, types of entertainment, reading matter, attitudes to children and their education. Each of these has been found to lend real substance to the distinction between the two "classes". Obviously then, to define the "middle class" is a complex business, with many pros and cons.

Most of the earlier modern writers took a negative approach. There is, they said, a small class of very rich people who are obviously above the middle class; but this class is at most only 1 per cent or less of the population. Then there is a very large section of the population who are not merely manual workers but wage-earners as well: in 1951, according to one estimate, they comprised 68 per cent of the male occupied population. Then, the argument went, the "middle class" consists of those between the very rich and the manual wage-earners, i.e. about 30 per cent of the population.[1]

[1] Bonham—*The Middle Class Vote*. Lewis and Maude defined the middle class similarly as those between the upper and working classes, comprising about 35 per cent of the population. Kahan, Butler and Stokes gave Upper-middle 3 per cent, Middle class 25 per cent, Lower-middle 4 per cent. (*British Journal of Sociology*, June 1966.)

Now, this definition, negative though it is, is not a bad one to start with. It is really based on occupation, because the figures come either from the Censuses or from the statistics of people at work published by the Ministry of Labour. And this is evident when, going on from this "negative" definition, these writers list the various sections of the middle class. With some variation, the main sections of the middle class are small employers and managers, professional people, those working on their own account and white collar workers.

This very indistinctness contrasts with the distinctness of the middle class when industrial capitalism was growing during the nineteenth century. Then at the top end came the independent professional, the clergyman, the schoolmaster, the doctor. Next came the bulk of the middle class—the shopkeepers and small tradesmen sentimentally described by Arnold Bennett and H. G. Wells. Lastly, there were the self-employed craftsmen and peasants, defined by Marx as the lower strata of the middle class. (By the present century, however, the small self-employed craftsman was probably regarded as no longer quite middle class.) The common distinguishable feature of the old middle class was that all its members were either self-employed, or employers on a small scale, with a personal or semi-personal relationship with customer or client. Whether or not the clerk could be regarded as middle class is a point of some importance, which will be discussed further. Marx, as we shall then see, regarded him as a worker. But *subjectively* the clerk a century ago regarded himself unquestionably as middle class. If we include him among the old middle class, therefore, the class included some "non-manual" *employees.* But at least the concept of the middle class in the nineteenth century was much clearer: it was based mainly on the idea of "independence" and self-employment.

During the second half of the last century, however, industrial capitalism began to create a new set of occupations. There were, first, the supervisors: "An industrial army of workmen, under the command of a capitalist, requires, like an army, officers (managers) and sergeants (foremen, overlookers), who, while the work is being done, command in the name of the capitalist. The work of supervision becomes their established and exclusive function."[1] There were also the ancillary workers, including clerks and warehousemen. And the professional engineers and technicians, some employed but many also independent members of the new and rapidly multiplying professions. Also the

[1] *Capital,* Vol. I, chapter 13. See also *The Communist Manifesto,* sec. 1.

State apparatus expanded, employing a growing army of civil servants and local government employees.

Marx later became conscious of this complication. As far as he was concerned, most of those employed in large-scale industry in the mid-nineteenth century belonged to the working class; but some did not. This, at least, is how I understand the passage in *Capital* which says:

> "The main cleavage is that between the workers who are actually employed at the mechanised tools . . ., on the one hand, and those who are mere attendants of these workers, children for the most part, on the other (presumably today's "labourers"—H.F.) . . . In addition to the two main classes, just mentioned, there is a staff of persons, few in number, whose business it is to look after the machinery as a whole, and to keep it in good repair: engineers, mechanics of various kinds, joiners etc. These comprise a superior class of workmen, some of them scientifically trained, and some of them skilled craftsmen; they are distinct from the class of factory operatives, and are merely aggregated with these. This division of labour is purely technical."[1]

In a footnote he pointed to the confusion in British official statistics, some of which excluded the last class of "workmen", while others included among "operatives" not only the engineers, etc., but also the managerial staff, clerks, warehousemen, etc. Thus, it would seem that Marx did not regard managerial staff, etc., in the same light as factory operatives, but *did* look at technicians as superior workmen. But more of that later.

The following table shows the changing proportions of the different sections of the so-called middle class.[2]

Group	*Percentage of whole occupied population*				
	1851	*1921*	*1931*	*1951*	*1961*
1. Clerks, shop assistants, etc.	3·5	12·1	13·1	16·6	19·0
2. On own account	4·5	5·3	5·2	5·0	4·2
3. Professional	2·6	4·2	4·4	6·0	7·0
4. Employers and managers	9·1	6·0	6·0	6·0	5·9
2, 3 and 4 Totals	16·2	15·5	15·6	17·0	17·0

[1] *Capital* I, Ch. 13, sec. 4.

[2] Estimates from the Censuses of Population and from Klingender. The figures cannot be regarded as exact, only as rough estimates, because of the changing categories used by the Censuses. They are, at best, a guide to general trends.

The table shows that the proportion of those working on their own account, mostly handicraftsmen and shopkeepers, has hardly changed over the century and stays at roughly 5 per cent of the occupied population. On the other hand, employers and managers (sections which the Registrar-General sometimes separates and sometimes lumps together) have declined, due mainly to the takeover or closing down of small businesses. But the lowest section of the middle class, chiefly clerks and shop assistants, has this century grown enormously. Professional people, also, have increased in proportion, especially since 1945. But perhaps the most interesting fact is that, *if clerks and shop assistants are excluded, the middle class has grown very little over the century*. The so-called expansion of the middle class, if expansion there has been, has been mostly in the *lowest sector*, the clerks and shop assistants, the worst paid and the sector of lowest social status.

The whole story of the middle class can only be appreciated, however, if we look at their history over the past century or so.

THE CLERK

Before the great commercial expansion of the second half of the nineteenth century, the clerk was in a distinctly different category of employee from the artisan.[1] He worked in a small office associated with some small enterprise. His relations with his employer were personal and he was expected to show, besides moderate education and a knowledge of book-keeping, qualities of diligence, tact and good sense. Salary and promotion depended entirely on the employer, to whom he was often tied for life. Uriah Heap was the servile archetype. Fairly early on during the nineteenth century, two tiers of clerks appeared: those employed in banking, the civil service and the more prosperous commercial enterprises, better-paid and hence more distinctly members of the middle class, and the rest, e.g. railway clerks and those in less well-paying firms, with nearly proletarian incomes. Despite income differences, however, both groups regarded themselves as above the working class, as "gentlemen" who rarely if ever argued about their remuneration. They imitated the ways of the upper class and regarded trade unionism and class struggle with abhorrence. Status was more important than money: Weber rightly pointed out that this situation was more feudal than capitalist in character.

But industrial and commercial expansion in the second half of the

[1] D. Lockwood, *The Blackcoated Worker* (1958).

nineteenth century and mass education brought about the spectacular growth of clerical labour to which we have already referred. Marx later noted that this brought about a steady fall in pay and the slow death of the personal relationship between employer and employed. The oversupply was aggravated, at the turn of the century, by amalgamations among banks, insurance companies, railways, etc. About 1895 Booth wrote: "Financially, the great mass of clerks are on a level with the great mass of artisans ... As in the legal profession, the eminence of a small minority dazzles the eyes of a large number whose talents might perhaps have been more profitably directed elsewhere."[1] About 1910 the National Union of Clerks estimated average salaries of all clerks to be 25/– to 30/– a week. Trade unionism grew among postal workers, railway clerks, local government officials and civil servants, but not among commercial clerks, who were in the main still scattered among large numbers of small offices, nor among the aristocrats of clerical labour in the banks and insurance companies.

The First World War and its aftermath were periods of sharp inflation, which hit the relatively fixed salaries of the white-collar workers. Trade unionism among them spread. In 1918 even those aristocrats, the bank clerks, formed the Bank Officers' Guild, although careful to declare in their first circular that the organisation was "... not a militant trade union, but a *guild*, conciliatory in its methods and broad enough to take in the whole profession from managers to junior clerks". By 1930 the average salary of all male clerks over 20 was 80/–, only just equal to the average earnings of all male skilled manual workers. In other words, the differentials now lay between higher- and lower-paid clerks, and between clerks on average and the lower-paid (semi-skilled and unskilled) manual workers.

But by the late 1930s even these differentials began to be squeezed; and this process continued during the Second World War and after, until the mid-1950s. *In 1956 average clerical salaries were roughly the same as average earnings for all manual workers.* Since then, as we have already pointed out, the male clerk's relative position has worsened. In October 1968 he got, on average, £18 12s. 5d. compared with the male manual worker's average of £23. (The female clerical worker was better off than her "manual" counterpart, with an average £14 8s. as against £11 6s.)[2]

Why, then, do so many young men prefer to become clerks rather

[1] Quoted in Klingender, *The Condition of Clerical Labour in Britain.*
[2] Figures supplied by the C. and A.W.U.

than factory workers? For a number of well-known reasons: the advantages that go with "non-manual" status, shorter hours, longer holidays and pleasanter working conditions. But even more important are the greater security of employment, the more individual relationship between employee and management and the greater chances of promotion. A manual worker can still be dismissed at a few hours' notice, must generally rely for higher pay on collective agreements and virtually his only possible promotion is to charge-hand or foreman.

Striking evidence of the different attitudes engendered by these different conditions was obtained by a study in 1956 of workers in a Scottish steel company.[1] The firm was nationalised in 1951 and denationalised two years later. The changes made no real difference to either clerks or manual workers. What was important was that it was an old, family-owned enterprise. The investigator interviewed, over a period of 18 months, 96 clerks and 118 manual workers, including 33 shop stewards and active trade unionists and obtained the following information. Of all aspects of their employment clerks unanimously regarded promotion as most important, while 90 per cent of the manual workers said it was pay. Clerks wanted promotion, had reasonable expectations of being promoted and prepared, or had prepared themselves for it by attending evening classes. The manual workers overwhelmingly did not want promotion, did not expect it and did not attend night school. Behind this lay the fact that, while promotion would not cause the clerks any difficulties either at work or at home, it would create both for the manual workers—they would be accused of going over to the management. The firm (under private ownership) was anti-trade union and this resulted in the clerks joining a staff association, even though it had virtually no power and the clerks themselves were contemptuous of it. This led the clerks to the contradictory view that unions were good in general and OK for manual workers, but not for clerks; while the manual workers believed that clerks *ought* to have a union. The clerks preferred bargaining individually, the manual workers collectively. The clerks regarded themselves as being on the management side of the firm; but the manual workers put them on their own (the workers') side. The clerks were overwhelmingly against nationalisation, while the workers were 80 per cent in favour.

[1] A. J. M. Sykes: Some differences in the attitudes of clerical and manual workers. (*Sociological Review*, vol. 13, 1965).

However, the post-war trend has clearly been towards greater mechanisation and larger concentrations of clerical workers in bigger and bigger offices. Already by the mid-1950s, one-third of all clerks were employed in units of more than 80 (as against manual workers, three-quarters of whom work in units of more than 100). While up to just after the war mechanisation was overwhelmingly ancillary to human effort (the manual typewriter, duplicator and so on), now more and more the machine is becoming the pacemaker in an electronic automated system and the routine clerk an auxiliary to the machine. As everyone knows, automation is being introduced to keep down the spiralling amount and cost of paper work. The clerk's increasing feeling of frustration is added to by the recent trend towards the recruitment of university graduates for management training. Thus there exists a wide spectrum of conditions for clerical workers, from those described in the steel company to those akin to manual workers'. In the steel company described above, the clerks did join the clerical workers' union some years later, precisely because promotion chances diminished owing to the company's introduction of outsiders as management trainees.

This trend produces in the clerical worker what Lockwood called "status ambiguity", or uncertainty as to one's position in the class structure of society. "This 'status ambiguity' . . . presents one of the most important obstacles to the mutual identification of clerk and manual worker."[1] The average clerk is no longer a member of the "middle class", but neither is he working-class; his position is "marginal", "ambiguous". For, despite some lowering of conditions and his relatively lower pay, the clerk still enjoys the advantages of "non-manual" employment mentioned above, and is on the whole still physically separated from the industrial worker. Nearly half of all clerks have had grammar-school or private education. In limitation of family size, attitude towards his children's education and in his leisure preferences, the clerk behaves like the "middle class". Lockwood argued, therefore, that the clerk is not a proletarian in Marx's sense and that this fact refutes Marx.

Even his turning towards trade unionism demonstrates this ambiguity. Trade unionism flourishes where there is a lot of bureaucracy, detailed and rigid job grading and limited chances of promotion. It is, therefore, strong in the civil service, local government and the railways, only moderately so in banking and insurance and weakest

[1] Lockwood, p. 133.

in commercial offices, where rises and promotion are still largely individually negotiated. Even where it is strong it is not generally "socialist", i.e. affiliated to the Labour Party or even to the T.U.C. Thus black-coat is quite different from manual-worker class-consciousness. Hence, Lockwood adds, although the Marxist insistence on class contains a basic truth, the Marxian idea of an "undifferentiated propertyless mass" is just not true.

Lockwood was, however, both unfair to Marx and premature in part of his conclusion. As readers will have noticed earlier in the present chapter, Marx did *not* consider all who were not capitalists, or even all who worked for wage or salary, as belonging to an "undifferentiated propertyless mass". Propertyless, yes, undifferentiated no. He was certainly aware of a discrepancy between the non-manual (and the manual) worker's objective class position and his subjective illusions. Who else invented the term "false consciousness"? What is true is that many Marxists have underestimated both the different objective position of the clerical worker, the power of this false consciousness, and how it can lead the clerical worker not merely to fail to understand socialism but to be hostile to it. (Of course industrial workers can also be deluded.) They have, in other words, thought of it only as a temporary obstacle, which real class-consciousness arising from propertylessness would overcome in a relatively short space of time; failing to take fully into account the power and persistence of this delusion.

Lockwood made the common mistake of seeming to think that nothing would alter very much in the future. On the contrary, the pressures driving the clerk towards a more proletarian outlook have increased. A few years after Lockwood's book was published, NALGO not only affiliated to the TUC, but seconded the famous T. & G.W.U. motion against the Government's incomes policy at the 1967 T.U.C. The National Union of Bank Employees successfully fought a major battle for recognition, increased its membership substantially and took industrial action over salary claims. All the evidence as to "market situation" (position as regards the sale of his labour-power), "work situation" (position as regards actual conditions of work) and status show this ambiguity under increasing pressure, and the clerk's behaviour converging towards the manual worker's, a convergence which, as we shall see, was later to be described by a group of British sociologists—including Lockwood himself. Even if the objective situations between clerk and manual worker differ—and they are bound to differ so long as the different types of work continue—and, with this objective difference, subjective notions also, this difference is no refutation of Marx. After all, subjective illusions (false consciousness) are not peculiar to the clerk, or to non-manual workers in general. At the same time, Marxists are bound to agree that, even with the "convergent" trend, the majority of clerks have this "ambiguous" attitude which Lockwood correctly pointed out. Nevertheless, the importance of the fact that *half of all clerks voted Labour* in the 1945 General Election can't be overstressed. It means that this half looked to "the party of the working class" for a brighter future. Even if this vote was largely "instrumental", i.e. simply for what they could get economically under a Labour Government, the vote constituted an important step from a political and sociological point of view. Although the Labour leaders betrayed their hopes, clerks must still be searching for another movement which will help realise them. They can move Left or Right: allies or enemies.

SALES AND SERVICE EMPLOYEES

To the 2,840,000 clerks must be added just over 2 million sales workers and 2¼ million employed in personal services (waiters, domestics, hairdressers, etc.). Nearly half of all sales workers and two-thirds of service workers are women, many so grossly underpaid that the State, through Wages Councils, was forced to lay down minimum rates of pay. Some, for example waiters in the posher restaurants, earn quite a lot: but even they, or salesladies in the more exclusive shops, could hardly be called "middle class". With the spread of the supermarket and self-service, the personal element has disappeared from a good deal of shop work: the saleslady becomes a shop assistant, the waiter an "impersonal dispenser at the display counter". With this trend, trade unionism grows as well, but slowly, a not uncommon feature among poorly-paid workers with a high turnover rate. Like the clerical worker, the sales and service employees' attitudes tend to vary with the degree of bureaucratisation of the enterprise. Weber's insistence on the importance of bureaucratisation is vindicated here also. But once again, sales and service employees can only be regarded as non-industrial *workers* with an ambiguous class attitude, hardly likely to become part of the spearhead of the revolution, but there to be won as allies or, at least, away from identification with the employing class.

THE SMALL MANUFACTURER AND TRADER

This hodge-podge assembly of "small men", so beloved of the Beaverbrook Press, was really the core of the petit bourgeoisie of the mid-nineteenth century. Mainly group 2 of our table (p. 183), as well as the smallest employers of group 4, they total today just over 1½ million persons. But, as the table shows, group 2 has pretty well remained the same proportion of the whole population since 1851. Together, however, small manufacturers and traders have declined as a proportion of the population as they have been steadily absorbed by bigger fish. This is what partly lies behind the decrease in group 4.

The overwhelming majority are self-employed. Thousands of people are always trying to make a go of shop or small business, but even in good times hundreds go bankrupt—in bad times thousands go to the wall. As Marx pointed out, they exhibit within themselves a contradiction of the capitalist system, for they are both capitalists and workers. In respect of ownership of their own capital (premises and equipment) they are capitalists; but part of what they get paid is merely wages for their labour. This curious situation in fact tends to make them feel separated from both capitalists and workers. Even if mortgaged to the hilt and dependent on the big companies for their supplies, they grip hard on to the illusion that they are "independent". They fear big business and its ally, the State apparatus, and socialism equally. Hence they exhibit that political vacillation which is the hallmark of the petit bourgeoisie.

THE PROFESSIONS

> "The bourgeoisie has robbed of their haloes various occupations hitherto regarded with awe and veneration. Doctor, lawyer, priest, poet and scientists have become its wage-labourers."[1]

Professional people, in marked contrast to the small manufacturers and traders, are not conservative,[2] but a product of, and directly helpful to, capitalism. In recent years their number has increased phenomenally. In 1931 there were 840,000 professional people, in 1951 over 1¼ million and in 1961 nearly 1¾ million. All sorts of groups are trying to acquire professional status and students of the subject have found it hard to

[1] *The Communist Manifesto*, sec. 1.

[2] "The lower middle class, the small manufacturer, the shopkeeper ... all these fight against the bourgeoisie, to save from extinction their existence as fractions of the middle class. They are therefore not revolutionary, but conservative" (*The Communist Manifesto*).

construct a permanent definition of a "profession". The main pre-war survey took the overriding characteristic to be the possession of a specific technique, but some "techniques" were at a fairly low level, e.g. opticians and secretaries. Other important characteristics were "a sense of responsibility", a tendency to form associations (professional not trade union) and payment by fee or salary and not by profit (although there were certain exceptions, e.g. the pharmacist).

The history of professionalism shows the evolution of two distinct types, plus many professions having some of the characteristics of both. Those which arose during the Middle Ages were either secular guilds (surgeons, apothecaries), or closely associated with the Church (law, teaching). Apart from teaching, however, all became free of religion by the sixteenth century; and they were unaffected by the bourgeois revolution, because they sold personal services which could be bought alike by feudal knight or capitalist burgess. The tradition of independence and superiority probably reached its height during the eighteenth century, when, apart from teaching, those older professions (and some of the new) came to be regarded as the occupations of gentlemen. That tradition has lingered on to the present.

But the Industrial Revolution brought about a tremendous change. Suddenly a host of new "professional" skills came into being or enormously expanded—chemists, engineers, surveyors and many others. The Institution of Civil Engineers was set up as early as 1818 and the Pharmaceutical Society in 1841. Industrial and commercial expansion in the second half of the nineteenth century saw the establishment of many more associations, including those of surveyors, accountants, company secretaries and teachers, all needed by capitalist expansion.

Within the last fifty years or so the most important changes have taken place in the economic and social situation of most professional people. On the one hand, the monopolies have grown enormously and the proportion of scientists, engineers, accountants and others employed by them has grown too. Some of these professionals have set up enterprises of their own; but usually they serve the big firms. Secondly, the growth of the State apparatus (the political, social and economic "management" of capitalism) has likewise brought an increase of professionals as employees of the State, especially those dealing with the public and social services. This employment may be indirect, but no one really doubts that most doctors, nurses and teachers are in fact salaried servants of the State. In 1961 it was estimated that three-quarters of all professional workers were salaried employees. The contrast to the situation in the eighteenth century, when the professional was a "gentleman", is quietly but dramatically shown by a recent writer's definition of a profession as "... a type of higher-grade, non-manual occupation".[1]

As soon as enough members of a particular "profession" want to get organised, they set up a professional association. In fact, "A profession can only be said to exist when there are bonds between the practitioners, and these bonds can take but one shape—that of the formal association."[2] The professional association's primary functions are said to be to maintain professional status for its members, to ensure that recruitment is selective, to retain exclusive control and to keep up and improve professional standards. The emphasis on status and standards has, in the past, gone with rejection of trade union methods of collective bargaining, including strike action. Indeed, the professional association is usually registered under the Companies Act, which specifically forbids it to undertake industrial action. But of course, its members are profoundly concerned about salaries; and the association usually performs this side of its activity indirectly, by providing employers with information and conducting public agitation and propaganda. In some cases, notably the doctors, the professional association is not afraid to call on its members to carry out what is, in fact, if not in law, strike action.

This brings us to the 64,000-dollar question: are professional people workers or not? On the one hand, three-quarters of them are employees and most of the rest are dependent on the big firms and State departments (including local government) for their livelihood.[3] On the other hand, they do not act like workers; they form associations, not unions, are more concerned about status than about pay and mostly vote Tory. Weber, rather than Marx, seems to have got it right in their case.

Weber, readers will recall, put "status" against "class": the former was, he said, more important in modern industrial society than the latter. But Weber also observed that, while status comes to the fore in static periods, *class becomes more prominent in dynamic times.* Why is this so, and how does it connect with the professional worker's apparently greater concern with status? K. Prandy, a sociologist who

[1] G. Millerson: *The Qualifying Associations*, p. 10.

[2] Carr-Saunders and Wilson, *The Professions*, p. 298.

[3] The Tory writers, Lewis and Maude, admit that without State intervention many professions—health, education, the arts—would have declined (*Professional People*, Ch. 5).

has thought deeply about this problem, concludes that people will be more concerned about their *status* in society *if they accept the existing social order*; and, naturally, the higher one's position in society the more one is inclined to accept it.

> ". . . society is seen by those in power to be stratified, not on class lines, according to the possession or non-possession of power, but on lines of status, that is, a set of superior and inferior grades in which every member accepts the validity of the status criteria, and thus his own place within the hierarchy. Status stratification is essentially harmonious, in the sense that it arises out of an acceptance of the authority structure. Individuals can compete with one another to raise their own status, but the validity of the criteria by which status is measured, the basis of legitimation, is not questioned."[1]

Predominance of a status view in the professional associations comes with two conditions. First, there is the long tradition among professionals that they are above the ordinary workers, i.e. manual and lower non-manual. Secondly, the favourable post-war situation as regards salaries, conditions and chances of promotion. The professional, especially the higher-grade, then tends to adopt the outlook of those in power: he considers ability to be well rewarded and existing society as just.

Willy-nilly, however, the inexorable pressures of capitalism force a steady lowering of real income and conditions of employment or, at best, a mounting struggle to maintain existing standards for all but those at the top. There are sporadic outbursts of resentment and militancy: the battle by junior hospital doctors against the power and advantages of the élite of consultants; the university teachers' lobby of Parliament over the reference of their pay claim to the Prices and Incomes Board; the nurses' militant campaign and, of course, the teachers' actions. The "brain drain" is a direct result of this worsening situation. Although pay differentials between the mass of professionals and the mass of workers sometimes widen, in the *long* term they steadily decrease. Negotiations with their employers become more and more impersonal as the employing groups get bigger and bigger. Employers' efforts to keep the salaries bill down get tougher as the demand for professional services and expertise increases. Less and less do the professional employees find themselves able to influence policy.

[1] K. Prandy: *Professional Employees* (1964) p. 37. Notice how this links status-view with functionalist consensus; and both with Marxian "false consciousness".

"Many more scientists are used, and more money spent on research, for defence work than for any other activity", Prandy writes. "If their influence in this area is weak, it is no less so than in others. There is doubt about the influence of scientists in the 'Office of the Minister of Science' and further doubt about the influence of the Minister himself. Outside the Government and within industry the position is no better and may be worse. The technologist has a good chance of reaching the ranks of management, and in certain cases even the board of directors, but there is a widespread feeling that their numbers are far too few and their influence far too small."[1]

There are, of course, still substantial differences in pay among professional employees. In February 1968 average incomes of solicitors employed in industry and commerce ranged from £2,200 at age 30 to £4,500 at age 55. Government economists and statisticians received from £2,300 at 30 to £4,600 at 55; graduate engineers (in 1966) from £1,800 at 30 to £4,350 at 55. But teachers in regional colleges (polytechnics and colleges of technology) teaching similar material as at universities and often carrying out original research, received (in 1968) from £1,980 at 30 to only £2,267 at 55. This reflects governmental policy of keeping the level of public expenditure low (except in the case of solicitors and other government advisers, where outside remuneration is very attractive). But the figures also show that the top salaries go to the oldest, who generally hold the most senior jobs. Progress to £4,000-plus is usually a slow business and these higher salaries are enjoyed, of course, only by a small minority. Inland Revenue classification of incomes for 1966/67 shows that, of all incomes before tax, only just over 2 per cent were over £3,000 a year. Even bearing in mind the criticisms of Inland Revenue statistics, it is obvious that the vast majority of professional workers have incomes at the lower ends of the scales.

The result is a growing disenchantment with the existing state of society among more and more professional workers, who turn from the professional association to the professional trade union, from a "status" to a "class" outlook. The ideal type of class consciousness, Prandy writes, is ". . . a rejection of the claims of those with power, and the belief that this power must be challenged".[2] Of course, between the extreme status and extreme class attitudes lies a whole range of mixtures of the two, sometimes glaringly self-contradictory. The

[1] Prandy, p. 28. [2] Prandy, p. 174.

mingling of class and status outlooks means that these professional workers adopt what Lockwood calls an "instrumental" approach to class tactics: the trade union becomes for them the instrument to maintain or raise their position. In other words they use a class weapon to maintain or improve their status.

But in doing so, they become infected, at least partly, with a growing class outlook. In the words of *The Communist Manifesto*: "If by chance they are revolutionary, they are so only in view of their impending transfer into the proletariat; they thus defend not their present, but their future interests; they desert their own standpoint to place themselves at that of the proletariat."

For example, even of the Engineers' Guild, a small professional association of men who are certainly at present in a very favourable market situation, Prandy comments: "A status ideology may be uppermost among Guild members, but class attitudes can be seen to be entering very strongly."[1] Among members of the Association of Scientific Workers (now merged with the A.S.S.E.T. to form the Association of Scientific, Technical and Managerial Staffs), three-quarters joined with the conviction that they ought to join a trade union and about half realised there was a necessary connection between trade unionism and politics. A.S.T.M.S. membership continues to grow, in the words of joint general secretary Clive Jenkins, at an "explosive" rate.

Of course, professional unions differ from "manual" unions as professional workers differ from "manual" workers. As a whole, professional workers, like other middle strata, tend at present to vote Tory much more than Labour. However, in proportion, more Left-wingers than Right-wingers are active in the unions; and, to prevent splits, the unions do not affiliate to the Labour Party. But, in criticising the existing system of society, they often advocate very radical and even outright socialist policies, particularly the reduction of military expenditure and the redistribution of wealth. In fact, some professional unions are well to the left of some industrial unions.[2] The broad tendency is, to use another of Lockwood's ideas, towards some "convergence". In Prandy's words,

> "(The) professional unions are different from those of manual workers, but the similarities are greater than the differences . . . There

[1] Prandy, p. 121.

[2] In this context, as throughout the section, "professional" includes technical employees.

would seem to be . . . a close parallel between the professional trade unions and the New Model unions of craftsmen in the mid-nineteenth century. The existence of unionism among this group is of greater significance than are the present differences with 'traditional' trade unionism."[1]

The ruling-class attitude towards the rank and file "middle-class" employee was crudely and bluntly put by the journal of big business, *The Economist:*

> "There is not much point in the salariat moaning that, because many of them are still worse off than their counterparts in 1938, it would be wicked for a Labour Government that applied an incomes policy to wages to apply one also to salaries. In 1938 there was a special historical reason for professional workers getting much higher rewards than manual workers, because the salariat had to spend a much longer period in full time education, often at the cost of much personal or parental skimping. Today, education has a smaller scarcity value than it had then; and the student is often kept in higher education in fairly congenial conditions at public expense, before moving into a more congenial job than the manual worker gets. A large part of the redistribution of incomes since 1938 from holders of salaried jobs to those of less congenial manual jobs is therefore natural and probably permanent."[2]

There was, unfortunately, little need for *The Economist* to advise the Government. The Salary Survey Unit reported that, during 1967, salary increases toed the Government line as laid down by the Prices and Incomes Board. According to official statistics, while average earnings of the salariat forged ahead during the late 1950s and the early 1960s, from 1965 onwards they kept in line with the more modest increases of wage earners.

PRODUCTIVE OR UNPRODUCTIVE?

Economically speaking, then, the gap between the bulk of the middle strata and the wage-earners has been narrowing; but there is still a widespread antagonism between them, based on the non-manual worker's feeling that the manual worker is below him and, contrariwise, on the manual worker's belief that the non-manual worker is a

[1] Prandy, p. 145.
[2] "Salaries: are you better off?" (*The Economist*, 1964).

parasite. Is it true that manual workers are productive, while non-manual workers are not?

In what was intended to be the fourth and last volume of *Capital* Marx defined in precise terms the difference between productive and unproductive labour in the capitalist system. "Only labour *which is directly transformed into capital is productive* . . ."[1] And further on: "*Productive labour* is therefore—in the system of capitalist production—that which produces *surplus value* for its employer, or which transforms the objective conditions of labour into capital and their owner into a capitalist . . ."[2]

Now the designation of labour as productive had, he added, *absolutely nothing to do with the content of that labour, with its special usefulness.* For example, according to this definition Milton, author of *Paradise Lost*, was an unproductive worker: his epic poem of Satan's fall into hell did not add to the stock of capital here on earth (old man Marx's sardonic humour). A self-employed tailor who makes a customer a pair of trousers does a *service* and is paid for his labour: as he creates no capital, he is unproductive. The customer creates no capital out of the trousers either; he merely uses them. From the customer's side the same would apply if he bought the trousers from a capitalist tailor-employer; but in that case the money would be transformed into capital *for the employer* and, for the latter, would be productive. Thus workers can be "productive" for the boss yet "unproductive" for the customer.

The self-employed craftsman could also be both productive and unproductive. In owning his tools, his machinery, he is a capitalist: as worker he is only his own wage-slave. When paid for the service he performs, he is paid partly for his labour, partly as tribute to his ownership of the means of production: the payment is partly productive, partly unproductive.

In Marx's time, professional people were mostly self-employed and therefore "unproductive" in his sense of the word.[3] The situation today, with the bulk of professional people employed, is very different. As employees of private firms they help either directly to create more surplus value or to lower costs, which amounts also to raising the rate of surplus value, i.e. they come increasingly into the category of those

[1] Marx: *Theories of Surplus Value* (ed. C. P. Dutt), p. 178.
[2] Same, p. 181.
[3] The scientist or engineer whose new process or machine was exploited commercially was, of course, often *highly* productive.

who help "transform the objective conditions of labour into capital". Even the visual artist is enrolled in the service of capital, stimulating sales (and hence profit) by attractive packaging and advertising propaganda. What the boss worries about is whether the ideas-man's output (how much he stimulates sales) covers what is spent on him—plus, of course, a reasonable "return". If the ideas-man covers himself successfully, he keeps his job (he is productive).

On the other hand, the distributive worker only helps the circulation of commodities and his wages are part of the costs of circulation. He is therefore "unproductive". At the same time he is exploited: the boss may employ him for, say, ten hours but pay him only for eight. But the surplus value is not transformed directly into capital; it only helps reduce distribution costs.

But from this very narrow point of view, both clerk and distributive worker are unproductive. Where, then, lies the difference between them? The answer used to be in *status*. The clerk had to be better educated and more neatly dressed. In return he enjoyed a higher level of pay and better conditions of work. But the differences are being steadily squeezed. What remains are differences in the nature of the work itself and work-relations: the distributive worker's work-position is more closely tied to that of the productive manual worker; whereas the clerk does not handle goods and services and is more closely associated with "management". Hence, in general, the distributive worker is classified as a "manual" worker and compares his pay with that of other "manual" workers, while the clerk is "non-manual" and, until his altered situation described before, considers his rate of remuneration from the point of view of how he can maintain his separation from the manual worker. This difference may have some relevance still in approaching them trade-union-wise, but as their status and conditions converge, emphasising the difference may indeed be harmful from a *class* point of view.[1]

Further still, Marx already began to see that the very distinction between productive and unproductive might be less and less important. He observed that book-keeping ". . . as the control . . . of (capitalist) process, becomes the more necessary the more the process assumes a social scale . . ."[2] Hence the growth of clerical labour, to which attention has already been drawn. But at the same time this growth

[1] We differ here from P. I. Seltman, whose analysis in *Classes in Modern Britain* is otherwise excellent.

[2] *Capital*, II, ch. 6.

causes alarm among the capitalists, who hastily introduce automation and computerisation to eliminate or at least check it. This very automation introduces, however, more non-manual personnel. Added to the scientific and technical personnel, who are increasingly employed directly in the productive process, the greatest growth in the non-manual sector is precisely the growth of persons most needed by the firm. The accountants (for example, Chambers and Weinstock) have the best chances among all the managers of becoming bosses themselves. The "unproductive" white-collar man has the best chance of controlling production. In the present era of intense competition, even competition between giant firms (oligopolistic competition), the salesman, ad-man, PR-man become increasingly important to the system. And we finally arrive at the situation where even the social service worker (teacher, doctor, nurse, etc.) once employed to salve the conscience of the rich and to prevent riots and revolution, is now more and more closely geared to the detailed, day-to-day task of fitting the worker to the toil, of keeping the system going. Even if strictly (economically) "unproductive", they are increasingly essential to the system.

At the same time, they are, wherever possible, subjected to increased exploitation. In industry, the introduction of automation increases the number of non-manual personnel, but neither they nor the manual operatives benefit to the full from the savings they make for the firm. In public service, staffs are not generally increased to meet the full increase in the amount of work and this is intensified by work-study and time-and-motion study, old stuff for the factory worker but new to the white-collar or the white-coated.

It is, of course, true that masses of clerical and distributive workers are not merely capitalistically unproductive; they are *socially useless*. Not only does capitalism breed work that is simply parasitical (betting offices, door-to-door salesmanship, private insurance and the like) but, even in necessary employment, competition breeds an excess to requirements (five different banks close to each other in every High Street). For this reason, the occupational structure, and especially the size of the white-collar force, is severely distorted under capitalism and is very different under socialism.

Unfortunately, these workers, whether "unproductive" or whose "productiveness" is hidden, cannot easily appreciate that they too are exploited. "The lathe operator sees what he is producing and can compare this directly with what he is paid. Neither the clerical workers nor the teachers can see so immediately their relationship to capitalism.

Among such workers, the economic struggle is always comparative, i.e. increased rates of pay to meet the costs of maintaining their social status in addition to meeting the increased cost of living. Because these workers are overwhelmingly non-manual, they are subjectively isolated from the process of commodity production as a whole. Their labour is an essential part of this process, but they do not *see* this directly as the manual worker does. A manual worker, such as a warehouseman, may be unproductive, but he directly appreciates the role of his labour in the process of production to a far greater extent than the clerical worker who is both unproductive and non-manual. This isolation has been a tremendous factor in recent years in separating off ideologically whole sections of the working population whose background and origins were rooted in the manual productive working class."[1]

The special characteristic of the "new middle class" in an era of great economic and technological change is their hope of individual advancement. A number of British researchers have noticed this growth of individual ambition and one has given the new ambitious individuals the descriptive name of "spiralists". In smaller communities they stand out more than in the large cities, because they tend to move out and live in the neighbouring villages, or move into expanding small towns. There they congregate apart from the older, local, "middle class", the shopkeepers, schoolteachers and others. "Spiralism" makes for the "Organisation Man", (the type described in detail by W. H. Whyte), who identifies himself closely with the firm, the "organisation". Naturally he will tend to adopt the ideology of the ruling class, the "status" outlook.

Nevertheless, in spite of all the forces making the salariat (for this is what most "unproductive" workers are) toe the capitalist line, large numbers, especially of technical, supervisory and professional people, are becoming or have become convinced socialists. (Conversely, among manual workers nearest to the point of production, large numbers never get beyond the sheer *economic* stage, the good trade-union man.) It is still true to say that these are, as yet, a minority and Seltman is correct when he writes that "... the general characteristics of these sections of workers are confusions as to their own positions, highly developed illusions about the advantages to them of capitalism and strong hostility, almost amounting to fear, of manual productive workers".[1] But, compare the situation today with a hundred years ago,

[1] Seltman, p. 63. [1] Same.

when Marx wrote, or even thirty years ago, and we realise that history moves and the "middle class" worker is not the same today as he was yesterday.[1]

"MIDDLE-CLASS" TRADE UNIONISM

This is particularly to be observed in the trade union field. The usual academic view, now slowly changing, was that white-collar workers only reluctantly joined trade unions and that, when they joined, they were even more reluctant to strike. Thus Routh writes:

> "... it goes against some deeply-held feelings—their sense of social equality with the boss, their privilege of payment for time lost through illness, their semi-permanent attachment to the firm, their sense of responsibility for the performance of their work (which accumulates while they are away), their hopes of promotion, their superiority to the manual worker".[2]

But this attitude is changing. In the last ten years or so there has been a march of civil servants to Parliament, a postal workers' work-to-rule followed by a threat to strike, strikes by airline pilots, nurses' demonstrations, the teachers' successful refusal to carry out school meal duties, and their magnificent campaign for £135 flat increase (still going on as I write); and many other actions. White-collar (including professional and technical) trade unionists number at least two million. Taking unions which are wholly white-collar (N.U.T., C. and A.W.U., etc.) we get a total in 1968 of 1,750,000. But many of the bigger manual unions, e.g. T. & G.W.U., have substantial white-collar sections. These figures, although encouraging, show that still only a minority, possibly about a quarter of non-manual workers, are union members. Organisation has still a long way to go.

[1] One interesting sociological aspect of this concerns the "middle-class" family. Up to recently, orthodox sociology distinguished the middle-class from the working-class family. The working-class family tended to be extended (included relations outside parents and children e.g. uncles, aunts and grandparents), the middle-class nuclear (parents and children only). This was due, it was said, to the fact that members of the middle-class family moved geographically towards the best material prospects, thus severing family ties. But a recent study of 120 middle-class families shows that mutual aid to maintain a respectable standard of living is still widespread, despite distance. In that sense family links are often as strong as in the traditional working-class family. C. Bell: Mobility and the middle-class extended family (*Sociology*, May 1968).

[2] G. Routh: "White-collar unions in the U.K.", in Sturmthal (ed). *White-Collar Trade Unions* (1966).

It is not always true, as Seltman suggests, that the nearer white-collar workers are to production, the more they are likely to organise into trade unions. Scientists, supervisors and technicians, who have recently combined to form a union of 100,000 members, claim that theirs has been the fastest-growing union in post-war years; and it is also one of the most militant. But teachers and local government officials are doing very well too—and they are not in the front line of production. So we have to refer to other factors, in particular the runaway cost of living, higher regard for their value to the economy, the increasing burden of work, as well as those laid down by Lockwood (increasing bureaucratisation, rigidity of function and lack of promotion), official encouragement to trade union membership by State organs and the role of the militants.

What of the future? Will white-collar workers' unions ever become as militant and politically-conscious as some manual workers' unions? First, it has to be pointed out that in 25 years' time, manual workers may be in a minority in the country's total labour force. But within the rapidly-growing white-collar force there will continue to be a chasm between the highest professional, managerial and administrative sections and the rest. The demand during the period of technological expansion for more technically-educated personnel has resulted in the gap between them and the lower manual/non-manual routine workers widening, as regards pay, conditions, status and way of life. But pressure is now being exerted, and will be exerted even more, to curbing these improvements, except, as we have already remarked, for the élite of these groups.

Strong indications of the continuing growth and militancy of white-collar unions in this sort of future are seen in the situation within the U.S.A. The United States is the first country to have more white-collar than "blue-collar" (manual) workers—43 per cent and 38 per cent respectively of the total working force. By 1964 only 11 per cent of white-collar workers were organised, but since then recruitment has speeded up, with manual workers increasingly trying to get their white-collar colleagues into their unions. As in Britain, white-collar unions in some occupations and industries are growing fast and professional associations are going over to collective bargaining. More and more mechanisation is producing more impersonality, less interest in the job and a growing split between the mass and the élite.

"The division between managerial duties, reserved to top and middle management, and the tasks performed by the employees is becoming constantly sharper. Whereas the employee could formerly hope to rise gradually in the hierarchy through a number of intermediate stages, he now finds himself confined to the role of mere operator . . ."[1]

Under automation, the white-collar worker almost becomes a blue-collar worker, because he mostly tends a machine and is therefore obliged to work shifts, is more isolated from his fellows and suffers an increasing sense of insecurity. Of course, there will continue to be, in the foreseeable future, significant differences between white-collar and blue-collar workers: in particular, the former will still continue to be promotion-conscious and more conservative politically. But in all aspects of employment and way-of-life there will continue to be a narrowing of differentials and even overlapping. And in the trade union field this will mean some white-collar unions will be more advanced "economically" (pay- and conditions-wise) and politically than some of the more backward manual unions. This is not to suggest that a complete merger will ever take place—certainly not under capitalism. There is likely to be as much variety among white-collar as among manual unions; but the trend is likely to continue so long as the dynamic instability of post-war British capitalism under competitive pressure persists. It is the *trend*, which Lockwood failed to see, that proves the Marxist view correct.[2]

Can one say that, because of this trend, the middle strata are becoming a class? The answer is still, No. Sturmthal says:

"The absence of a clear and simple trend is suggestive of the tremendous variety of occupations covered by the term 'white-collar'. They represent neither a closed nor a homogeneous class. Their jobs show a bewildering variety of degrees of difficulty, of social ambience, of responsibility, of educational and training requirements etc. No wonder, then, that these groups demonstrate very different responses to the phenomena of industrial development and technical change which affect them in very different ways. It is also not surprising that the attitudes towards enterprise, society and

[1] From an article in the O.E.C.D. bulletin *Trade Union Information* (no. 35) quoted by Kassalow, *White-Collar unionism in the United States*, in Sturmthal (ed) *White-Collar Trade Unions* (1966).

[2] Of course, we can't discount a right-wing reaction, especially if a right-wing extremist government is in power and uses State forces and the mass media against the Left.

union of this so heterogeneous group run the whole gamut of possible responses."[1]

Yet even this excellent summary statement suffers from the static bourgeois approach. It does not compare the present day with a generation or a century ago and therefore, ignores the important basic trend, the "convergence" taking place between the more advanced groups of white-collar and manual workers which will increasingly draw the former to a more "class" outlook.

HOW CONSERVATIVE ARE THEY?

If, then, there is little homogeneity among the so-called middle class, but rather a growing basic division between mass and élite, the implication might be that, in time, the mass of non-manual workers would become proletarianised and all we need to do is sit back and wait for this to happen. But objective class changes don't immediately reflect themselves in political thinking; and the psephologists remind us of this when they point out that the "middle class" in Britain vote mostly Conservative. In fact, during the 1950s, psephologists pointed to the trend towards the Conservatives and away from Labour as "proof" of the growing middle-classness of the British electorate. The following figures illustrate voting changes 1945/51:[2]

Section	*Conservative %*		*Labour %*	
	1945	*1951*	*1945*	*1951*
Managerial	47	65	23	19
Higher professional	58	78	15	6
Lower professional	41	52	23	24
Higher office worker	49	63	20	13
Lower office worker	33	48	30	29
Whole adult population	29	40	35	41

Yet the picture is not as pessimistic for the future of socialism as some of the commentators imagined. First, the swing to the Tories was no greater among the middle strata than among the electorate as a whole, including the manual workers. The working-class vote "floated" just as much as the middle-class. Even in 1951, when Labour was thrown out of office, the middle strata gave Labour two million votes, nearly

[1] Sturmthal, p. 374.
[2] From Bonham: *The Middle Class Vote*, p. 129.

a third of what they gave the Tories. Nearly a third of all lower-office, and nearly a quarter of all lower-professional workers voted Labour. Only the higher middle strata voted overwhelmingly Tory. Bonham estimated that only about a seventh of the increase in the Tory vote between 1945 and 1951 came from the middle strata, compared with their proportion (30 per cent) of the total electorate. It should not be forgotten either (though it usually is) that in post-war years they voted Labour more than ever before. The following table[1] for the 1966 General Election shows that as much as 30 per cent of the "lower middle-class" voted Labour, though they constitute only 22 per cent of the total electorate.

1966 General Election: percentage votes by social class

		Social Class			
	All %	*M/c AB* (*12*%)	*Lower M/c C1* (*22½*)	*Skilled manual C2* (*37*%)	*Unskilled & very poor DE* (*29*%)
Conservative	41	72	59	32	26
Labour	49	16	30	59	65
Liberal	9	11	11	8	7
Other	1	1	1	1	2
Swing (L %) from 1964	3	5	4	3	5

This General Election saw a swing back to Labour. Although statistical comparisons are difficult, the evidence points to a return roughly to the 1945 position as far as the middle strata are concerned, with 30 per cent of the lower-middle (class C1 in the Readership Survey classification), voting Labour, 59 per cent Conservative and 11 per cent Liberal. Middle-class support for drastic social change, shown by the substantial minority votes for Labour in 1945 and again in 1966, would almost certainly have grown had their expectations from the Labour governments been met. But this support is falling away today, as it fell during the last years of Attlee's government.

Voting behaviour is, in fact, only partly related to social class position, as many commentators have been eager to point out in order to "refute" Marx. What does voting behaviour indicate? According to Bonham, it is related to social class as a "political idea", which is found on examination to be subjective self-rating, i.e. what social class

[1] From Butler and King: *The 1966 General Election*. The percentages in brackets show the proportion of each "class" relative to the total electorate.

people *think or feel* they belong to. Voting behaviour reflects how electors believe the political parties *cater for that social class and for their kin*. But there is no more an "electoral man" than there is an "economic man". All the influences exerted by bourgeois and anti-socialist propaganda help distort his judgement. To interpret the large number of the middle strata voting Tory as indicating simply worker-bourgeoisification means that they were bourgeoisified in the 'fifties, but de-bourgeoisified in 1945 and again in 1966, which is absurd. Voting swings indicate rather a largely "instrumental" attitude on the part of those who change their party preference, while long-term historical development shows a zig-zag movement towards socialism. If the bourgeoisification theory were correct, it would, conversely, mean that, because in 1951 and again in 1966 a third of all skilled manual workers (class C2) voted Conservative, the Tory Party is becoming, as its propagandists claim, a party for all classes or for no class. The interpretation of voting behaviour leads to no such conclusion. For the way people vote is determined by a mixture of class and personal interests, and the whole weight of the created environment of a capitalist society, in which the propagation of revolutionary socialism is difficult and is only rarely allowed in the pro-capitalist mass media.

Because of the powerful, anti-socialist propaganda from the mass media and the weight of class ideas throughout the whole political, social and cultural set-up, the battle for the minds of the masses oscillates from reaction to progress and back again. The 60 per cent of the middle strata who still vote Tory may, therefore, support an extreme right-wing régime actively or passively. So could the $\frac{1}{4}$–$\frac{1}{3}$ of all manual workers who have given the Tories half of all Tory Party votes, mostly, as we shall see later, from a feeling that the Tories will do more for them than Labour. "Mass politics" feeds on both these large slices of the population—and on those whose belief in a Labour Government has been, or is being, steadily destroyed. In a situation of crisis, as happened in Europe in the 'thirties and may happen here, the failure of "liberal democracy", as Kornhauser and the theorists of mass society tell us (or remind us), may turn these masses to racialism and fascism. Nothing more strikingly illustrates the great need for a Socialist Government with a truly socialist policy than the size of these mass potentials for a reactionary régime in Britain and the particularly dangerous role played by those leaders who are making "socialism" a dirty word.

SUMMARY AND CONCLUSION

The "middle class" is therefore not a class, because it is not a homogeneous body with common interests distinct from other classes; and in fact there is no visible trend in this direction; rather the other way, towards growing identification in certain respects with manual workers.

The "middle class" consists of strata based mainly on criteria of occupation, income and way of life. The occupations are mainly non-manual, but their incomes, way of life and voting behaviour are spread over a very broad band indeed. At the lower end they overlap the upper working-class, at the top they reach into the ruling class. The bulk of the middle strata are nearer the working class on the more objective criteria, nearer the ruling class in subjective behaviour.

It consists of several strata. Professional people have become mostly employees, either of private firms or public bodies, and, except for the spiralists, who have become the élite or are on their way up, more and more trade-union and class-conscious. Possibly their most distinctive characteristics—again excepting the lowest range—are higher incomes and prestige, greater job satisfaction and promotion prospects. And though they are still mostly workers, these differences account for their dislike of the word and their preference for classification as "employees". Only the shopkeepers and small businessmen are clearly "middle class" in the classical sense, like the petit bourgeoisie of the nineteenth century, but are under pressure from the monopoly-capitalist system. Clerical workers are proletarianised to a considerable degree but, because of certain factors, lack that class consciousness which is more evident among the more "manual" distributive workers—although among their upper ranks they resemble professional employees. It is more difficult, generally, to make them conscious of what capitalist society is and their position in it, because they tend to be removed from direct contact with production and the manual worker. They are often ambivalent in their political attitudes. But the fact that they tend, except for the lower end, to have had better educational opportunities, makes the question of their understanding the nature of capitalist society a particular challenge.[1]

[1] The great American sociologist C. Wright Mills was right when, in his classic *White Collar* (1951), he exposed the mechanical sort of Marxism which argued that, because white-collar workers were being proletarianised economically, they were automatically members of the proletariat. Unfortunately, his conclusion was pessimistic, first because his approach was academically passive and secondly because he, too, broadly assumed post-war conditions would continue unchanged.

The future will see further movement among the middle strata. Individual strata will rise and fall. As non-manual labour increases proportionately to manual, the likeness between the lower strata of the former and manual labour will increase both economically and status-wise. Class-consciousness and trade unionism will increase; so may left-wing political consciousness, though always qualified by that vacillation that Lenin spoke of. But by sheer size they are of increasing political importance and potential allies (or enemies) who can help make (or mar) the social revolution.

7

THE PROLETARIAT, THE WORKING CLASS AND THE POOR

DEFINITIONS

After the last war, critics of Marxism were all firmly of the opinion that the proletariat—Marx's nineteenth century proletariat—had vanished. How could it be otherwise? The brutal conditions producing those millions of grossly exploited, half-starved wretches had gone. The working class today enjoyed incomparably better conditions, much higher pay, good housing, better family life and was increasingly comfortising that life with a host of button-starting gadgets. Not only was there absolutely no comparison between these workers and the mid-nineteenth-century proletariat, but some writers, pointing to post-war changes—equalisation of manual and non-manual incomes, mechanisation and the reduction of physical labour, growth of management-labour collaboration, changes in life-styles of workers through affluence—even came to the conclusion that to speak now of a "working class" was nostalgia: the workers were becoming part of a vastly bigger middle class and really the "working class" either was disappearing fast, or didn't exist at all. Even if this wasn't accepted in its entirety, most people, while agreeing that there were still "workers", were likely, so the critics said, to deny the existence of a working *class*. Classes, they said, were disappearing.

The terms, working class and proletariat, are often interchanged; but it is necessary to understand precisely what each one means, or we shall be getting into the same muddle as the critics of Marxism. The word proletariat derives from the Latin, meaning those whose only property is their children (proles). Proletarians have therefore existed in systems other than capitalism, e.g. slaves in ancient societies. Under capitalism, however, the term specifically refers to those (without property) whose only means of existence is the ability to sell their labour-power. Or, more strictly, a proletarian under capitalism refers to the individual who is legally free but economically compelled to sell his labour-power on the market. In Marx's time the proletariat were in the main the industrial workers. There were, as we saw in the last chapter, other proletarians, but for Marx, who was well aware of their existence, they were politically unimportant.

If the original meaning of the word is taken, there certainly is a proletariat today. In the mid-1950s, according to Lydall and Tipping, eleven-twelfths of the adult population (32 million people) shared 22 per cent of the wealth. The lower half of these, 16 million people or roughly half the adult population, owned on average less than £50 each. According to *The Economist's* Survey, 88 per cent of all taxpayers in 1959/60 owned an average of only £107 each and, all together, less than 4 per cent of all the personal wealth of the country. It can be assumed that the bulk of the 31 million *non*-taxpayers, mostly children, housewives and pensioners below the tax limit, owned little or nothing. Or, even taking the Inland Revenue figures for 1967, which the department frankly admit have wide margins of error, two-thirds of the population have no wealth at all. In addition, 5·4 out of the 17·3 million who own anything at all, share between them £2·8 thousand million, or just over £500 each, which can hardly be called property in any real sense. This therefore increases the propertyless and near-propertyless to 40·4 million, or 77 per cent of the population. Thus the proletariat today constitutes about three-quarters of the population.

Again, in 1966, out of a total population of 52·3 million, 40 million persons were aged 15 or over, i.e. of working age. Of these 20·1 million[1] were employees, i.e. just over half the population of working age. This ties up roughly with Lydall and Tipping's half the adult population who own little or nothing. And it also fits roughly the *Economist's* estimate of 88 per cent of taxpayers who own little or nothing, since 88 per cent of taxpayers in 1966/67 is equivalent to 19·2 million persons. This figure of 20·1 (or 19·2) millions does, of course, exclude dependants including a large proportion of the 15 million "economically inactive", mainly children of the proletariat.

But there are many who, though outside the ranks of "other employees" are, whatever their opinions—and we shall deal with this problem later—near-proletarian. In 1937 Briefs, a German sociologist, defined a proletarian as "... a wage earner (or salaried worker not in a permanent position) whose exclusive, or at least indispensable, source of income is found in the sale of his labour power in a shifting and insecure labour market".[2] Briefs added that even members of the professions might be proletarians if their incomes were so low as only to cover current needs, obliging them to be constantly at work,

[1] Or 19·2 million, calculated by counting all employees and excluding managers, foremen, apprentices, professional employees and family workers.

[2] G. A. Briefs: *The Proletariat*, p. 24.

especially if their work were controlled by another person or persons.

In a sense, Briefs had a good point when he argued that the proletariat was a Weberian ideal type, because there were many borderline cases. Such cases, which he called "proletaroid", consisted of those who, though owning some property, had constantly to sell their services; for example, the small farmer or shopkeeper. Marx also frequently referred in his historical writings to certain classes who, though generally politically opposed were economically close to the proletariat.[1]

In fact, we are beginning to see the source of confusion about whether there is or is not a proletariat today. The confusion arises from the level at which the question of class is considered. The issue of the division of society, the system of gradation, depends on the criterion. In the terminology used by the Polish sociologist, Ossowski, the scheme of gradation may be "simple" or "synthetic". Simple gradation is based upon one objectively measurable criterion, e.g. wealth or education or birth. Synthetic gradation occurs when a range of criteria is taken, for example, style of life. When Marx divided capitalist society into two main classes, using the single criterion of wealth, he did so for a very sound reason. But he also recognised the existence of other classes determined by other, and in his view subsidiary, criteria. For the dichotomic (two-class) scheme is more fundamental from the point of view of understanding capitalism as a general system. Multi-divisional schemes are more useful for unravelling the details of the social structure, the position and the minutiae of behaviour of the different sections. As Ossowski writes: "The dichotomic scheme is intended to characterise capitalist society with regard to its dominant and peculiar form of relations of production, while the multi-divisional scheme reflects the actual social structure."[2]

As we saw in the discussion on professional workers, the question of *time* is very important, in two ways. First, as we have already discovered and as Ossowski stresses, *membership* of a class is relatively permanent. Briefs stressed that (at least when he wrote) the proletariat was distinctive because, over the long period of industrialisation, it had developed distinctive *attitudes*, for example, feeling itself below other classes. But —and this was Weber's major challenge—status divisions arise side by

[1] "The 'dangerous class', the social scum, that passively rotting mass thrown off by the lowest layers of old society, may, here and there, be swept into the movement by a proletarian revolution; its conditions of life, however, prepare it far more for the part of a bribed tool of reactionary intrigue." (*The Communist Manifesto*, I.)

[2] S. Ossowski: *Class Structure in the Social Consciousness*, p. 83.

side and intertwine with class divisions. Status is acquired by usurpation, by seizing upon and exploiting certain social estimations of honour, e.g. birth, education. With status comes certain privileges, for example, the right to use a title, have a special place in public functions or wear special costumes. The stronger the restriction on market forces, the stronger the status feeling. During the early 1950s, when the power of organised labour had wrested for wage-earners the highest proportion of personal income in British history, status, according to Zweig and others, was far more important than class: the wage-earner's car and "telly" were more prominent in the mind than insecurity of employment. But, as Weber himself observed, *every economic and technological change threatens status and brings class forward*. Hence, even if, at certain periods, status appears more prominent than class, status is more subject to change, more temporary. And it follows that, since social estimations of honour have a strongly subjective element, status *criteria* can change quite rapidly and status *estimations* often seem absurd, as in the case of Centers' American enquiry. Also, status divisions must be more numerous than "simple" (using Ossowski's term) class divisions. Hence, looking at present, "Western" (i.e. industrially advanced) capitalist society from a status-division point of view tends to reveal a picture of continuous gradations, of a *continuum*, starting with the poor, or the least educated, or the homeless and up through whatever scheme is being considered, from whatever group of criteria, to the top, the "Establishment", the Government, the élite or other group. It follows that the proletariat is more permanent than a status division characterised by "way of life" or even by occupation. Secondly, within the two broad classes, real changes, subdivisions and mergers nevertheless take place over time. The major change in the proletariat since Marx's time is the inclusion of millions of lower-paid non-manual workers, the major change in the ruling class the fusion of landed aristocracy, capitalists and top managers, the emergence of "monopoly" State capitalism. And because it is felt that the criterion of propertylessness is no longer as important as it was in Marx's time, the term proletariat (which has an ancient ring anyway) is out of fashion.

The reader will recall Prandy's conclusion that a status view is linked with defence of the existing order, a class view with its rejection. The ruling class has to try to persuade people that the proletariat doesn't exist today, because to admit that it does means that capitalism still exists. It has already been shown that Marx and Engels were well aware that there existed more than two classes; but, as practical revolutionaries, they had to emphasise that the two essential classes were the capitalists and the proletariat. The latter, brought into being by capitalism, was in their view to be the prime instrument of its abolition. Therefore we may say that while there may be a good reason for not using a rather archaic word like "proletariat" today, the right-wing theorists throw it out for a more directly political reason.

IS THE WORKING CLASS DISAPPEARING?

Let us talk about the working class instead. Has it disappeared, or is it in process of disappearing?

From one point of view, it may seem to be doing just this. In all advanced industrial societies the size of the manual working force is diminishing. Routh estimates that, due to the rapid expansion of the white-collar working force, manual workers in the U.K. will in 25 years' time be in a minority.[1] On this ground it is often argued that the working class is shrinking quite rapidly. Now, this depends on what proportion of the labour force is "working-class", an issue we tried to resolve in the last chapter. Fortunately, by dividing the labour force into wage- and salary-earners, the Censuses provide us with another way of looking at the matter.

Now, no one would disagree with the proposition that wage-earners as such must be working-class. We then have the following facts. The number of *industrial* wage-earners fell from 9,800,000 in 1951 to 9,600,000 in 1961. Not much of a fall, for at this rate there would be a drop in 25 years of only about half-a-million. If agricultural workers are added, the totals are 10,550,000 in 1951 and 10,100,000 in 1961, a much more severe fall due to the sharper decline in the number of agricultural workers. Even then, the fall in 25 years would only be just over a million. However, there are also *non*-industrial wage-earners, for example local government manual workers like refuse collectors and park keepers. Those *increased* between 1951 and 1961, from 2¾ millions to over 3 millions. Adding these we obtain grand totals of all wage earners of 13,310,000 in 1951 and 13,240,000 in 1961. At this rate, the fall in 25 years would be less than 200,000. There was a sharp increase, in fact, of the number of wage-earners between 1961 and 1966 (bearing in mind the discrepancies that are likely to arise

[1] G. Routh: White-collar unions in the U.K. (in *White-Collar Trade Unions*, ed. Sturmthal).

because both sets of figures are based on 10 per cent samples). By 1966 the number of wage-earners jumped to nearly 15 million, nearly 1¾ million *more* than in 1961. In terms of proportions of the total economically active population, however, wage-earners were

1961	61%
1966	60·5%

showing virtually no change. (This 60–61 per cent still excludes "economically inactive" dependants, including children and old-age pensioners; and in chapter 4 we pointed out that, taking the *whole* population, nearly 80 per cent come within the three "social classes" comprising the working class.) It is this mistaken emphasis on "industrial" as opposed to "non-industrial" wage-earners which is responsible for this picture of the advanced capitalist state's population rapidly becoming absolutely different structurally from the nineteenth-century capitalism of Marx. It will be a very long time indeed before *wage-earners* become a minority of the British working population; and the working class consists of all wage-earners, at the very least.

HIGH AND LOW WAGES

What about the argument that present-day high wages have transformed the worker into a member of the middle class? Certainly, the worker may own little property, and may still depend for his and his family's existence entirely on the sale of his labour-power. But what a price he can get now! He and his family enjoy a middle-class standard of living.

As some reference to wages has already been made, the main points only need to be repeated. Basic rates are often very low. In 1968 the minimum rates for men were: in agriculture £11 11s., baking £10 8s., municipal bus drivers £12 17s., chemical manufacture £11 15s., engineering and shipbuilding skilled men £12 17s.[1] On the other hand, there were many higher. But *earnings* were very much higher; for example, earnings at October 1968 were: vehicle building £26 9s., paper, printing and publishing £26 19s. Nevertheless, the average for all male manual workers (excluding agriculture, where earnings were only £16 12s.) was £23. This compares with an average of only

[1] *Statistics on Incomes, Prices, etc.* June 1968 (H.M.S.O.). All the figures are at April 1968, unless otherwise stated.

£18 12s. for male clerical workers, but of £29 9s. for all male salaried employees. It is useful to point out, moreover, that only a small minority of wage-earners enjoy the high wages the yellow press cackle about. In October 1960 (the latest figures available), when average earnings for men were £14 2s., nearly 50 per cent earned less than this and *less than 9 per cent earned £20 or more.*

Wage-earners make up their earnings in two ways. First, overtime. In October 1968 average hours men worked were still 44·6 a week, much more than average office hours and usually in less pleasant conditions. Earnings, especially piecework, also depend on speed and increased work load. Thirdly, there is shift-work.

There are, moreover, many sub-divisions of wage-earners. The divisions of skilled, semi-skilled and unskilled are often bitterly contested. Skilled workers often complain that differentials are inadequate, the unskilled that their wages are too low for a decent standard of living. Employers constantly try to cut skilled men's rates and to demote skilled to semi-skilled. Basically, all these wages are regulated by the "labour market", meaning the power of the biggest combines, curbed to some extent by trade union strength. Considerations of humanity rarely enter, if at all.

There are also *regional* differences in pay. In the South-East, skilled fitters on P.B.R. knocked up (January 1969) £27 7s. a week, in the North-West £25 1s. Labourers on time-rate in the South-East got £18 18s., £20 5s. in Wales, but only £16 10s. in Yorkshire. These differences, plus the regional variations in unemployment (dealt with later), account for the population drift to the South-East. Despite the fact that, on the one hand, this drift is itself part of a vicious circle (economic depression—population drift—lowered morale—depression worsened) and, on the other, it increases the problems of an already congested South-East, the ruling class can do very little to prevent it, despite ever bigger subsidies to private firms. In spite of the praiseworthy efforts of local planners, the situation glaringly illustrates the anarchy of capitalism and the way the capitalist class exploits local economic depression to keep wages lower than elsewhere.

It is generally believed that wage-earners have narrowed the incomes gap between themselves and the salariat. How true is this? The following table shows different, long-term trends among the seven occupational "classes" defined by Glass and his L.S.E. colleagues:[1]

[1] from Routh: *Occupation and Pay in Great Britain 1906–1960.*

Occupational class		*Average earnings 1960 as percentage of earnings 1913/14* *Men*	*Women*
1A	Higher professional etc.	620	—
1B	Lower professional	546	680
2	Managers	925	1,250
3	Clerks	689	949
4	Foremen	898	1,056
5	Skilled manual	804	898
6	Semi-skilled manual	842	678
7	Unskilled manual	849	1,000
	Average	874	866

The table shows that *the pay of male manual workers has not kept up with the average over this long period and that skilled workers have fared worse*. Among women workers the skilled have done a little better than average and the skilled much better, due, of course, to the greatly increased employers' demand for the type of unskilled factory work which is largely performed by women at lower pay than for men. On the other hand, the semi-skilled are being squeezed out and their improvement has been much lower than average. To say, therefore, that wage workers have done enormously better than the salariat is a gross exaggeration. Once again we repeat that what has brought more money into working-class homes since the last war has been the expansion of employment (full employment) and particularly of women on largely "unskilled" (routine) work.[1] Basic rates being far too low for an acceptable standard of living, male workers are forced into an undignified scramble for overtime.

As for the "fantastic" rise in the level of wages (and salaries) Norman Atkinson has now shown how much truth there is in this. By making up working-class budgets for 1938 and 1968, Atkinson shows that in those 30 years the cost of basic necessities went up 370 per cent, compared with the official Index's 270 per cent. Then there have been very big increases in direct taxation (income tax and national insurance) and a much higher cost of housing. Taking these and the rise in the national product, Atkinson argues that a worker should be entitled to a 4½-times

[1] Norman Atkinson points out that while the percentage of total personal income going to wages and salaries was 55 per cent in 1938, by 1967 it had gone up to only 63 per cent, despite a 41 per cent increase in the total working population (N. Atkinson: *Whatever happened to our wages?* Tribune Publications 1969, 1/6d).

higher minimum wage or salary than he or she got in 1938; and shows that very few indeed (even with high take-home pay) have got near this, although most have kept up well with the higher cost-of-living.[1] That the workers *have* been able to raise their share of national output is causing our Tory and Wilsonite politicians, big businessmen, financiers and bankers at home and abroad increasing concern.

But, finally, what *are* wages? They are, of course, payment for work done. In production for profit, as Marx showed, wages pay for only part of the work the worker does. If we deduct from the value of a factory's final output the cost of the raw materials (or parts) and other necessary factors of production like fuel, the remainder is known as "value added". Wages form only part of this. Suppose, for example, an article whose final value is £10 used up raw materials worth £4 and fuel, etc., £2. Then the value added is £10 less £6 = £4. If wages take £2, the surplus is £2 also. This surplus value, two-tenths or one-fifth the final value, the capitalist appropriates. Of course, the whole £2 does not necessarily go to the producing capitalist: part goes in rent, part in interest on money borrowed. Part also goes in taxation (already discussed in a previous chapter and again later in connection with social welfare).

The ratio of wages to value added ought, if capitalist propagandists are right about the growing power of the workers and their unions, to have changed a lot over the years. But, according to figures supplied by the Director of the Statistical Office of the United Nations, the share of wages *and salaries* in *manufacturing* in a large number of countries has averaged 50 per cent over the post-war years. In the U.S.A. the average over the years 1889–1965 was 52 per cent, with not much variation from that figure except in a slump, when the share tended to go down and during a boom, when it went up a few per cent.[2] In Britain since 1958, according to official statistics, it has been over 60 per cent. Without the statistical material available to students today, Marx himself reckoned on a 50:50 division.

Another way of looking at the division of the national product is by means of the figures of national income. In 1967 the Gross Domestic Product (value of total production in Britain) was £33,882 millions, of which income from employment (before tax) amounted to £23,471

[1] N. Atkinson: *Whatever happened to our wages?*

[2] P. J. Loftus: Labour's share in manufacturing (*Lloyds Bank Review*, April 1969). It is necessary to point out that the share is roughly the same, or less, in the socialist countries; but what happens to the surplus value is quite different. None goes as private capital.

millions, or 69 per cent of the total. Income from self-employment was £2,623 millions, or 8 per cent of G.D.P. The amount going off in rent, interest and profit amounted to £7,788 millions, or 23 per cent of the whole. This is larger than in 1947, when the share going to employers and landlords was 20 per cent (£1,871 millions out of total G.D.P. of £9,308 millions). Although the situation is more complicated than this simple division suggests, the figures do indicate by how much the working people (manual and non-manual workers) are robbed.

CLIMBING OUT OF THE WORKING CLASS

But perhaps the worker's chance of climbing out of the proletariat or out of the wage-earning class is greater today than ever before? In the 1930s, everyone agrees, there was little of what the sociologist calls upward mobility. As Briefs wrote in 1937: "Wage-earners ... particularly constitute a caste, in which not only they but their children after them remain."[1]

Shortly after the war, Glass and his colleagues at the London School of Economics undertook their pioneering investigations into social mobility in Britain. Their results, which were referred to earlier in this book, were inconclusive about the mobility of the working class. But their more reliable data seemed to show high mobility among sons of skilled manual workers, least mobility among unskilled manual workers.

In the United States, however, Lipset and Bendix found surprising immobility, surprising because the U.S. is supposedly the land of greatest opportunity. Their study of nearly 1,000 wage-earners in Oakland, a San Francisco residential suburb, revealed that all manual workers had spent 80 per cent of their working lives in manual occupations and all those in non-manual employment had spent 75 per cent of their careers in such positions.[2] Generally the "opportunities" offered to the manual worker were in the lower non-manual jobs, chiefly salesmen and small shopkeepers. They claimed the situation was roughly the same in all industrial societies. But in fact they meant *total* mobility, up *and down*. When upward and downward mobilities were taken separately, their figures showed considerable variation, even between different capitalist countries.

[1] Briefs: *The Proletariat*, p. 18.

[2] Lipset and Bendix: *Social Mobility in Industrial Societies*, ch. 6.

Miller's later study, also referred to earlier, in fact showed wide differences in mobility; but in most countries there was more downward movement from non-manual to manual than upward from manual to non-manual, France and the U.S.A. being outstanding exceptions. In Britain movement down was much greater than up. But when all was said and done, the most movement, just as Lipset and Bendix found, was from manual to no higher than non-manual, specifically excluding the top or élite. In all capitalist countries the chances of a member of the working class moving into the élite were very small. In this respect Britain was among the worst.

THE END OF THE WAGE SLAVE?

According to the apologists of capitalism, however, the position of the worker today has been fundamentally transformed by full employment. In the view of writers in the 1950s, full employment was here to stay; it was part and parcel of the new social-democratic, "post-capitalist" order. (Of course, in those days the Conservatives also pledged themselves to maintain full employment.) To quote Engels' remark in the eighteen-fifties, that the English working class was becoming bourgeoisified, became quite fashionable. Not only had mass unemployment been abolished for ever, but with it much of the old competitive antagonism between class and class. Class co-operation was now widespread. These had been achieved without the need for the workers to seize power. In fact, enough was enough: the workers had already sufficient power. (As for further nationalisation, this was not merely unnecessary but unpopular.) How had the workers achieved great power? Through their unions, of course. True, they were largely excluded from actual management and they ought to be drawn into it. But *not* workers' power, for they had no right to run, nor were they capable of running, modern industry. Today's worker was no longer the Marxian wage-slave: the theory of wage-slavery, wrote Crosland "... has no relevance to present-day conditions".

What was wrong with this picture? Apart from such unproven prejudices as the worker's incapacity to manage or help manage an enterprise, the simple answer is that improved economic situation was confused with alteration of class relations. The workers' *class* position had not fundamentally changed. The left-wing writer, Ken Coates, put it this way:

"A wage slave does not cease to be a wage slave when he can buy a refrigerator. Roman slaves can be thin or fat, sad or cheerful, employed to entertain their masters' lions as dinner or their masters' wives as lovers: wage slaves too come in all sizes and conditions. Some even drive to work in motor cars. As they trod the grape harvest, the Roman slaves on the *latifundiae* probably ate some too. You cannot tell a wage slave by his looks. You can tell him by the fact that on Monday he says 'Roll on Friday'. He is defined by the fact that he lives in little islands of freedom called 'leisure'."[1]

An exaggeration? Hardly. Anyone who has ever worked in a factory knows the feeling. Here is the heart-cry of one such wage slave.

"I work in a factory. For eight hours a day, five days a week. I'm the exception to the rule that life can't exist in a vacuum. Work to me is a void . . . .

"People who speak grandiosely of the 'meaning of work' should spend a year or two in a factory. The modern worker neither gives anything to work nor expects anything (apart from his wages) from it. Work, at factory level, has no inherent value. The worker's one interest is his pay packet.

". . . Mechanisation, though it has played a part in the achievement of a shorter working week, has led to jobs that are both dull and monotonous. The loss of dignity and restriction of talent compatible with modern factory life cause a lack of quality in the factory worker. My workmates have a sameness about them: there is an overall apathy and shortage of sinew."[2]

Although the impression given is one-sided, ignoring such features as class and political consciousness (which will be discussed later on), the writer vividly describes the "alienation" characteristic of the routine worker in capitalist society. To alienate means to estrange; and sociologists have lately been very concerned with this phenomenon, which has now extended beyond manual to other workers.

In his younger days Marx was deeply interested in the subject of alienation. His detailed analysis of alienation, in the *Economic and Philosophical Manuscripts of 1844*, was made when he was only 26 and still very much under Hegel's influence, before he really decided to embark on his life's work of examining the *economic* working of the

[1] Article "Wage Slaves" in *The Incompatibles*, ed. Blackburn and Cockburn (Penguin ed. pp. 74–5).

[2] Article "Factory Time", by D. Johnson in *Work*, ed. R. Fraser (Penguin ed.). See also Jackson: *Working-Class Community*, ch. 5.

capitalist system. It is not true to say that thereafter he dropped the subject of alienation altogether: he referred to it again in *Capital*. Although many philosophers and economists, from Adam Smith on, have remarked on this distortion of the human being, present sociological theory bases itself mostly on Marx.[1]

Marx distinguished four aspects of the process of alienation. Brought up to date they can be described roughly as follows:—

(1) The worker has no control over the *work process*: it has become *meaningless* to him. He is an accessory to the machine, not the machine to him. He falls into a machine pattern, dehumanised, robot-like.
(2) The worker is estranged from the *product* of his labour. He works only for his wage, while the world of objects seems hostile to him. Against this world he feels *powerless*.
(3) He becomes increasingly *self-alienated*, divorced from his total being. He lives only for his animal needs—eating, drinking, sleeping, procreating. Intellect and feelings become stunted.
(4) He feels *alienated from others*. He confronts them solely from the worker's standpoint. Life becomes a struggle against others.

These aspects of alienation are vividly illustrated in this extreme description by one man in a department of a large print works:

"Some people might expect workers doing such undemanding work—one 60-year-old worker in my factory has been pushing a pile of periodicals into positions on a cutting table for the past 40 years—to develop outside interests or creative outlets. The contrary is generally true; the work in all but a few cases has a brutalising effect. Many are racialists, anti-semitic and intolerant of minority opinion. Most would like hanging brought back, many even flogging. I don't

[1] Also on the French sociologist, Durkheim (*The Division of Labour* 1893, *Suicide* 1897). Like other nineteenth-century, bourgeois sociologists, Durkheim wanted to defend bourgeois social foundations; so, in opposition to Marx, he argued that the division of labour under capitalism acted as a unifying, not as a disturbing, force. But many people exhibited *anomie*, or normlessness; they felt alientated from society and, in extreme cases, could commit suicide (and homicide). Durkheim argued that this was due to a collective tendency in each society, i.e. a social-psychological force. According to Durkheim, then, since no society was perfect, anomie was a "natural" phenomenon and could never be entirely eliminated; and his theory was, therefore, the forerunner of all those theories which say that no society, capitalist or communist, can abolish alienation. To reduce a high rate of suicide Durkheim recommended the setting up of "occupational corporations" —an idea later seized by fascist leaders.

have to wonder how in past elections so many workers have voted Conservative. The majority don't read their own union reports. I have often tried to describe to my work-mates some of the possibilities of a Socialist Britain, only to find that they are either incapable or unwilling to see any alternative to their present way of life. The typical reply is that it wouldn't work 'because the business-men wouldn't allow it'. In the end you can only discuss politics with a few people; for the rest, you talk about horses or football or something abstract of that sort."[1]

But when bourgeois sociologists discuss alienation today, they almost invariably try to get away from its intimate connection with the capitalist system. Marx himself forewarned about this, when he wrote:

"Political economy (by which he meant bourgeois economics, and this would include sociology—H.F.) conceals the estrangement inherent in the nature of labour by not considering the direct relationship between the worker (labour) and production."[2]

This appears to be the reason that Marx dropped further discussion of the subject. As the U.S. sociologist, Bell, says:

"... Marx, had, in effect, repudiated the idea of alienation. The term, because of its Hegelian overtones, was, for him, too abstract. And, because it carried psychological echoes of ideas such as 'man's condition' it was too 'idealistic'. Estrangement, for Marx, had to be rooted in concrete social activity; and Marx felt that he had found the answer in the idea of exploitation, the economic precipitate, so to speak, of alienation."[3]

How terribly the printworker's account illustrates the truth of Marx's denunciation! Why has the old worker spent nearly 40 years just pushing piles of periodicals, when a simple machine could do it? Because of his fear of unemployment.

Bourgeois sociologists who are reluctant to challenge the present

[1] R. Doyle: "The Print Jungle" in *Work* (Ed. Fraser). For a fairly full discussion of alienation from the bourgeois sociologist's viewpoint, see R. Blauner: *Alienation and Freedom*, especially ch. 2.

[2] *Econ. and Phil. Manuscripts.* (Lawrence & Wishart Edition), p. 71.

[3] Bell: *The End of Ideology*, ch. 15. A short but useful Marxist article is Professor Struik's *Introduction* to the U.S. edition of Marx's *E. and P.M.* (Lawrence & Wishart, 1970).

system therefore slide away from Marx's emphatic association of alienation with capitalism. Either they merely analyse in more and more detail the different aspects of alienation, dissociating it from its economic base. Or, worse still, they assert that *all* industrial societies, capitalist or socialist, produce alienation. This becomes part of the ammunition in the fight to prove that communism is just as bad as capitalism. Applying such defensive analyses of alienation means trying by various manipulations to abolish alienation without abolishing the system of private ownership. (Examples of this will be found in the next section.) It is, of course, true that Marxists did, in the past, assume that alienation *would automatically* disappear with the overthrow of capitalism; that socialism would free the worker from exploitation and that he would find himself again (unity of subject and object). That alienation would persist under socialism, because life, including work, can still be harsh and many serious management mistakes take place, is something we have come to know since. Only under the higher stage of communism can it be assumed that men will be really united within themselves because they will be at one with their society.

Alienation in class society produces reactions at different levels. Some of the qualities that man has lost are felt to exist in another world, the world of magic and religion. The spirits or gods possess all power, the meaning of all things is clear to them, they can aid the distressed believer and bring peace to the world. On a much more earthly level, workers find the satisfaction they fail to get in work in day-dreaming and leisure-time activities; but, whether it be day-dreaming, the "telly", or car-obsession, the worker does it partly to get some satisfaction out of life.[1] Others, like Doyle's fellow print-workers, transfer power and knowledge to the very capitalists responsible for their subjection. In extreme cases, the individual can drop out (anomie), turn to crime or even commit suicide. On a higher level, the worker, realising that all he can get out of the system is his wage, combines with his fellow-workers to get a better share of the product, a higher wage, more material comforts and more time away from the drudgery and his fellow-drudges. But because the trade union in this sense and at this level doesn't reject the system of wage-slavery, it seeks only to

[1] I am far from suggesting that all leisure-time activities are wasteful and would begin to disappear under socialism. Many would, and do, continue under socialism, the more wasteful ones because alienation still persists under socialism, others because they add to the stock of man's culture.

extract more out of the system, sometimes taking part in actions that can have elements of farce as well as tragedy. Tragedy when it's a question of extracting better redundancy payments or higher dole; farcical, as in the print world, when jobs that don't exist are still paid for.[1]

Finally, as even pessimistic workers like Doyle admit, there is a minority which sees an alternative; and the continuous propaganda against socialism proves that the ruling class, despite all claims that Marxism is out of date, dead, irrelevant to the "post-capitalist" epoch, still regard it as the greatest danger of all. All the contradictions of capitalism driving the wage-worker to thought and to action demand greater expertise by the capitalist class to repress or divert this movement; and it calls up its servants, the industrial sociologists, to provide them with answers.

ENTER THE INDUSTRIAL SOCIAL SCIENTIST

The end of the last century was the classical period of industrial capitalism in the United States. The capitalists see the world as a universal machine producing exchange-values, as an endless flow of input units and output units, with labour as one of the input components. All these should obey the will of the capitalist class. The laws of reality are their laws. The future unrolls before the bourgeoisie in this form for ever, although external dangers threaten.

This vision brought into being the "classical" type of management theory of F. W. Taylor and his followers. Taylor, an American engineer of considerable ability, began to look for solutions to the problems of inefficiency and low productivity in the better use of labour. He looked at labour-power mechanistically, to be manipulated, easily satisfied by more money. Described as "Scientific Management", Taylorism symbolised the confidence of early American industrialism. It believed not only that the worker was pliable, that his sole interest was to have a definite task and a satisfactory reward (the donkey and the carrot), but that every industrial problem had one best solution. Taylor's follower, Gilbreth, invented Motion Study; and Time Study followed soon after. In its crude form it led to speed up, massive intensification of work and violent reactions by workers. Even the U.S. Government's *Hoxie Report* condemned Taylorism for, among other reasons, denigrating skilled labour and turning the worker into an automaton and a moron.

[1] See R. Doyle: *The Print Jungle.*

"Scientific Management", Hoxie declared, in the version of his report which he submitted to the American Federation of Labour, "not necessarily science in management—is a device employed for the purpose of increasing production and profits; and tends to eliminate consideration for the character, rights and welfare of the employees." Also: "It looks upon the worker as a mere instrument of production and reduces him to a semi-automatic attachment to the machine or tool."

Events shattered this mechanical-deterministic view. The worker, it was realised, was not simply a mechanical unit; he had feelings and emotions which, although "irrational", had to be taken into account. This new view was developed by Elton Mayo and the school of "Human Relations".

Probably the most influential of the pioneering investigations by this school were those conducted at the Hawthorne Works of the Western Electric Company, which commissioned Mayo and his team from the Harvard School of Business to investigate certain problems and their connection with output. Their first experiments, which consisted in varying lighting in the factory, couldn't be explained on the ordinary hypothesis that the better the physical conditions the higher the output; because production went up, not only in the control room where the lighting remained unchanged, but in the experimental room when the lighting was actually reduced. Similarly, when rest periods were tried, production went up *and continued to go up even when the rest periods were abolished.* Mayo and his team concluded that production kept on rising because the workers felt they were being recognised by the management, were participating in the production process and were no longer isolated units but a team with common aims, free and unforced.

The second stage of Mayo's work consisted in what are now called open-ended interviews, a skilled interviewer asking the worker questions and listening while the worker talked his problems out. Even if nothing could be done about the problems, the fact that the worker felt he had someone he could talk to helped.

Thirdly, the Hawthorne Works investigation revealed the key importance of "informal relations" between the workers. The investigator observed the way the workers of the shop under observation got together, set their own output norms irrespective of management and operated their own system of sanctions against offenders.

The conclusions Mayo drew were (1) workers did not behave as a mass of isolated units (a "horde") but as a group, (2) "human relations" in management were more important as incentives than sheer cash, (3) participation and co-operative effort must be encouraged.[1]

The "Human Relations" approach in overcoming worker hostility and alienation spread rapidly across the Western world. Today in Britain it forms an important part of management-worker relations in the nationalised industries and public services, as well as in giant firms like Esso and I.C.I., with elaborate systems of worker representation and joint consultation. But essentially it is, like Parsons' structural-functionalism, a consensus approach, which assumes that once Mayo's principles are in operation, the problems will disappear.

Conservative reaction to "Human Relations" argues that, if workers are encouraged to take an ell, they will demand a mile. But these critics admit that the old "Scientific Management" approach needs modification because it fails to realise that management is a much more complicated business than Taylor supposed. Management functions not merely by ordering downwards but also by organising efficient channels of communication upwards; also firms are organised not only "vertically" (i.e. from management down to workers), but "laterally" (i.e. between different departments and employee grades on the same level) and conflict may occur between levels with the same degree of authority. The critics also refer to the problems of bureaucracy, which Human Relations ignores; they, like Weber, feel that bureaucratic organisation offers the advantage of laying down precisely what job each section and every individual has to do.

Critics from the side of conflict theory stress that Human Relations fails to solve all industrial problems because, as in any consensus theory, it assumes that workers and management can always co-operate, regards trade unions and government intervention as unnecessary, a managerial élite essential and industrial conflict as pathological.

"... the Goliath of industrial warfare cannot be slain by the David of human relations," a conflict theorist retorts.

"If we want rather to preserve the freedom of association (i.e. of unions, H.F.) we must run the risk of industrial warfare. ... The crucial issue is not to avoid all conflict, but to contain that conflict within the limits of a broad pattern of common purposes." ...[2]

[1] E. Mayo: *Social Problems of an Industrial Civilisation.*

[2] Bendix and Fisher: The perspective of Elton Mayo (*Review of Economics and Statistics* 1949). Note how conflict must be contained, it is implied, in the "Western" pattern.

Even further, Human Relations is criticised as "plant capitalism", based on the idea that worker-management problems can be entirely solved within the plant or factory. But subsequent studies have found that, in spite of all the efforts of Human Relations experts, the overwhelming majority of factory workers do not regard their work as their main life interest. Factory workers, particularly those on routine work, find their jobs so monotonous and their prospects of promotion so minute that they spend much of their time day-dreaming. The class struggle continues all the time in daily battles with the time-and-motion study men or the rate-fixer. For most factory workers the main interest in work is still the money at the end of the week (or security, where employment is uncertain—but then, this is also a question of money, and morale, for very few people like to be idle). Hence there has been a plea for the bosses to attack the problem of industrial relations by going outside the factory, and approaching the worker through his leisure-time activities. Unfortunately for the employers, workers do not want to be reminded of their employment once they have passed through the factory gates. Human Relations, the progressive critics add, ignores the whole external environment, quoting, as an example, W. F. Whyte, who allegedly found the solution to industrial relations in a big Chicago plant between 1937 and 1950 without referring to the effects of the World War, the Taft-Hartley anti-trade union Act, the cost of living or even the economic position of the industry.[1] How, they asked, could managers be forced to develop good human relations? What about the self-employed and the unemployed? What should be done with workers and unions in conflict with management? And one of the leading American researchers on the left, Alvin Gouldner, defended workers' "informal" organisation and strikes, not as irrational aberrations, but as logical defence mechanisms against employers' irrationality, bureaucratic incompetence and to protect the gains achieved outside formal agreements. Finally the British critics, Eldridge and Cameron, defended "unofficial" strikes (over 90 per cent of strikes in Britain are "unofficial") as being mostly against unjust agreements between management and unions. There is, in Gouldner's telling phrase, an "iron law of democracy": the worker's claim to fight must be recognised.[2]

Modified "Scientific Management" rejects Taylorism's crude,

[1] Kerr and Fisher: "Plant Sociology", in *Common Frontiers of the Social Sciences*, (ed. M. Komarovsky).

[2] See also T. Lupton: *On the Shop Floor.*

mechanistic approach, but it does believe management to be a science. It takes off from Weber's complimentary assessment of bureaucracy. "Precision, speed, unambiguity, knowledge of the files, continuity, discretion, unity, strict subordination, reduction of friction and of material and personal costs—are raised to the optimum point in the strictly bureaucratic administration. . . . The fully developed bureaucratic mechanism compares with other organisations exactly as does the machine with the non-mechanical modes of production."[1] But it recognises that Weber overlooked the dysfunctions of bureaucracy, some of which we have already described. Modern "Scientific Management" theory particularly concerns itself with conflicts within the organisation, expressed as differences between departments and individuals. In the view of one of its founders, Chester Barnard, the organisation must be seen as a "system of co-operation" and the "management function" to bring co-operation about by both financial and non-financial incentives. He also urged managements to accept the existence of "informal organisations". More recent theorists stress the fundamental problem of reconciling the individual's hope to use the organisation to further *his* own goals with the hope of the organisation to use the individual to further *its* own goals. In attempting to fuse these opposing tendencies, "Scientific Management" joins with "Human Relations" in the current craze for "Behavioural Science", which aims to reduce conflict and to promote "co-operation" by viewing the organisation as the interaction between worker and management. But, in spite of their achievements, industrial social scientists have failed to find a comprehensive theory which will succeed in limiting conflict and promoting co-operation everywhere. As Miss Joan Woodward, one of the leading Establishment figures in "management science" declares, no one theory of management can solve all problems (of capitalist enterprise).[2]

The simple fact is that, with certain honourable exceptions, industrial social scientists fail to go to the heart of the problem because they are unable to. A leading critic explains:

> "The reason that an understanding of human relations assumed such monumental proportions was that, in an age of governmental regulations and more powerful unions, costs continued to rise. American management came to believe in the importance of under-

[1] Gerth and Mills: *From Max Weber: Essays in Sociology*, ch. 8.
[2] J. Woodward: *Industrial Organisation* (1965).

standing human behaviour because it became convinced that this was one sure way of improving its main weapon in the struggle for power, the profit margin.

"Sociologists, too, tried to make clear what they could do if they were given the chance, though they were usually more restrained than the psychologists.

"Hired by management to solve specific problems, they had to produce ... Demanding that the social scientists in their employ concentrate exclusively on the narrow problems of productivity and industrial loyalty, managers made of industrial social science a tool of industrial domination."

After all, "... managers, as managers, are in business to make money. Only to the extent that industrial social scientists can help in the realisation of this goal will management make use of them."

Management need not have feared. "... throughout their professional history, industrial social scientists, without prodding from anyone, have accepted the norms of American managers".[1]

There are exceptions, of course, but few: and one of the first post-war British investigators of industrial disputes, K. J. C. Knowles, writing in the early 1950s, pointed out that, while there was a variety of immediate and longer-term causes, including the trade cycle, the *underlying* causes were the worker's propertylessness, his lack of mobility and insecurity, and *the basic difference of economic interest between workers and "management"*.[2] These causes are, of course, inherent in capitalism itself.

THE EFFECTS OF AUTOMATION

Recently, however, the introduction of automation has brought about some "revolutionary" new management-union agreements, hailed as the pattern for the future. Long term agreements concluded provide for very big wage increases, shorter hours and other improvements. In addition, automation, it is stressed, takes the physical drudgery out of work and transforms the manual worker into a white-coated, button-pressing technician. The demand for skilled men increases. They become "multi-craftsmen", able to do a variety of skilled jobs. Each man, once he starts on a job, is able to complete it. This makes the work

[1] Baritz: *Servants of Power*, pages 191–197.

[2] K. J. C. Knowles: "Strike-proneness and its determinants" (*American Journal of Sociology*, 1954).

more interesting and reduces alienation. Even if some manual workers are displaced, the demand for *non*-manual staff, mainly technicians, supervisors, and programmers, increases; and quite a number of manual workers change over to this type of work. Physical working conditions improve. It is almost as if an Omo-white future with minimum alienation is at hand, without altering capitalist property relations.

The most widely quoted settlement of this kind is the 1960 agreement at the Esso Refinery at Fawley. The Esso Company offered its 2,400 wage earners a 40 per cent wage increase (2/6 an hour for craftsmen) spread over 2 years, in exchange for redeployment of craftsmen and the upgrading of some, relaxation of demarcation rules, more management freedom in the use of supervisors, reduction of the working week from 42 to 40 hours and a cut in overtime. The results of this pioneer agreement were that the productivity of the men most concerned went up by over 50 per cent, the average working week fell from 50 to 42½ hours, and average hourly earnings rose by 35 per cent.

The workers' paradise? Well, there is the other side. A simple calculation shows that, taking into account the sharp fall in hours, *weekly* earnings must have risen much less than (the hourly) 35 per cent: in fact by just under 7 per cent. Of course, a substantial reduction in hours, *plus* more money, was a godsend to the workers. But the bosses got a *50 per cent increase in productivity*. Within two years from the start of the scheme, there was a £12 million increase in plant operated and maintained by *200 fewer workers*. Another case, the 1968 productivity agreement of the nationalised Steel Company of Wales provides, in return for consolidation of cost-of-living bonuses, improved fringe benefits and protection of the jobs of those who remain, for a *halving* of the labour force by 1971, foregoing of national craft union pay awards during this period, job evaluation and work study.

From these and other agreements on productivity under automation,[1] the aims and achievements of the employers are clear. There is always a substantial reduction in manpower. In the best firms, specifically the nationalised industries and most famous giant combines, the sack is softened by spreading it over a longish period, aided by good severance pay. Productivity is enormously increased and the main benefit goes to the bosses. Christensen found from a survey of a number of companies that, with the introduction of programmed machines, earnings

[1] See E. Christensen's survey: *Automation* and *the Workers* (L.R.D., 1968).

increased between zero and 15 per cent, but the drop in labour costs was between *55 and 90 per cent*. The overall result, as Professor Meade has pointed out, is that as automation proceeds, the share of the national product going to the workers must fall and that going to the employers must rise.

It is important to state that fears about mass unemployment due to automation have not been confirmed, at least for the present. But this needs qualification. Automation requires less semi-skilled and unskilled manual labour, but it does boost skilled manual and non-manual employment. The overall result, called "displacement", means that many unskilled and semi-skilled workers have to find other jobs. Because the general increase in productivity and pay brings higher consumer demand, the "displaced" can usually find jobs—at least for the time being. But all this movement puts the interest of the "displaced" worker last; the capitalist state does not guarantee employment and the worker's insecurity remains.

Experts claim that alienation diminishes under automation. Not only does the worker get more pay; his status rises; the work is more interesting and more responsible.[1] But, as Blauner, one of its leading advocates admits, to express satisfaction with the job is not a real guide. The worker may be satisfied and yet still be alienated. Work satisfaction, a favourite phrase with the industrial sociologist, is not the same as absence of alienation. The two are like objective class situation and voting preference. The worker may be only partly conscious of his alienation, as he may be of his class position; and he may express satisfaction simply because he prefers alienating work to *no work at all*.[2]

The fact is that bourgeois sociologists look at alienation as only or primarily a *subjective* attitude, whereas for Marx and Marxists it is not only what the worker thinks and feels about his job, but the objective situation underlying it and its effects, of which the worker may or may not be conscious. While alienation is least in small-scale craft work, in large-scale capitalist industry, especially where the division of labour is greatest, alienation is at a maximum. But, being human beings, workers can take defensive action to reduce dissatisfaction (which is not the same as alienation). Zweig, who discussed the problem with many workers, concluded:

[1] But chances of promotion from shop-floor to managerial grades are probably less the more advanced the technology. (See Goldthorpe etc.: *The Affluent Worker in the Class Structure*, p. 80).

[2] Blauner: *Alienation and Freedom*, ch. 2. Other investigators claim that work satisfaction *decreases* under automation. The conflict of opinion reinforces our main point.

> "A man who feels dissatisfied and uncomfortable in his job will try to change it, but if he decides for one reason or another to stay put, he will develop a compensatory mechanism by accepting the job and making the best of it, if he is a healthy-minded person, i.e. a person with full power of adjustment."[1]

In that case, according to Zweig, there is little alienation. But what he means is little overt dissatisfaction. His claim that he noted little sign of alienation among the hundreds of workers he interviewed shows that he does not understand what alienation is. From the figures he himself supplies it turns out that 60 per cent of all those workers read nothing at all or only the lightest fiction, that among them all there was a terrible waste of human intelligence and capability and that money-mindedness "... plays an ever-increasing part in a man's attitude to his work". *That* is alienation.[2]

The problem of alienation cannot be separated from the wider society. Industry in every advanced capitalist country tends towards bigger and bigger combines, first confined to the particular industry, but recently more and more towards "conglomerates", which spread their tentacles towards any firm, in whatever industry, that appears to show a very profitable future. International big-business link-ups are increasing. In this situation not only does the physical separation between workers and bosses grow greater; impersonal indifference towards the individual worker increases. If business conditions demand, thousands are simply sacked, as recent events in the GEC-AEI-English Electric combine and the Rolls Royce company, not to mention the National Coal Board, show. Sociologists' advice to firms to involve the workers in decision-making becomes so much more difficult to implement. As Touraine, writing for the W. European capitalist leaders, points out, alienation is spreading and with it resistance to change; it is spreading also to higher and higher levels and is finally becoming a criticism of the social, economic and political system.

> "The study of workers' attitudes with regard to change is inseparable from a more general analysis of the policies of management and thus necessarily leads to the more general theme of the

[1] F. Zweig: *The Worker in an Affluent Society*, p. 191.

[2] Readers may recall that the American sociologist, R. K. Merton, criticising Weber's assessment of bureaucracy, also had something to say about the pressures to conformism in U.S. society today. In such a situation, he wrote, the goal (mainly money) may become more important than the means of getting it and anomie, demoralisation, can set in. (See Merton: *Social Theory and Social Structure*, ch. 4.)

representation, in the firm and at a higher level, of the interests and social forces which are affected by these changes; in other words, to the problems of industrial democracy."[1]

FULL EMPLOYMENT AND THE UNIONS

All parties after the war agreed that full employment must continue. At first the Tories were quite proud that post-war Britain maintained full employment, because it showed that "Western democracy" had solved its biggest pre-war problem. But, while the Labour Party continued officially to support full employment until 1966, already some years before that one noticed in Tory publications twinges of regret that it was putting the working man in the position of being able to push wages up too much.

It was not much of a surprise, therefore, to socialists when the Tories brought back their traditional method of lowering (or trying to lower) wages, i.e. unemployment. In the winter of 1962/63 unemployment suddenly increased, at a rate not seen since the 'thirties, to a record 878,000 in February 1963. Popular reaction forced the Government to take counter-measures. The Conservatives learned then that drastic deflation didn't work because (*a*) while in theory it might hold wages down, in practice the working class and salariat didn't easily give up their claims even under the threat of unemployment, (*b*) it had a bad effect on production and (*c*) it was politically unpopular.

No such wisdom marked the policies of both post-war Labour governments, especially the Wilson administration. With a suicidal impetus resembling the lemmings', the Labour leaders insisted on trying to solve British capitalism's economic problems in the way now associated with Labour governments: restrict wage increases, make a show of price control and cut workers' consumption. The Wilson Government added one more: if you (the workers) don't let us carry out this policy, they said, we will put a million or more of you out of work. So, not only are wages and salaries barely keeping up with prices and taxation, but the number of registered unemployed, which topped half a million again in November 1966, has been kept at that level since. Anti-Marxist theorists who claimed that Marx's "industrial reserve army" was a thing of the past are now remarkably silent. Crosland himself wrote about the "... profound significance not only of the fact of full employment, both for individual welfare and the balance of

[1] A. Touraine: *Workers' Attitudes to Technical Change* (O.E.C.D. 1965), p. 161.

class power, but also of the explicit acceptance by governments of responsibility for its maintenance. This constitutes," he declared, ". . . a major victory for the Left, as important as any in the social revolution of the last two decades."[1] Crosland now acquiesces in the policy of a permanent pool of unemployed, strongly backed as it is by the Tories, who thereby play a double game by at the same time exploiting Labour's unpopularity over this issue.

Over the long term, then, capitalism cannot permit the indefinite continuation of full employment. It must have the pool of unemployed as a lever to try and keep down wages.[2]

What about the power of the unions? Much has been said about this power, not only by the extreme Right but by sober economists like Galbraith. Crosland took this line too. ". . . Even under a Conservative Government the Trade Unions remain effective masters of the industrial scene", he wrote.[3] Of course, the unions have power, which they used during and after the war to improve pay and conditions in many fields of employment. But it is now clear that, whatever benefits they have brought, they have not been able substantially to alter the power of the capitalist class to appropriate a large slice of the national wealth, or its power to employ or not to employ,[4] let alone the existence of that class. As Galbraith himself admitted, the power of the unions varies: they are stronger during inflation, weaker during deflation. The right-wing academic economists who dominate the Wilson Government so love deflation (for, additionally, in the short run, it stimulates share prices and profits) that they turn a blind eye and deaf ear to its consequences on the Labour Movement which brought them to power.

Academic argument about whether unions have improved the workers' lot has pretty well ended. It is now widely agreed that, if they have done so, the achievement has been marginal. On the other hand, it is equally certain that without unions the workers would have been very much worse off. From a purely economic point of view, therefore, they have been largely defensive organisations, able to prevent sharp deterioration in living standards in periods of depression (though not, of course, for the unemployed) and pushing them up during booms.

[1] *The Future of Socialism*, p. 54.

[2] "The industrial reserve army that at the beginning of the century appeared mainly at times of economic crises has been replaced by a permanent unemployed army." (E. Varga: *Twentieth Century Capitalism*, p. 121).

[3] *The Future of Socialism*, p. 94.

[4] See, for example, T. E. Chester's admission in his important article, "Industrial conflicts in British nationalised industries", in Kornhauser, Dubin and Ross (eds.): *Industrial Conflict*.

Even that set of attitudes has changed. The argument that another fellow's outside, ready to do the job for less, cuts much less ice now. Wage-earners and salariat demand their rights and are rather more successful in getting their increases. The capitalist class' reaction is to raise prices, intensify labour exploitation and increase taxation in various ways, as well as to try and curb unions by legislation. So the standard of living goes up or down or stays put for different *sections* depending on the organised strength of that particular section of the working class. "Wage disputes", as a leading bourgeois economist tells us, "are more likely to settle the distribution of the wage-bill between one section of labour and another, or between one industry and another. . . . Broadly speaking, therefore, wage disputes are disputes over *relative* rates of wages."[1]

But if this were the whole story, we might despair of trade unions altogether. What's the point of devoting so much time and energy to work in the unions if it only results in a squabble over the crumbs from the rich man's table? The answer is, of course, that they are also schools of battle, of class struggle, of political education. The limitations of trade unions have been correctly and eloquently analysed by Perry Anderson:[2] they operate in the work-place only, they are sectional, they are part of capitalist society and their ultimate weapon is only negative (withdrawal of labour). A socialist party is its opposite: it works everywhere, it unites the working class, it is opposed to capitalism and its weapon is (or ought to be) positive—revolution. But the unions can and do fulfil a unique, preparatory role: they are, in Lenin's famous phrase, "schools of Communism": every gain strengthens the workers' self-confidence and helps bring socialism that much nearer. That is why there is continuous conflict within the trade union movement between those who would like to suppress or contain the leftward move, to keep the unions strictly for the role of getting a slightly better share of the spoils of capitalism, and those who want to develop the preparatory role also.

However, under capitalism the attempt to get a "fairer share" (what did Attlee mean exactly when he talked of "fair shares"?) merely builds up capitalist opposition; and, where not actually suppressed by terror, there is increasing pressure to shackle the unions "voluntarily" or by legislation. This is the trend in Britain today. If a "voluntary

[1] Cairncross: *Introduction to Economics* (3rd ed.), pp. 361–2.

[2] P. Anderson: "The limits and possibilities of trade union action", in *The Incompatibles* (Penguin 1966).

incomes policy" does not sufficiently restrain the workers' demands, as it failed to do also under Attlee and Cripps, the law must be brought in to do it. And what the Labour Government has started, the Tories aim to extend. The recommendations of the Royal Commission on Trade Unions (the Donovan Report) do not satisfy the Tories or the Wilson Government by any means. Social-democratic "voluntarism" does not work, either, as the experience of even such a highly-organised state as Sweden has shown. The honeymoon image of a Capital-Labour marriage always fades as Capital, revealing that the "marriage" was only a temporary convenience, insists once again on being master in the house.

After all, something similar to the post-1945 period took place 100 years ago. In the period 1846/1866, real wages as well as money wages rose, as a result of the expansion of trade and falls in the prices of basic foods. There was an immediate reaction from revolutionary Chartism. The English trade unions renounced class warfare and used their new-found strength only to get a better slice of the national wealth. But this honeymoon period ended too, as ours today has ended.

Some sociologists produced figures during the 1950s purporting to show a decline in the use of the strike-weapon in N.W. Europe.[1] As far as Britain is concerned, the statistics do not bear this out. While the number of stoppages in 1966 was much lower than in 1956, the numbers of *workers involved* was slightly greater, as was the number of *days lost*. Besides, as everyone now knows, industrial disputes have increased tremendously since 1966, as the following figures show:

Year	*No. of stoppages*	*No. of workers involved (thousands)*	*Working days lost (thousands)*
1966	1,951	544	2,398
1967	2,133	734	2,787
1968	2,390	2,258	4,690
1969	3,051	1,620	6,772

WORKING-CLASS POLITICAL ATTITUDES

But, if these merely show that the workers only want a fairer share out of the system, what measures political dissatisfaction with the system?

[1] Ross and Hartman: *Changing Patterns of Industrial Conflict* (1960).

One measure of political development is voting in parliamentary elections. The following table shows the numbers and percentages of all votes for Labour in selected elections from 1900 onwards:

Year	*% of all votes cast*	*No. of votes (to nearest 100,000)*
1900		62,000
1910		500,000
1918	21·4	2,300,000
1935	38·1	8,300,000
1945	48·3	11,600,000
1950	46·1	13,300,000
1951	48·8	14,000,000
1955	46·4	12,400,000
1959	43·8	12,200,000
1964	44·1	12,200,000
1966	47·9	13,000,000

What Britain has witnessed, therefore, is a fairly swift rise (historically speaking) of the Labour Party to the position of being able to form a majority government after just under fifty years of existence. This must be regarded as a triumph of British working-class political progress.

But the failure to increase, or even completely maintain, the Labour vote is, of course, the subject of much argument. The right-wing claim it is because Labour has not thrown out its cloth-cap image and its old dogmas, the left-wing because the parliamentary leaders have overthrown the principles and aims on which the party was built.

Examination of reasons for voting Labour is revealing on this issue. Students have found two types of Labour voter (which are to some extent Weberian ideal types), the one who votes Labour out of traditional solidarity and the one who believes simply that a Labour Government is more likely to deliver the goods as far as the working class is concerned. The latter attitude (called "instrumental collectivism") seems to be on the increase; in other words, traditional solidarity with Labour is waning.

That this does *not* mean diminishing *class* feelings is shown by the results of an investigation among higher-paid workers in Luton in 1962. Despite a good deal of confusion, 81 per cent of all respondents considered society in Britain to consist of only two or three classes. But more significant than this (since the definitions of the classes varied) is the fact that over half of all respondents regarded "money" as being the most important determinant of class and that the largest class embraced the bulk of wage *and* salary earners.[1]

The following percentages also declared that in Britain there was still one law for the rich and another for the poor:[2]

	%
Manual workers	72
White-collar workers	59
Labour voters	78
Conservative voters	48

But the Labour Government has lost many of (*a*) its "traditional" supporters, because they regard the Government's actions as a betrayal of socialism, and (*b*) its "instrumental collectivists", too, because the goods (higher standards of living etc.) have not been delivered. What is needed is a radical reversal of existing policies. "Such a strategy", declare Goldthorpe, Lockwood and their co-workers, "would entail a reversion by Labour to a clear commitment to the interests of the mass of wage-earning, rank-and-file employees, and an endeavour to advance these interests not merely by promoting general economic expansion but also by thoroughgoing egalitarian measures over a wide front."[3]

But surely, it is said, the fact that as much as one-third of all working-class votes goes to the Tories shows widespread pro-capitalist attitudes among workers. Certainly it does; but it conceals much more.

Actual studies of working-class Tories are very revealing.[4] The overwhelming characteristic of these people seems to be their reactionary political views, rather than any wish to lift themselves up out of their class. They support judicial flogging and the barring of coloured immigrants and oppose any further nationalisation. They dislike or distrust trade unions. Far from being "lumpen", they are often better informed politically than Labour voters and are as well-integrated into the community. They believe the Conservatives can get things done, are less concerned about class and think the Tories are far superior to Labour when it comes to foreign policy, Commonwealth relations, national prosperity and sense of patriotism.

[1] Goldthorpe and others: *The Affluent Worker in the Class Structure*, p. 147. "Money" meant differences in incomes, wealth and material standards.

[2] Goldthorpe and others: *The Affluent Worker in the Class Structure*, p. 193.

[3] Goldthorpe and others: *The Affluent Worker: Political Attitudes and Behaviour* (pp. 26–7).

[4] For a short account see article by R. MacKenzie and A. Silver, *The Observer*, 6th September 1964.

When working-class Tories are analysed, they seem to fall into two groups, "deferentials" and "seculars". "Deferentials" (about 30 per cent of all) are those who believe the upper classes have a natural superiority and were born to rule. "Seculars" (about 40 per cent) support those who have got to the top the "hard" way. The remaining 30 per cent are a bit of each. One of the important findings is that "deferentials" tend to be poorer and to include more women. Just as religion in the socialist countries is today largely maintained by older women, it can be inferred that the "deferentials" are more likely to remain loyal to the Tory Party than the "seculars", whose support, like that of the "instrumental collectivists" for Labour, is based more on what the party can *do* than in the innate superiority of the upper classes. The investigation shows, in Marxist language, the "false consciousness" among "deferentials" and supports the conclusion that the Tories will continue to receive support from the "seculars", who see the Labour leaders making a mess of running the system. It is also evident that at least the "seculars", who are the majority, concern themselves primarily with their own interests and support the Tory Party not on principle but for purely pragmatic reasons. This majority of all working-class Tory support is, therefore, Tory not on principle nor for social-climbing reasons, but pragmatically. Theirs is certainly not an *innate* support for the capitalist system.[1] The working-class Tories still look on themselves as working-class.[2]

WORKING-CLASS CULTURE AND THE THESIS OF EMBOURGEOISEMENT

In 1957, Richard Hoggart, himself the son of a manual worker, lamented, in his famous book *The Uses of Literacy*, the passing of working-class culture. Basing himself on memories of his own childhood, Hoggart looked back nostalgically on old working-class family life centred around the mother, the father's authority, the strong class feelings and a working-class culture which, however crude, was

[1] One "secular" working-class Tory gave as reason for supporting a lorry driver's son as Prime Minister: "He has struggled in life. He knows more about the working troubles of the ordinary person. Those who inherit money rarely know anything about real life." (from the *Observer* article).

[2] The effect of the mass media on people's attitudes and opinions is a big subject in itself. They tend not so much to create attitudes and opinions as to reinforce those already there. But, as millions of people continually question our society, reinforcement of bourgeois ideology is critically important; and that is why the material it puts out implicitly or explicitly supports the "Western way of life". (See either of two books, both entitled *The Effects of Mass Communication*, one by J. T. Klapper (1960) the other by Halloran (1964).)

anyway distinct. Comparing it with today, Hoggart saw family ties dissolving, the father without authority, a working class whose class feelings had wilted and, above all, whose distinctive culture (home, pub, music-hall and working-class press) had been replaced by passive time-wasters like bingo and the "faceless" culture of the mass media, which reduced all news and major events to triviality and chit-chat about individual personalities. With great sincerity, Hoggart saw the main enemy in the commercial mass media and later played a leading role in the Pilkington Committee, which publicly attacked commercial T.V.

While Hoggart was regretting the disappearance of working-class culture, other writers were taking the line that we were witnessing today the transformation of the working class into the middle class through their new-found affluence. Everywhere in the advanced industrial countries, whether capitalist or communist, the workers were losing their old class-consciousness and were becoming interested more and more simply in their homes, families and material comforts.

"Working-class life finds itself on the move towards new middle-class values and middle-class existence", wrote one of the leading exponents of this point of view.[1]

This became the official Tory Government line. Macmillan, then Prime Minister, declared that the class struggle was "obsolete"; Tory propaganda invented the slogan, "You've never had it so good"; and the working class seemed to prove it true by voting the Tories back into office a third time in 1959.

Of course, the unprecedented expansion of consumer-goods production, advertising and sales resulted in the transformation of homes, habits and customs. But, although the popular press, financially interested in the consumer boom (through advertising), vigorously promoted this notion of the "classlessness" of the new Britain, more cautious voices began to be heard. Unfortunately, they were only a minority, chiefly academics, without access to the mass media. Their reaction to Hoggart's book was that it was too personal and based too much on observation of only one area. It also tended to idealise the past and to paint the present in excessively sombre colours. Zweig's work was, on the other hand, conducted mostly in prosperous areas of the country during a period of economic expansion and where about 40 per cent of all wives went out to work; and so could be said to describe only the new "aristocracy" of labour.

[1] F. Zweig: *The Worker in an Affluent Society* (1961), Introduction.

Anyone reading Zweig's book will, in fact, find that the responses he got from the hundreds of workers he interviewed do not fully bear out the simple conclusion we quoted above. Their attitudes and behaviour were far more varied and complex. Most important is the fact that the great majority of interviewees, in spite of their higher earnings and home-centredness, still placed themselves in the working class. Indeed, two-thirds declared they were still working-class (more among the skilled, rather less among the unskilled) and only 16 per cent (less than one-sixth) middle-class. Zweig's conclusion was at variance with his own statistics.

Many studies of working- and middle-class life were made in the 'fifties and early 'sixties,[1] from a mining community, through village and small town life, to Bethnal Green and the London suburb of Woodford. Summarising the studies of working-class life, Josephine Klein described the changes somewhat as follows. Due to the various forces (full employment, higher wages, rehousing, growth of the mass consumer-goods market), the working-class had changed radically. From being always hard-up, accepting the situation as it was, the family network very close, family authority lying in the father, the son following the father's occupation and social life centered on small communities (the street or local area), they now experienced greater affluence, more partnership, marriage, family network loosened by greater physical separation, greater preparedness to move for the job with more money, social life centred far less on the community and much more on the home.

Klein appeared to be less concerned with the alleged change in class consciousness and class culture. Frankenberg, however, who is a Marxist, concentrated attention more on the class aspect. Some of the more important conclusions he drew from all the studies were:

(1) There were still distinct sections in British society, which might be defined as upper class, middle class and working class;[2]
(2) Within these there were sub-divisions, which sometimes cut across and within class barriers, e.g. the division in rural areas and small, growing towns between "locals" and "cosmopolitans"

[1] Summaries may be found in Klein: *Samples from English Cultures*, and Frankenberg: *Communities in Britain* (Penguin).

[1] To give Crosland his due, he agreed strongly with the view that there were still deep *social* class divisions in post-war Britain, but they had little connection with capital ownership.

(outsiders who had moved in through the establishment of new industries);

(3) Within the working class there were sub-divisions, especially the "traditional" working class and the "deprived" (alternatively known as "respectables" and "roughs");

(4) Because of movement to new countil estates, traditional working-class life approached suburban, middle-class life in being less neighbourhood-centred and more family- and home-centred.

Frankenberg drew up an elaborate scheme of social organisation along a continuum from rural to urban society. While stressing that the economic factor was still most important, other relationships, such as family and kinship, were also important, more so in villages and small towns than in cities, and these often cut across class lines, as did changes described in proposition (4). But neither Klein nor Frankenberg settled the issue.

It was left to two of Britain's ablest, younger sociologists to put forward a clear answer to the popular propaganda of growing "middle-classness". Also using the evidence afforded by all the local studies, Lockwood (of *The Blackcoated Worker* fame) and Goldthorpe[1] have argued that not only are the objective situations of manual and non-manual worker still largely different, but so are their attitudes and behaviour. Even in high-earning areas manual workers, as even Zweig showed, still regard their jobs without much *positive* satisfaction,[2] are mostly interested only in the money, work a lot of overtime to get it and have little chance of promotion. They expect any advancement to come, not via promotion, but by trade union negotiation of higher rates of pay for their present jobs; whereas white-collar workers' attitudes and expectations are the opposite, with greater work satisfaction and promotion prospects. Studies of working-class adolescents have shown how these limited expectations, and hence aspirations, carry on from generation to generation. Working-class youngsters rarely have ambitions above their class. This is so even in the United States. "Handicapped early in life, working-class boys and girls limit

[1] Lockwood and Goldthorpe: "Affluence and the British class structure" (*Sociological Review*, July 1963), and "The affluent worker and the thesis of embourgoisement" (*Sociology*, January 1967).

[2] When the American sociologist, Blauner, claimed that only 13 per cent of all U.S. workers whose attitudes had been investigated were dissatisfied with their jobs, he included all grades, from unskilled manual to professional. But a breakdown of the figures shows that the overwhelming majority of manual workers were *not* satisfied. (See Blauner's article in *Labour and Trade Unionism*, ed. by Galenson and Lipset.)

their aspirations and barely secure even their minimal goals."[1] As regards life outside work, segregation is still the rule, both as regards where workers live and the sort of organisations they belong to. Kin are important to both manual and non-manual workers; but, with the former, neighbours are closer than non-neighbour contacts, (workmates and fellow-members of organisations), with the latter the other way.

Voting behaviour (see Chapter 6) shows that, while a substantial minority of manual workers still vote Tory, the Labour Party is still seen as the party for the working class. (Whether, one might add, recent events electorally mark the beginning of the end of this belief, has already been suggested. In any case, it doesn't affect the main argument, indeed reinforces it.) The "middle-class" tendencies, Lockwood and Goldthorpe add, i.e. more home-centredness, plus rising aspirations for children, are not common to the whole working class and in any case constitute only part of their total behaviour pattern. In other respects they are *not* becoming middle-class. The key criterion as to whether or not the working class are becoming middle-class is whether they are not only abandoning their own class but becoming accepted by and assimilated into the middle class; and this, they claim, *is definitely not happening*. And finally, they stress (as this present book has done) that the so-called middle class is not a single class and is more highly stratified than the working class.

Despite all the forces for change bearing on the working class, everyday observation plus a number of sociological studies still pick out, despite variations, certain characteristics common to manual workers, which clearly arise from their socio-economic position in industrial-capitalist society. Besides being largely "instrumental" in attitude towards his job, the manual worker feels less secure than the non-manual worker, lives more for the immediate present, is down-to-earth and more conservative in his attitude to change, very class-conscious, morally stricter. He is very keen on all types of mass sport (mainly to watch) which excite or which bring companionship with others of his class. His leisure-time tastes, apart from sport, are still chiefly the pub and the "telly", with others depending to some extent on the area he lives in, e.g. brass bands, pigeon fancying, dog racing,

[1] Shostak and Gomberg: *Blue-Collar World* (p. 121). A recent British study, with similar conclusions, is described in the article, "Class differentials in educational opportunity", by D. J. Lee (*Sociology*, 1968). See also Goldthorpe and others: *The Affluent Worker in the Class Structure* (1969), table 17, p. 135.

the workingmen's club.[1] Working clothes are different. And, of course, language: the language of the working class being, in Bernstein's description, simpler, more direct, more virile and of wider metaphoric range, than the middle class. For example, the working-class father might say, "Hoppit", when the middle-class parent would say, "I wish you'd go away".

A study of over 700 Nottingham mothers with babies one year old showed striking divergences in behaviour in respect of their infants as between the different social classes. These are given in the following table:

Class Differences in Infant Rearing[2]

	Social class and percentage				
	I & II	*IIIW*	*IIIM*	*IV*	*V*
	%	%	%	%	%
Mother aged 21 or less at birth of first child	24	25	40	46	53
Breast-feeding at 6 months	20	12	11	11	7
Bed-time at 8.0 p.m. plus	7	12	20	23	26
Child sleeps in room alone	54	42	20	18	3
Diet inadequate	5	10	13	13	32
Frequent tantrums	9	8	14	15	23
Family with 3 or more children	28	27	40	44	64

(IIIW = III non-manual, IIIM = III manual)

The table shows that the working-class mother tends to be younger at the birth of her first child, goes in less for prolonged breast-feeding, lets the children stay up later, does not generally give the child a room on its own (cannot, more likely), feeds the child less adequately and tends to have a larger family, than the middle or upper classes.

These attitudes and patterns of behaviour not only *reflect* the basically unchanging relationship of the manual worker and his family to the system of production (property) relations; they also *reinforce* these relations. For example, as Bernstein tells us in the matter of language and education, ". . . the linguistic form is a powerful conditioner of what is learnt, how it is learnt and so influences future learning."[3] And, in the wider context, the worker's outlook of more immediate gratification, planning less for the future because the future is unpredictable, means that the working-class child has less chance and lower expectations (aims). Thus the structure of capitalist society not only

[1] B. Jackson: *Working Class Community* (1968) esp. pp. 155–166.
[2] From J. and E. Newson: *Infant Care in an Urban Community* (1963).
[3] B. Bernstein: "A public language" (*British Journal of Sociology*, 1959).

produces these characteristics, but the characteristics react upon the worker and upon society. This is precisely what Marx and Engels meant in their well-known analysis of base and superstructure. And it is important to note that the lower *non*-manual workers share some of these characteristics. This is how Brian Jackson summarises working-class life.

> "Working-class community rests on the division of labour in society. The working-class family has few, if any, financial assets. The man has nothing to live from except his labour and his skill. His job is unlikely ever to give him enough money to build up capital, let alone employ others. His earnings probably reach their peak in his early twenties and thereafter—except for trade booms—they will hold still, or decline. His chances of promotion from the shop floor are negligible. And though he may earn more or earn less than his neighbours, the range of income in a working-class area is very tiny compared with the range and forms of income amongst a middle-class group. Contrast this with the middle-class man whose income tends to rise through his life, who is usually on some promotion ladder, who may build up a small amount of capital, and who knows that many in the middle class might be ten, twenty, thirty times as rich as he is. This single economic division, whatever else it does, pulls the working class together as a group; and as a self-conscious group—whereas it splits the middle class into much more separate households, even if joined by common bonds of interest."[1]

The worker's *position* in the capitalist system then leads to a "style of life". This is characterised by, first, work, carried out because without work you starve and degenerate into something less than a human being. Dependency on work leads to class solidarity, though the degree can vary. There is the eternal struggle of making ends meet, a life cycle starting with temporary affluence as an unmarried teenager, the growing economic burden of parenthood, relief as the children grow up but resuming as one gets older, finally ending in the hardship of living on pension. There is the community feeling, often enforced by actual physical crowding together and lack of privacy, but on its positive side welding them together. Class solidarity is the most important expression of the worker's way of life; and with it goes

[1] B. Jackson, same, p. 155. I disagree with Jackson's joining the £30,000-a-year company director with the clerk earning £20 a week in a single "middle class". So, I suspect, would Goldthorpe and Lockwood.

ingrained hostility to employers, suspicion of police, bureaucracy, politicians and a natural scepticism. Workers, as Goldthorpe and his colleagues show, still mostly see present British society as class society determined by wealth and related criteria.

Of course, working-class life has changed. Most of all it has changed for those who were born and reared under the Welfare State; but this improvement has been exaggerated. However, it has meant that workers demand and expect more; especially it has meant considerably greater freedom and opportunities for women, although the opportunities are still those of second-class citizens. But it has meant more companioniate marriage between equals, no longer father-dominated households. The housing situation has improved for those in council housing, but it has also meant the disruption of many traditional communities and difficulty in establishing new ones, leading to more "home-centredness" and insularity. The rise in production of mass consumption goods has been both symptom and cause of higher living standards. But, although both they and the mass media (especially the TV) have altered consumption habits to some degree, it cannot be said that either has transformed workers into members of the "middle class".

> "In most ways", Jackson concludes, "working-class life is undoubtedly far, far better than it was. But in essence it *feels* the same, offers the same kind of *experience*."[1]

What, then, is the social and political significance of the post-war alterations? Lockwood and Goldthorpe have offered the theory of "convergence", which argues that the more affluent workers have adopted *some* "middle-class" ways, while the lower paid and newer categories of white-collar workers have taken on some of the characteristics (attitudes and behaviour) of the manual workers. But, they emphasise, this convergence doesn't imply identity: ". . . for the 'new' working class, convergence largely means an adaptation of ends, . . . for the 'new' middle class an adaptation of means".[2] The "new" (more

[1] Jackson, same, p. 166. American sociologists have carried out a great deal of research into the attitudes and behaviour of manual workers. From one of the most authoritative investigations, Richard F. Hamilton concludes that the skilled workers, even though they tend to be an autonomous group within the larger working class, are nearer in behaviour and attitudes to the semi-skilled than to the white-collar workers. (See R. H. Hamilton: "The behaviour and values of skilled workers", in Shostak and Gomberg (eds.) *Blue Collar World*). Also Goldthorpe and others: *The Affluent Worker in the Class Structure* (1969), pp. 118–121 and generally throughout the book.

[2] Article in *Sociological Review*, July 1963.

affluent) working class do not want to be, nor are they being absorbed into, the "middle class", or even to fuse with lower white-collar workers: they only want to improve their standard of living; while the "new" middle class are using traditional working-class methods, especially the trade unions and the Labour Party in Parliament and local government, to protect themselves, to prevent themselves being pushed down, more economically than status-wise, to the level of wage earners.[1]

A last word of caution is necessary. In their praiseworthy effort to prove that the workers were not becoming part of a vast middle class, the sociologists quoted have, if anything, tended to play down the degree of convergence between manual and white-collar workers. For example, as the following table shows,

	Assemblers & machinists	*Craftsmen & setters*	*Process workers*	*White-collar*
Level of pay given as *only* reason for staying	27	7	9	4
Level of pay given as *one* reason for staying	46	58	39	26

craftsmen, process workers and white-collar workers in Luton are very close in rejecting the idea that pay was their *only* reason for staying in their present employment; while, on the other hand, more than one-quarter of all white-collar workers gave pay as *one* reason for staying. Broadly, there is great need to find greater and greater common ground between manual and white-collar workers; and continued emphasis on their differences does, in the long run, weaken the anti-capitalist forces.

THE POOR AND THE POOREST

Apologists for the "post-capitalist" society claimed the abolition of poverty as one of its greatest successes and perhaps the most dramatic refutation of Marx's theory of the growing impoverishment of the proletariat. As late as 1962 Crosland wrote:

"Marx's prophecy of increasing inequality, which has been falsified

[1] And, incidentally, these various studies contradict Weber's claim that all classes were becoming more status- than class-conscious. While it is true of the upper sections of society, with their status illusions, it is certainly not true of wage earners.

in respect of internal *class* divisions, has ... been unexpectedly realised in the field of external national divisions."[1]

So, while admitting the international division in the non-communist world between rich and poor nations, Crosland assumed that poverty within Britain had been wiped out. Indeed, in that book he hardly mentioned the subject of poverty at all.

At the back of this widely-held belief lay a series of investigations conducted over fifty years by B. Seebohm Rowntree. The Rowntree family's connection with York is well known, so it is not surprising that B. S. Rowntree's very thorough investigations were of families in York itself. In 1901 he showed that over one-quarter (28 per cent to be exact) of the population of York were in poverty; in 1935 18 per cent; but in 1950 less than 2 per cent (mostly old people). These figures tied up with current statistics about high wages and low unemployment and were convincing evidence that poverty had been virtually wiped out. Marx's doctrines could safely be buried alongside his corpse.

Some social investigators were not so sure about this figure of under 2 per cent (or less than 3 per cent of all working-class families). They pointed to a further 11 per cent of York's population living, according to Rowntree's own report, *just above* the poverty line: this stratum had, in fact, increased slightly compared with 1936. They also questioned Rowntree's *criterion* of poverty, suggesting it was dated, because *standards* had altered. Also, it was very harsh; for example, the basic diet which Rowntree laid down as the necessary minimum was virtually the same in 1950 as in 1936 and for man, wife and 3 children under 14 years old cost (October 1950) only 47/4. Six shillings a week were allowed for household sundries and total family outlay was only £5. The Ministry of Labour's own *Enquiry into Household Expenditure 1953/54*, designed to help frame a proper cost-of-living index, revealed that over one-quarter of all heads of households earned less than £6 a week! But these statistics in an official report got little publicity in the capitalist press at the time. After all, the Tories were then "setting Britain free" and little discrepancies like these would disappear in time. Indeed, both Liberals and Conservatives were already calling for the winding-up of some of the social services and for greater reliance on "private provision".

By the early 1960s, the team of social investigators built up at the London School of Economics under Professor Titmuss was exposing

[1] Crosland: *The Conservative Enemy*, p. 104.

the real situation. A study of the circumstances of old people found that in 1962 nearly 1¾ million elderly men and women (about half of all elderly single and widowed persons) had incomes of less than £4 a week and 400,000 couples (just under one-quarter of all) less than £6 a week. *Together there were nearly 25 million aged poor*; while another ¾ million lived just above the poverty line, which was taken as the total benefit available to persons under (the then) National Assistance scheme. About half of all the aged had no assets or assets totalling less than £100. One-third of all were utterly dependent for their standard of living on State benefits. Very few had substantial pensions from their previous employment. Last but not least, single women were worse off than men or couples in every way: the median (middle average) income of all women living alone was £3 2s. a week.[1]

The study that really caught the headlines came out in the same year (1965) and was the first comprehensive investigation of poverty in Britain since the war.[2] Using a combination of Rowntree's and National Assistance scales, and taking data from the Ministry of Labour's own *Household Expenditure Surveys*, they compared the position in 1953/54 with the position in 1960. The results, which shook millions of more fortunate people when they saw the figures in their daily papers, are summarised in the table below:

Numbers of household and persons in poverty 1953/54 and in 1960

Total income or expenditure as % of basic N.A. scale plus rent or housing	*% of households*		*% of persons*		*Estimated no. of persons (thousands)*		*Estimated no. of children (thousands)*	
	1953/54	*1960*	*53/54*	*1960*	*53/54*	*1960*	*53/54*	*1960*
up to 100%	2·1	4·7	1·2	3·8	607	1,990	300	660
up to 140%	10·0	18·0	7·8	14·2	3,948	7,438	1,330	2,250

The table shows two levels of poor: those whose incomes were less than N.A. scales plus 40 per cent (marked "up to 140 per cent" in the first columns)—these were the "poor"; and those with income less than the N.A. scales alone (marked "up to 100 per cent")—these were the "poorest".

If these figures were true, they showed an alarming increase in the number of poor between 1954 and 1960 and a degree of poverty never thought possible in the affluent, post-war Britain. For, while in 1954

[1] Townsend and Wedderburn: *The Aged in the Welfare State* (1965).

[2] Abel-Smith and Townsend: *The Poor and the Poorest.*

there were nearly 4 million poor people, by 1960 the figure was almost *7½ million*, or *one-seventh of the total population*. Of these, *2¼ million* were children. The *poorest* numbered over 600,000 in 1954, but nearly 2 million in 1960, including *two-thirds of a million children*. And all this despite the supposed lavish benefits of the Welfare State.

For some time the newly elected Labour Government said nothing. But, spurred by the Child Poverty Action Group, they published a document two years later roughly confirming Abel-Smith's and Townsend's figures.[1] According to the Government survey, over one-quarter of a million families, including nearly one million children, were below National Assistance level in 1966. But, as new Supplementary Benefits were introduced soon after, thus slightly raising the N.A. level, the numbers went up to 345,000 families, including *well over 1 million children*. Allowing for various additions, the survey concluded that nearly half-a-million families, with up to 1¼ million children, had incomes below N.A.-plus-Supplementary Benefits level. These figures show that, if anything, Abel-Smith and Townsend under-estimated the numbers of the "poorest" and probably those of the "poor" also. The staggering conclusion is that the proportion of poor people today is only slightly less than in 1935, a year of mass unemployment. Then, the poor were mainly families on the dole: today they are, not only the unemployed, but the old, the chronic sick and large families on low incomes. The categories may change, but the poor are still with us.

Of course, as we pointed out before in connection with wages, there are wide regional variations. London and the South are better off than the North, so that in some areas there is likely to be a very high level of poverty. For example, two recent surveys in Nottingham, one of a slum area, the other of a council estate, showed that more than a third of the families were poor. Of the poor people, nearly half were children.[2] The standard used was the Townsend-Abel-Smith National Assistance-plus-40 per cent.

At a teach-in on poverty held in London a few days before Christmas 1966, speakers stressed that the situation was worsening. Abel-Smith claimed that after 1960, at which his and Townsend's book stops, poverty was still increasing, chiefly because the number of large families was growing. A year later Townsend renewed the attack. In a Fabian

[1] Ministry of Social Security: *Circumstances of Families* (July 1967).

[2] The studies, by Ken Coates and Richard Silburn, are published by the Department of Adult Education, Nottingham University, 1967 and 1968.

Tract, *Poverty, Socialism and Labour in Power*, he accused the Government of failing to tackle the problem. Even by conventional standards, he wrote, the extent of poverty was under-estimated; yet the Government had done little. He repeated that between 7 and 8 million people, or one-seventh of the population of Britain, were living below the official subsistence level.[1]

Many people, including some who ought to know better, argue that these are the large families of the ignorant and, worse, the feckless and the workshy. The Nottingham, as well as the national, surveys do find that the poor families tend to be bigger and ignorant. But feckless and workshy, no. Even *The Times* said:

> "The growing realisation of the extent of child poverty in Britain is hurting the public conscience. Feeling is the stronger and more widespread because it cannot be escaped by blaming the laziness or irresponsibility of the children's parents. A good many of the families are poor in spite of the fact that the breadwinner is hard-working and industrious. They are poor plainly and simply because his earnings are not large enough to keep them above subsistence level. . . ."[2]

Malnutrition is, therefore, widespread. Government reports base themselves on standards of nutrition laid down by the British Medical Association and give the impression that most people are well above the minimum. But a notable study recently published[3] points out that this B.M.A. standard was designed mainly to help food manufacturers and distributors. By 1960, Dr. Lambert estimated, *at least a quarter and perhaps as much as a third of the people of Britain failed to attain all the desirable levels of dietary intake*. The famous nutrition research unit at Queen Elizabeth College, London, claimed that standards of nutrition were actually worse in 1967 than in the Crippsian "austerity" period of 1950. Families got less protein, calcium and some of the vitamins in 1967 than in 1950. In all, about half the families with children are thought not to get the protein and calcium laid down as necessary even by the B.M.A.; and these standards are some way below those of the U.S.A. and the U.S.S.R.[4] About 10 per cent of the population suffer

[1] In an article in *Tribune* (13th October 1967) he pointed out that under a Labour Government, Britain was spending less on social security than most other West European capitalist countries.

[2] *The Times*, 10th July 1967.

[3] Royston Lambert: *Nutrition in Britain 1950–1960*

[4] *Sunday Times*, 6th August 1967.

chronically from malnutrition, is the estimate of Dr. Geoffrey Taylor, chairman of the Liberal Party's medical committee. This includes a sizeable minority of the aged, probably more than a million. Bread and jam, baked beans, chips, tea, with meat sometimes on Sundays, form the staple diet of the half-a-million children who live below the minimum subsistence level of National Assistance. Their mortality rate is three or four times that of children of professional people. Finally, alongside this material poverty go the spectres of social and mental deprivation. According to the authors of the recent Penguin book, *Children in Distress*, (one is Sir Alec Clegg, chief education officer of the West Riding of Yorkshire), nearly one in eight of Britain's children are in desperate need of social, medical or psychiatric help.[1]

But if this is so, surely the evidence would appear daily before our eyes? We should see them on the streets hollow-eyed and with bloated bellies. But such children as we see in newsreels of Africa do not suffer from the type of malnutrition we are talking about; they are starving to death. The malnutrition in Britain, variously estimated, as we have shown, between 10 per cent and a third of the population, according to the criterion used, reveals itself in what Dr. Lambert calls "concealed deficiency states", or failure to reach optimum health and development. In other words, such people are simply not as fit as they should be, nor do they thrive and grow as they ought to.

Yet Social Security benefits seem, even though they are lower here than in most other West European countries, quite reasonable. Under the 1967 system of benefits a family with four children can receive up to £16 13s. a week (if the breadwinner is out of work). But this compares with average gross earnings of adult male manual workers of about £23 and the trade union campaign for a minimum £15 a week for every adult worker which, incidentally, the TUC now (end of 1969) appears to consider inadequate.

It is however, difficult, not merely to keep a large family on £16 13s., or whatever it might be, but to decide on priorities under a "free enterprise" system, where people are subjected to pressures to spend for the profit of individual firms. People do not know the nutritional value of the foods they buy: the manufacturers and distributors are not obliged to tell. The sole aim is to sell and to do this tastiness takes priority over food value. "It is now possible for the food manufacturer to separate palatability from nutritional value", wrote Dr. Yudkin, a well-known expert. "As a result, man is increasingly

[1] Clegg and Megson: *Children in Distress* (1968).

exposed to food of high palatability but of low or undesirable nutritional value."[1]

But, more than this, comes the question of what people regard as more important even than food; and here we return to Marx's point about changing subsistence levels. The Nottingham council estate study found that 90 per cent of the poor had a television set, 60 per cent a washing machine, 40 per cent a vacuum cleaner and a very few (5 per cent) even a motor-cycle or car. "It seems very plain", the report declared, "that there are numbers of people who would endure malnutrition rather than sacrifice the television set, or even the family car. It is quite pointless to moralise about such matters: new needs have been created, partly by inchoate social pressures, partly by deliberate manipulation through advertising, and partly as a result of the changing demands of the labour market itself."[2]

Finally, a recent survey shows that reformist social-democracy has failed in its most crucial field, that of helping the bottom dog, the lowest-paid. About 10 million workers, full-time and part-time, had (October 1967) gross weekly earnings of under £15. Most of them were employed in leather manufacture, clothing, services like laundries and motor repair and public administration. In the three years from October 1964 the earnings of manual workers in general increased by 21 per cent; but the earnings of the four lowest groups rose by 15, 19, 21 and 20 per cent respectively. This means that even the most successful of the lowest groups only just managed to keep pace with the general rate of increase. But, on a purely cash count, they were all worse off. These low wages—most women and juveniles have low pay—tend to occur in areas of high unemployment, so that, while substantial unemployment continues, so will the relative worsening.[3]

While all this goes on, the stock market booms. Taking the *Financial Times* share price index (July 1935=100) as our guide, we get the following figures:

	F.T. Share Index	*Average earnings* *Men*	*Women*
October 1949	104·9	142s. 8d.	78s. 9d.
October 1967	393·1	437s. 9d.	210s. 10d.
% increase	375	307	268

[1] Quoted by Lambert. [2] *The Morale of the Poor* (1968).
[3] Edmonds and Radice: *Low Pay* (Fabian Society, 1968).

But the rise in share values only crawled in the period 1949 to 1967. Share prices absolutely rocketed after October 1967, partly due to devaluation. By August 1968 the Index was nearly *100 points higher*, a quarter of the whole rise over the previous thirty years.

Society is, therefore, still very much polarised; only the structure is rather different from what it was a century ago. In Marx's time, the proletariat was the industrial working class, sharply divided socially and economically from the petit bourgeoisie, who were in turn well below the upper classes, still largely aristocracy and capitalist bourgeoisie, although beginning to merge. But Marx also wrote of numerous other strata, so that there was even then something of a continuum from the poorest beggars and outcasts up to the wealthiest aristocracy. Today there seems to be also something of a continuum, ranging from the poorest (those living below National Assistance level) up to the wealthiest; but this is an illusion, for the range between upper and lower is widening.[1]

Also parts of the lower middle strata and the upper working class are "converging". Even though the mass production of consumer goods has raised the whole continuum in respect of consumption, inequality in every major respect is just as great as before the war.

HAS CLASS CONFLICT DISAPPEARED?

When Labour swept the board in 1945 there was a wonderful feeling of elation among not only staunch working-class Labour voters but among millions who believed this was really the beginning of the social revolution. Even old stagers on the left were swept away on a wave of optimism. Any criticism was lost in the deluge of pro-Labour sympathy. This was the period when many people thought that Britain was being suddenly but peaceably transformed into a socialist state via the ballot box. The class struggle manifested itself, it seemed, only in some rather feeble Tory opposition to nationalisation. To that extent class and the class struggle were just petering out.

Bewilderment followed as the Attlee Government first devalued the pound under pressure from the U.S.A. and then insisted on continuing wage restraint as prices were rising sharply. When the Tories returned in 1951 they, true to the instincts of businessmen, returned to the "free" operation of the market. Long pent-up demand resulted in an almost

[1] Industry and finance now produce far greater wealth than landownership, which, though great, has declined compared with a century ago.

continuous boom and Britain plunged into the years of "affluence" "Socialist dogma" was shown up and Macmillan could say, contradicted only by fanatics (!) of the left, that the class struggle was obsolete. And so it was—for several years; until market forces began to build up the contradictions of capitalism, some of which previous chapters have described. This was the high-tide period of consensus theory.

As the people found themselves faced with mounting difficulties, one explanation became quite popular: the growth of bureaucracy due to growing State and quasi-State institutions. Revolt became revolt against "bureacracy", against "authority": in intellectual circles the theory of Dahrendorf challenged consensus theory and "old-fashioned" Marxism. The spirit of Weber reappeared in Crosland's claim that the bureaucratic authority of State, nationalised industries, courts, church, press and trade unions were ". . . of greater significance than the economic power to control production and distribution . . .".[1] Thus the underlying power of wealth (capital) and of those State and quasi-State institutions acting for the preservation of private capital was completely hidden.

As we know now, class will out and the bourgeoisie are determined to suppress the class struggle, or, rather, the class struggle by the ruling class against the working people must be waged more strongly, the struggle by working people for a bigger share of the national cake suppressed. As Clive Jenkins wrote: "What is now being envisaged in Britain is a State capitalism which enshrines privilege and borrows some of the representative features of the corporate state. Already the employers are offering the bait of compulsory trade unionism and the commercial advantage to the unions of a check-off of union contributions. At the same time the Prices and Incomes Act and a ready flow of finance from the Government are components in a circle which is beginning to form. This perimeter will squeeze and constrict trade union liberties—which means the right of an ordinary citizen to combine against the overwhelming economic power of an employer controlling the product and the market."[2]

The class struggle has not only not disappeared, but is being intensified—by the ruling class. The Wilson Government's attempt to push through anti-union legislation will, it is promised, be strongly carried forward by the next Conservative Government. The Conservatives, re-

[1] *The Future of Socialism*, p. 40.

[2] Clive Jenkins: "We haven't got enough", in *The Incompatibles*, ed. Blackburn and Cockburn. Notice that to "the employers" we should now add "and the Government".

lying more on the "free" market, will raise the cost of living by reducing State expenditure on public and social services.

> "Marx's theory of class consciousness depended upon the class becoming more and more aware of its objective class interests as it engaged in struggle. Under neo-capitalism the struggles which are likely to occur over the share of labour in the national income are exactly calculated to foster a more far-reaching class consciousness than any we have witnessed hitherto."[1]

Mr. Blackburn's words are coming true.

SUMMARY AND CONCLUSION

Far from the proletariat having disappeared, it is now proportionately about the same as in Marx's time, but numerically it is much bigger. For Marx, as for us a hundred years later, the core of the proletariat is the industrial workers. In Marx's time the rest of the proletariat consisted of agricultural workers and domestic servants. Today, taking the word in its strict meaning of those without property, *The Economist* 1959/60 survey, giving 88 per cent of the population with an average of only £107 each, means that more than 80 per cent of the population are strictly proletarian. And this means, further, that the lower-paid sector of white-collar workers are strictly proletarian. But, since they do not display the same attitudes and behaviour, particularly the same class consciousness, as the manual, and especially the industrial, working class, it is useful to adopt for them Briefs' term "proletaroid".

Examination of Census and other statistics also gives the lie to the notion that the working class is shrinking because the non-manual sector is increasing. We find instead that the number of wage-earners has stayed much the same since the end of the last war; and that the non-manual sector has grown mainly by the employment of much larger numbers of women, chiefly in clerical work.

As regards working-class incomes, Routh's researches on changes in pay over the last 50 years do not support the popular notion propagated by the mass media that workers have shot ahead. On the contrary, they have hardly made average progress. Only the unskilled, particularly unskilled women, have done better than average. Studies of

[1] R. Blackburn: "The new capitalism", in *Towards Socialism*, ed. P. Anderson and R. Blackburn (1965).

occupational mobility show that the most that workers usually expect and achieve in the way of promotion is to foreman level.

Contrary to the opinion that today's worker is somehow different from his father and grandfather before him, descriptions by workers themselves, as well as studies of workers by researchers in the field, demonstrate that the worker today is still a wage-slave. Most workers think only or mainly of the money; the job itself is far less important, except that it remains important for the minority of skilled craftsmen. Marx's theory of the alienation of the worker under industrial capitalism is, unhappily, only too true today also. The capitalist class and their managers have tried to overcome this alienation, tried to draw workers into "one happy family" with the bosses (a "consensual" industrial society) by employing industrial sociologists. However, no industrial social scientists, from Taylor to Miss Woodward and beyond, have been able to achieve this; with the result that "conflict" theorists have declared that conflict within industry is inevitable and must be accepted.

Automation under capitalism seems, as one might expect, to have contradictory effects. It reduces the physical burden, only to increase mental strain. It may reduce alienation, because the worker is more conscious of the whole process and his part in it, or it may not. On the other hand, the benefit he gains is far less than the benefit passing to the employer. And there is always the steady reduction in numbers employed, except that the number of technicians and other non-manual workers usually increases. It is the less skilled who often suffer. The problems of automation under capitalism lead workers more and more to questions about the wider society they live in.

Nor can Tories and Labour right-wingers boast any more about full employment. That Marx was wildly wrong when he predicted a permanent pool of unemployed (the industrial reserve army) seemed proved by the long period of full employment which followed the last war. Now this period has ended; and the Wilson Government, backed by the Conservatives, have re-created a permanent army of unemployed of more than half-a-million workers.

The propagandists declare that the trade unions are "masters of the industrial scene". But not only can the unions do nothing about the re-emerged "industrial reserve army"; it seems their achievements and power in respect of wages are much less than the anti-union propagandists claim. The unions have increased the share of the national wealth going to wages by a few per cent; and their power is more defensive than offensive, more preventing a worsening of the worker's position than really improving it. This heightens the importance of the unions as "schools of Communism (socialism)".

Many sociologists and political hacks after the last war also argued that the British worker was becoming "middle class". But Lockwood and Goldthorpe have countered with their well-substantiated theory that the workers are still largely distinct, economically and sociologically, from the "middle class", except that a slow process of *convergence* is taking place in certain respects between the more affluent manual workers and the lower white-collar workers. This convergence will continue, though possibly with variations; but the bulk of the (manual) working class, including most "affluent" workers, remains deeply class-conscious.

Another success claimed for the "post-capitalist" society was the abolition (or, at least, sharp reduction) of poverty. But the work of Townsend, Dorothy Wedderburn and Abel-Smith show that as much as a seventh of the population are in poverty; and the Government have confirmed this in a Ministry of Social Security report. It is certainly not diminishing, and may even be increasing, alongside the increasing wealth of the ruling class, proving that our society is still polarised, even if there are many in between rich and poor.

The whole argument of "revisionism", from the early Fabians to Crosland and beyond, rested upon the alleged reduction and eventual abolition of inequality, capitalist ownership and exploitation by constitutional steps, against the idea that it could only come about by a revolutionary take-over. We have found that, despite real improvements won by popular pressure, revisionism has not only failed to bring these changes about, but is now actually working away from them. The same goes for the class struggle. Reformists and reactionaries who, in the 1950s, made jubilant speeches at its graveside, found in the 1960s that their judgement was too hasty. Now they are just as unsuccessfully trying to bury it by sitting on the coffin lid while the body is alive and kicking.

In one respect, however, the reformists seem to have achieved much—in the growth of State intervention to correct the abuses of uncontrolled "free enterprise". In the next chapter we shall examine to what extent they have been successful.

APPENDIX 4

That the working class still constitutes a majority of the adult population is confirmed by two important population surveys. First, in the *Hulton Readership Surveys*, classes D and E comprised the following proportions of the population over the age of 16:

Year	*Class %* D	E	*Total* D & E
1947	55	10	65
1950	63	9	72
1955	64	7	71

D = working class. E = the poor.

showing that, if the poor are included, the total proletariat, excluding the "lower middle class", increased a few years after the war. In 1966 the Institute of Practitioners in Advertising, continuing the Hulton Survey, combined classes D and E and estimated the combined class DE (over 16 years of age) as 33 per cent; but the skilled workers had been separated into a new class, C2, comprising 36 per cent of the adult population; combined with DE the working class now comprise 69 per cent still over two-thirds.[1] Secondly, the recent estimates of Kahan, Butler and Stokes, using the main Census criterion of occupation, gave the following:

	% of population
Upper working class	10
Working class	53
Lower working class	4
Total	67

Thus the working class, excluding any "lower middle class" element, constitutes at least two-thirds of the population.

[1] I.P.A. *National Readership Surveys.* (Their "classes" are normally based on occupation.

8

"PRIVATE AFFLUENCE AND PUBLIC SQUALOR"

SOCIAL INSURANCE

Although implicit in all social-democratic ideology, the Welfare State was not in fact brought into existence by a Labour Government, although Labour leaders had a hand in its birth. If anybody started to set it up it was surely the wartime Coalition Government under Churchill, which in 1942 received a report from Sir William Beveridge, a Liberal and former professor of economics at London University, on plans for a comprehensive scheme for social insurance.

Beginnings of State help to those worst off can be traced back to at least the poor laws of Elizabeth I; but a nation-wide (or partly nation-wide) scheme came only in 1911, when the Liberal Prime Minister, Lloyd George, adopted the method common to trade unions and friendly societies of obtaining contributions on a national scale to provide payments for temporary interruption of work due to sickness or unemployment. It is even ironic that the two men who made the biggest steps in social insurance were Liberals, believers in minimum state interference. They did so to meet popular demand and to prevent worse happening (i.e. social upheaval).

Adopted in principle by the Coalition Government, Beveridge's scheme was a landmark because of its *universality:* it covered everyone over school-leaving age. In return for their contributions, everyone was entitled to certain benefits against interruption of earning power and to special benefits at birth, marriage and death. "Social insurance", Beveridge wrote, "should aim at guaranteeing the minimum income needed for subsistence." Retirement pensions should rise to full subsistence level over the twenty years 1945/65, to reach the same rate which he proposed for sickness and unemployment, £2 for a couple, 24/- for a single person.[1] As a Liberal, Beveridge declared that private pension schemes should continue and even increase, because the State scheme provided only *minimum* (subsistence) benefits and people

[1] But children's (or family) allowances should come direct out of tax revenues, not out of the social insurance fund.

should be encouraged to make private provision for anything above subsistence. He stressed that Want, which social insurance was designed to eliminate, was only one of the five giant social problems, the others being Disease, Ignorance, Squalor and Idleness. He recommended "full employment" (not more than 10 per cent unemployment!) to combat Idleness and a National Health Service to fight Disease.

The social insurance scheme very soon came up against the fundamental problem, which the Liberal Government of 1911 also had to face; and the Coalition and subsequent governments came down on the same side as Lloyd George. Put simply the dilemma is: shall a social insurance scheme (in a capitalist society) be "soundly financed" or not? In other words, should the benefit money paid out be limited to the contributions paid in (always keeping them as low as possible), or should the benefits be enough to meet people's needs adequately and the deficit in the insurance fund made up by, say, an extra Government contribution? All governments, like Lloyd George's, plumped for the first alternative; and this has meant that, in spite of every increase, *basic benefits have never been at even subsistence level.*

The impossibility of reconciling universal social insurance with "sound finance" restates one of the contradictions of capitalism. The capitalist class is forced to introduce social insurance, but resents having to do so. The capitalist philosophy is basically individualistic: everybody looks after himself and the devil take the hindmost. But, if forced by public pressure to spend money on social insurance, our rulers ensure that (*a*) most of the money comes from the working people (manual and non-manual) (*b*) the government contribution is kept to a minimum and (*c*) expenditure is kept as far as possible on a level with income. It follows that, in a society where basic wages for millions of people are low and there is permanent, large-scale unemployment, large-scale poverty can never be eliminated.

All sorts of dodges are tried to avoid a rising deficit in the insurance fund; and the history of social insurance over at least the last ten years shows closely-related thinking in official Labour and Tory circles. In May 1958 the Labour Party outlined a scheme for wage-related pensions; i.e. the more you earn the more you pay and the higher the benefits you are entitled to. The Tory Government put this into effect the very next year in the shape of the Graduated Pension Scheme. But this device fails to solve the contradiction, for the simple reason that people object not only to the high *additional* contributions but to the fact that the Government continues to increase the *basic* contributions as well. Employers' objections carry, naturally, a good deal of weight; so the next step, currently advocated by Tory spokesmen and openly accepted by some Labour leaders, is "selectivity", the jargon for restricting benefits to those considered to be in "greatest need". Some sort of selectivity is bound to come: the stepping-up of family allowances for bigger families is the first such measure. Perhaps the bigger, poorer families will benefit; and this is to be welcomed. But the mass of working people will not: for them the same old round of higher contributions with some raising of benefits will continue. The Child Poverty Action Group have canvassed the excellent idea of a negative income tax, whereby those with incomes below tax level obtain cash allowances. If ever operated by a Tory or right-wing Labour Government, the burden (by way of reduction of income-tax allowances) will still fall on the majority of working people, without ever abolishing poverty. For under capitalism social insurance has to race merely to keep up with its problem.

Beveridge's Liberal insistence on the value of private insurance schemes has led to a second interesting feature, first exposed by Titmuss. Under existing tax laws these schemes, mostly occupational (i.e. arranged between employer and employee), are in fact State-subsidised, because they enjoy tax reductions. Moreover, the lump sums paid out are tax-free. In 1955 Titmuss reckoned they cost the Exchequer (in tax loss) £100 millions a year, substantially more than the cost of all State pensions: today the tax loss must be far greater. The schemes particularly benefit the wealthy, the "top executives". Readers may have read of the £28,000 "golden handshake" and £2,000-a-year pension paid to Sir Stanley Raymond when he was sacked from the chairmanship of British Railways. But even these sums are small compared with some paid to ex-directors of very big private companies. The firm "deducts" the premium from the individual's salary; or the rich individual pays a part of his income straight to the insurance company: either way the tax liability is reduced. Another device is to split one's scheme into a number of smaller policies, which in total enjoy a bigger tax reduction. Of course, the insurance companies also benefit: the new Company Law requiring publication of directors' emoluments show those of the insurance companies to be among the best. Insurance companies' profits and share-values rise fantastically: £100 invested in the Legal and General Assurance Society in 1951 were worth £1,744 by 1961. Head offices of these companies are among the most imposing in all the big cities.[1] The Government is deprived of this huge slice of the national wealth, which could help reduce or even abolish the whole unnecessary system of compulsory contributions to the State scheme.

THE NATIONAL HEALTH SERVICE

A similar development took place with regard to the National Health Service, which Beveridge urged and which the first Labour Government set up in 1948. From the start the N.H.S. was never "free": in addition to the compulsory weekly contribution from all at work, patients had to pay for spectacles and towards dental treatment, not to mention the notorious prescription charges, over which, as everyone knows, Bevan and Wilson resigned from the first post-war Labour Government and which Wilson reintroduced after he became Prime Minister. Only a few health centres were built, despite the fact that the doctors themselves considered centres to be absolutely essential to the service. By 1960 4,000 were needed, but only 14 had been built. The (1969) Minister of Health, Kenneth Robinson, promised a lot more, but how many more must depend on Britain's creditors, the International Monetary Fund bankers, to whom the right-wing leaders have put Britain in pawn. Finally, the public as a whole has very little say in how the service is run.

For some time the yellow press (the *Daily Express* in the forefront, of course) sounded off about the rising health bill and the wild extravagance of supplying everyone with "free" spectacles and "free" false teeth. The Tory Government reacted by setting up the Guillebaud Committee, which in turn commissioned Titmuss and Abel-Smith to undertake a cost investigation. To everyone's surprise the investigation revealed that, although the total cost of the N.H.S. had gone up steadily since 1948 (and what cost hadn't?) its cost per member of the population was the same in 1954 as in 1949. The cost as proportion of the country's Gross National Product had actually fallen in the same period from 3¾ per cent to 3¼ per cent. And this despite the enormous increase in the quantity and scope of work, with more staff, more patients, wider services, more appliances, prescriptions and medical

[1] Not to mention the terrible waste of manpower and building-space by this superfluous business. Beveridge himself estimated that administration costs in private insurance accounted for as much as 7/6 in every £ received in premiums. Weber should have lived to examine this monstrous bureaucracy.

research. Even by 1967, examination of public accounts shows that the cost as proportion of G.N.P. was only just 4 per cent, fractionally more than in 1949.

Just as the private insurance companies make millions from the defects in social insurance, so the N.H.S. provides a bonanza to the big drug firms. The famous *Sainsbury Report* (1965/67) declared that the profits of some were "much higher than can be considered reasonable". Total profits of British companies selling N.H.S. products rose from £20 millions in 1961 to £34 millions in 1965. This also represented a rise in the *rate* of profit from 14 per cent to 22 per cent. The wasteful and sometimes dangerous sales promotion of new drugs by firms' representatives cost the nation an additional £250 per doctor per annum. All that has happened as a result of the Report is a little bit of cut-throat competition between some of the firms. The Wilson Government made the patient pay towards these profits, at the rate of 2/6 per prescription item!

In the meantime, despite mounting expenditure (in 1968 over £1,500 million), the N.H.S. is constantly verging on breakdown. Queues of patients get longer and waiting lists for hospital beds are such that it may take up to a couple of years to have a minor operation. All the time the shortage of money, equipment and opportunities, the low pay and excessive hours are driving a fantastic number of young doctors to seek salvation abroad: in 1962 as many as one-third of the total output of the medical schools. The hospitals rely more and more on nurses and domestic staff from abroad. In 1960/61 total expenditure on hospitals was £24 millions; but the Shell building in London erected about the same time cost £33 millions. Currently, hospital building has gone up to over £100 millions; but property speculators will be making about £22 million clear profit on the Euston Road office colossus alone. Private medication booms. Full planning permission was recently received for a luxury private hospital, where patients will pay basic charges of at least ten guineas a day. All meals, except breakfast, will be extra, as will medical attention. The "post-capitalist" sick will not have to join the half-a-million on the public waiting lists, thank God!

Sociologists argue that the relationship between health and social class has altered, that it is not as simple as a century ago. Then, incidence of sickness and death rates were higher the lower the social class. Today, it is not quite true: certainly sickness and death rates fall as you go up the social scale, but above certain incomes they level off, showing that the wealthy are not so immune as they used to be. These higher sickness and death rates among the higher income groups are due to diseases which have become quite acute among such people, particularly coronory heart disease, brought about, as one authority puts it, by gluttony, sloth and emotional stress. It is still true, however, that sickness (as measured by the number of days off work) is much higher among the poor than among the rest and that the "lower" classes suffer and die more than the upper from certain widespread scourges, especially bronchitis and pneumonia. At the same time experts feel that the higher sickness rate among the "lower" classes may be partly due to the fear of going off work, leading to neglect and worsening of the illness.

Again, the issue of mental illness is more complicated today. In 1948 the Americans, Hollingshead and Redlich, carried out an extensive survey of mental illness and found that the lowest class (V) (measured by occupation, education and type of residence) had a much higher percentage of mental patients than the other four classes. Also the higher the class the smaller the proportion of patients. Neuroses were more prevalent in the higher classes, psychoses (insanity) in the lower. The explanation for this difference was that the lower classes were more reluctant to go for psychiatric treatment, mainly for economic reasons, so that their illness worsened.[1] British studies show that mental subnormality is very much higher in the lower than in the upper social classes. This difference may be due to genetic factors or to the environment, but the evidence favours the latter together with family influence.[2] The work of the Clarkes shows how poor cultural environment lowers measured intelligence (I.Q.) and change to a stimulating environment raises it.[3] While, therefore, cultural factors enter into the question of mental illness, the evidence indicates the underlying importance of the economic factor.

THE HOUSING QUESTION

Nearly a hundred years ago Engels wrote that capitalism could never solve the housing problem and that its solution for the masses was "Buy your own house". "The essence of both the big bourgeois and petit bourgeois solutions of the 'housing question' is that the worker

[1] Hollingshead and Redlich: *Social Class and Mental Illness* (1958).

[2] Susser: "Social medicine in Britain", in *Society*, ed. Welford (1962).

[3] A. D. C. Clarke, "Genetic and environmental studies of intelligence", in *Mental Deficiency—the Changing Outlook*, ed. Clarke and Clarke (1958).

should own his own dwelling."[1] Yet the public sector has become very large, sometimes exceeding the private; together the number of dwellings built annually runs into hundreds of thousands and is presented as evidence of the end of capitalism. But has the rising rate of house-building solved the "housing question"?

In the first few decades of industrial capitalism in Britain city life was abominable. Improvements in medicine, water supply and sanitation introduced at the beginning of the Industrial Revolution were swept aside as the builders threw up huge, cheap estates for the rapidly increasing urban proletariat. The worst housing conditions occurred, then, about the middle of the century, as described by Engels in *The Condition of the Working Classes in England in 1844*. In such conditions what the ruling and middle classes feared most was epidemics; and housing policy was summed up in the single word, "drains". Only later in the nineteenth century did demands come from both reformers and workers for local authority house-building. To these demands the First World War acted as a tremendous spur. For perhaps the first time, society generally woke up to the existence of a "housing shortage", i.e. public conscience was roused; and Lloyd George made his famous promise of "homes fit for heroes to live in". Came the first housing subsidies, which have continued ever since.

But Lloyd George did not fulfil his promise. In the "bad old days" between the two wars, the aristocracy had their castles and the upper middle class their comfortable bourgeois homes. But the mass of manual workers lived in rented accommodation in old houses or tenements in city centres, often far from open spaces and even further from the countryside. Suburban ribbon-development estates spread outwards and here lived the lower middle strata, with some better-paid artisans, buying on mortgage. The Building Societies (they are, of course, simply money-lending businesses) expanded to such an extent that by 1935 the British public owed them £530 million and was paying off the loans at the rate of nearly £80 million a year. This growth might be regarded as a sign of a general rising standard of living; but, as Cole and Postgate shrewdly observe, it was rather a sign of growing differentiation among the employed. "The Building Societies grew most in the relatively prosperous South, where the proportion of non-manual workers was largest and where industry had been immune from the extremes of depression. The workers in the depressed areas could not afford to buy their houses; more often they

[1] Engels: *The Housing Question*. Preface to 2nd German Edition.

failed to keep the ownership of houses which they had bought in more prosperous times."[1]

The Second World War gave a much greater boost to the demand for better housing. Coupled with the decay and physical destruction of the war, market laws began to operate, house prices began to rise steeply and private building expanded enormously. But this was no solution to the problems of the lower paid, whose homes in the city centres were harder hit by enemy bombing and who couldn't afford to buy. Hence there was also a big expansion in local-authority building under the first post-war Labour Government. When the Tories returned to power in 1951, this rate of building was more or less retained; but later, when they tried to cut back on council building, their unpopularity rose. Since 1945, therefore, a high rate of both private and council house-building has been retained more or less; and competition for the highest building record has always been accepted as electorally important to all parties.

Yet everyone knows that the housing question is far from solved. A survey in the late 1950s by P.E.P. found that housing came second only to ill-health as the chief source of worry and that nearly a quarter of all people questioned had a serious housing problem. Official housing statistics show a pretty good reduction in the amount of overcrowding, the density of occupation falling from an average of ·74 persons per room in 1951 to ·66 persons per room in 1961, or an average of just over three persons to a five-roomed house (in Greater London five persons to such a house). What, then, are the sources of worry about housing?

The worst features are the age and condition of a great deal of British housing. While new homes are being built to accommodate the rising population and meet its demands for better standards, old dwellings are becoming uninhabitable. Private house-building offers accommodation only to those who can afford it; council building is never enough, because under capitalism it is always regarded (especially by the press) as providing cheap housing for feckless families with Jaguars parked outside. It is never expanded to meet all needs.

In its *White Paper on Housing, 1965–70*, the Government spelt out the facts of the situation, which are:

1 million slums, i.e. unfit for human occupation (and this number increasing)

[1] Cole and Postgate: *The Common People 1746–1938*, p. 615.

2 million more not worth improving

3 million dwellings without one of the basic amenities (w.c., cold water tap, hot water supply or bath).

In addition, it is estimated that 1½ million families in England and Wales are living in overcrowded conditions. In April 1968, the Ministry of Housing published a revised estimate of dwellings unfit for human occupation: 1,800,000 instead of the original under-a-million. Nearly 6 million houses, more than a third of the whole stock in Britain, were built in the last century and are approaching or have passed the end of their normal life.

The situation is bound to be most acute in the great cities or conurbations, because people are continually moving into them from the countryside (although there is also a movement out from the city centres to the suburbs). The startling Millner Holland *Report on Housing in Greater London* (1965) revealed that more than one million out of the 2½ million households in the London conurbation either lacked, or had to share use of, one of the basic amenities (w.c., hot and cold water supply, bath, sink or stove). Of these 1 million, more than half were entirely without the use of a bath.

> "Small, dark rooms, walls so damp that mould appears and wallpaper will not stay in place, woodwork that has not seen paint for very many years, or is broken or even rotten, windows that cannot be opened, uneven floors, defective lavatories, bulging or broken plasterwork, obsolete and defective and sometimes positively dangerous appliances and fittings, old-fashioned scarred and chipped shallow sinks served by a single cold water tap shared by a number of families, damaged roofs, broken or missing gutters or drainpipes, and many other examples of neglect and decay. The misery, which living in conditions like these imposes on those who have to endure them, hardly needs stating. Their existence provides an unending battle for Public Health inspectors. . . . One, showing us round a particularly bad area of his borough, told us: 'If I had my way I'd take a bulldozer to the lot.'"[1]

The Millner Holland Committee found that no private landlord was building houses or flats to let at less than £400 a year. The promise of such big returns has two pernicious effects. First, only the well-to-do can now afford to rent a new dwelling in Greater London. Secondly,

[1] *Report on Housing in Greater London*, ch. 5.

Rachmanism, or the use of every trick, including force and intimidation, to get tenants out and re-let at sky-high rents. As regards council building in Greater London, rents are rapidly climbing because of high land prices and interest on money borrowed. In 1967/68 the Greater London Council paid 61 per cent of all housing expenditure on interest charges. Finally, to buy a house in the London conurbation at, say, £5,000 (and rising) means that, at the present interest rate of 8½ per cent p.a. over 25 years, the buyer will repay a total of about £12,300 (an average of £10 a week) or *nearly two-and-a-half times* the price of the house. No wonder that by 1965, of the 14½ million dwellings in England and Wales, 45 per cent were "owner-occupied", 30 per cent privately rented and only 25 per cent local-authority rented. As Engels remarked, housing is very profitable to the capitalists.

Because in a capitalist system rents in urban areas would, if let free, rocket up, the State is obliged to restrain market forces in the interest of maintaining social stability. Control in Britain was first introduced during World War I, when the workers of Glasgow demonstrated against rising rents. This rent control, designed in the first place to prevent disruption of the war effort, has continued in some form or other to this day. It goes almost without saying, therefore, that rent control is not synonymous with socialism (although, taken the other way about, socialism does imply low rents). But the bourgeoisie hate rent control and are continually trying to reduce it. The Tories rebelled against the widespread control imposed during the Second World War and in 1957, as we all know, decontrolled dwellings above certain rateable values, on the argument that if landlords of bigger properties were allowed to raise rents, they would be ready to offer more accommodation. But this has just not happened; and the Tory Government, expecting a massive increase in available rented accommodation, had to reverse their decision to cut back council house building.

To see what the 1957 Act accomplished, let us look at two contrasting areas, Lancaster and the London borough of St. Marylebone. In St. Marylebone rents doubled between 1958 and 1961, as against an average national increase of 8 per cent. With the increased rents came a distinct improvement in amenities, but the tenants became responsible much more for repairs and decorations, a further concealed rent rise. Since the borough borders on and even includes bits of the West-End of London, flats are much sought after by people with higher incomes. The Act allowed a large measure of decontrol, with the result that working-class tenants could no longer afford their tenancies, which were taken up by more well-to-do people. More and more housing has been going over to childless, middle- and upper-middle class couples; and most families living in slums have been rehoused *outside* the borough.[1] But, while in St. Marylebone most "landlords" are companies making fat profits, in Lancaster, a typical provincial town, over half the landlords are fairly poor, old folk; and the Rent Act has not benefited them. Rather than raise rents and make themselves unpopular with their tenants, they have tried to sell their houses.[2] In short, in the heart of the big conurbations rents have soared; elsewhere the pressure towards "ownership" (i.e. indebtedness to the building societies) continues. In 1967 the total indebtedness to building societies reached a staggering £1,470 millions, roughly the total cost of the whole National Health Service.

Naturally, overcrowding and homelessness, despite average national figures, worsen in the big cities. The Censuses, as was mentioned before, show a reduction in overcrowding between 1951 and 1961. But in the first place, there is some doubt as to whether the Census measure is good enough. The 1951 Census Report itself admitted that measuring density of occupation by the number of persons per room "... may be valid when applied as a statistical average to summarise the general conditions of a large group of householders ... but it cannot be used to determine whether a particular household is overcrowded."[3] Secondly, like all averages, these conceal wide differences, spotlighted by the Millner-Holland Report. For, while the reduction in the amount of overcrowding over the whole London conurbation between 1951 and 1961 was as much as 22 per cent, in the nine worst districts, the inner boroughs of Paddington, Kensington, Islington and others, overcrowding actually increased. The number of persons who could not find a home at all, already 7,000, was increasing rapidly, the chairman of the G.L.C. Housing Committee warned. New legislation, brought in by the Labour Party when it returned to power in 1964, giving tenants some security and setting up Rent Tribunals to determine "fair rents", welcome though it is, has done very little to alter the overall position.[4]

[1] *Essays on Housing:* Donnison and others (1964). [2] Same.

[3] *1951 Census Housing Report*, p. lxiv.

[4] "Rachmanism—the harassment of tenants in private property—was continuing in London, Mr. Michael Morris, chairman of Islington Housing Committee, told the National Housing and Town Planning Conference here today.

"In a debate on the fair-rent machinery set up under the 1965 Rent Act, Mr. Morris

As well as overcrowding there is under-occupation. This goes not only for the rich, but for many not-so-well-off older people, who own their own homes but are afraid to change to smaller, rented accommodation because of high and ever-rising rents and fears of insecurity of tenure.

Perhaps the greatest scandal of all is the price of land. Even bourgeois economists regard the price (sale or rent) of land to be monopoly extortion, for which the owner contributes nothing: the price simply reflects demand. In the Midlands selling prices vary from £6,000 to £14,000 an acre, in the Southern Counties £11,000 to £21,000. But in Greater London the price can be as much as £65,000 and more per acre. The Rover Motor Co. recently sold 63 acres of land for over £1 million, or nearly £16,000 an acre: cost per house £1,350. In 1966 the overall cost of a dwelling built by the Dartford (Kent) Council was £3,800, of which the cost of land came to £1,200 or nearly a third of the total. The combination of land and other costs, including interest, has nearly doubled the average price of new houses in Britain during the last ten years; and the trend is still upwards.

In this situation of rapidly rising profits in building, the speculator sharks thrive; and gobble one another up. Among the mergers now taking place with increasing rapidity, most supported by the Labour Government, a notable case is the £65 million paid for the Clore-Wolfson City Centre Properties by Sir Harold Samuel's £400 million Land Securities Investment Trust.[1] Only under capitalism can individuals become unbelievably rich by exploiting the human need for a home.

It will be said that a housing shortage is not peculiar to capitalism. The answer is that this is true, but that under capitalism, the shortage, particularly in the cities, is aggravated. "What is meant today by housing shortage", wrote Engels, "is the peculiar intensification of the bad housing conditions of the workers as the result of the sudden rush of population to the big towns; a colossal increase in rents, a still further aggravation of overcrowding in the individual houses and, for some, the impossibility of finding a place to live in at all."[2] Despite all the improvement, and there *has* been an enormous improvement since Engels wrote, because people demanded it, the statement does, with

said that the level of harassment was about the same as before, though today neither illegal eviction nor harassment was quite as blatant." (*The Times*, 30th October 1968.)

[1] See Chapter IV, sec. 8.

[2] Engels: *The Housing Question*, Part I.

certain modification (especially "rents *and* house prices"), remain largely true.[1] And we can therefore fittingly end this section with another comment by Engels: "In order to make an end of *this* housing shortage, there is only *one* means: to abolish altogether the exploitation and oppression of the working class by the ruling class."[2]

"PRIVATE AFFLUENCE AND PUBLIC SQUALOR"

The struggles for adequate social security, for the National Health Service and for enough housing at low rents are just examples of the contrast summarised in the famous phrase, "private affluence and public squalor", coined by the leading liberal economist of the United States, J. K. Galbraith.[3] Galbraith, frankly affirming that profit is the prime motive of American capitalism declared that, therefore, its enormously increased power of production can only continue if people can be persuaded to keep on buying personal goods. Conversely, the expenditure of money on public, "non-productive", services, is regarded with distaste, for it results in higher taxation. In a capitalist society, therefore, public expenditure, though rising, is kept to the lowest possible level that people will tolerate, while personal wealth soars and personal possessions accumulate.

> "Such attitudes lead to some interesting contradictions," he writes of the U.S.A. "Cars have an importance greater than the roads on which they are driven. We welcome expansion of telephone services as improving the general well-being but accept curtailment of postal services as signifying necessary economy. We set great store by the increase in private wealth but regret the added outlay for the police force by which it is protected. Vacuum cleaners to ensure clean houses are praiseworthy and essential in our standard of living. Street cleaners to ensure clean streets are an unfortunate expense. Partly as a result, our houses are generally clean and our streets generally filthy."[4]

How these words, written about the United States a few years ago,

[1] "Solution to the housing famine in Britain is no nearer", is the title of an article by Adam Ferguson (*The Times*, 14th February, 1969). "The housing situation in the problem areas is not getting better but far, far worse", Mr. Feguson declares.

[2] Engels, same.

[3] *The Affluent Society* (1958).

[4] *The Affluent Society* (Penguin ed.), p. 116.

currently apply to our own country! Who doesn't know that cars are choking the streets of every city, bringing about the destruction of tens of thousands of homes for the sake of roads for more and more vehicles? Who doesn't see them parked outside millions of old houses, while the litter left by a reduced refuse-collecting system lies around the wheels and on the pavements and public transport continues to deteriorate, bringing ever-increasing strain to its users? At the 1968 Conference of the Town and Country Planning Association, Dr. Mark Abrams, chairman of Research Services, warned that in a mere 15 years Britain, except for parts of Scotland, Wales and N. Ireland, could become almost bereft of unspoiled countryside and its highways a nightmare with 20 million cars. In the near future, Britain (or at least England) could become a country of concrete and carbon monoxide. Dr. Abrams might have exaggerated, but we are certainly going that way. And advertising? The hoardings are plastered with appealing advertisements urging the passer-by to buy these cigarettes, that car, this American petrol. On TV cosmetics adverts, car adverts, detergents-and-soap adverts bombard the viewer. All-in-all, advertising costs the public over £500 million a year, all of which, one way or another, goes on to prices. The more doctors and Government warn about the dangers of smoking, the more numerous the tobacco adverts, the higher go the tobacco sales and profits.

Some figures reinforce this contrast powerfully. In 1967 over £1,500 million were spent on tobacco. The Churches' Council on Gambling recently estimated that gambling has a total annual turnover of over £2,000 million and "challenges all other industries in its rate of growth."[1] There are 16,000 betting offices, 2,000 bingo clubs and 1,000 gaming clubs. The most popular form of gambling is betting on horses and dogs, with a turnover of over £1,200 millions; then come gaming clubs with a turnover of £750 millions. It is interesting to put these side-by-side with some amounts spent annually on the social services at about the same time:

	million £'s		*million £'s*
Alcoholic drink	1,558	Education	1,779
Tobacco	1,512	National Health Service	1,437
Betting	1,200	Housing (public)	973
Gaming	750	All local welfare services	64

We live, moreover, at increasing pressure, bringing more illness,

[1] Quoted in *The Times* report, 27th September 1968.

especially mental illness, and more crime. We have moved away from purely heredital explanations of crime to explanations which, while admitting the importance of individual characteristics, emphasise their inseparability from the society in which the individuals live and which moulds them. So we find, in Britain, that the number of persons found guilty of offences has risen considerably in recent years, especially in the crimes of murder, attempted murder, manslaughter and assault, theft and forgery and illegal drug-handling. In 1964 the number of known crimes topped the million mark: twelve years ago the number was about half-a-million.

Marxists believe in freedom. In rejecting bourgeois morality, Marx and Engels also rejected the liberal notion of "freedom" in a capitalist society, pointing out that this was merely a cover for the exploitation by one class of all other classes. This is happening today in newer and more persuasive ways by those experts, the advertisers. Raymond Williams has pointed out that the "permissive society" was launched by the advertisers to help the producers of consumer goods break new sales ground. Williams goes further; he places the so-called "permissive society" within the context of the Tory–Wilson campaign for the "modernisation" of Britain. "... the whole modernisation programme is the bourgeois attack on all institutions and habits of mind that limit or hinder the aggressive and expanding operations of the market, which is seen as the only important social process."[1] The sudden liberation from old restraints is not freedom as Marx and Marxists understand it, although it may and indeed does overthrow some old and undesirable shibboleths; it tries to fill the minds of many, both young and not-so-young, with new brands of sex and violence, cynicism and anti-humanism, which the commercial mass media seize on to make bigger and better profits.

The Pilkington Committee, which examined broadcasting in 1960, condemned commercial TV's bias. In a representative week's evening programmes, commercial TV gave practically no time to serious drama. Compared with the BBC, it gave less than one-third of the time to topical discussions, nearly three times as much to crime, three times as much to comedy serials and more than twice as much to "Westerns". The ITA's power to control the companies, once they were appointed programme contractors, was ". . . illusory and negligible. The companies hold the initiative, and the Authority has

[1] R. Williams: "Towards a socialist society", in *Towards Socialism* (ed. Anderson and Blackburn), Fontana ed.

no real power to ensure that they use that initiative so as to realise the purposes of broadcasting."[1]

The Committee also attacked the ITA and commercial companies on other counts. The commercial press held such large blocks of shares that in several cases they owned or dominated the company; e.g. the Mirror Group held 26 per cent of ATV shares and the Thomson Organisation (Lord Thomson) nearly all the shares of Scottish TV. The companies were also condemned for excessive violence on the screen, showing the more serious programmes far too late in the evening, the triviality and poor quality of many programmes and, of course, excessive advertising, much of which was undesirable in content.

Certain changes have been made in the contracts awarded, but these have not led to the improvements hoped for.[2] And pressure to cut back on public expenditure is now endangering that island of minority, quality radio, the Third Programme.

As C. Wright Mills so well pointed out, the freedom which Marx (and Marxists) demand is moral, rational and humanist. If Marx regarded religion as a trap, he substituted moral principles, which Mills described as "radical humanism", against all forms of exploitation, material or spiritual. Marx believed in the supremacy, not of our most primitive and exploitable drives (sex and hunger), but of human reason. His understanding of alienation went hand-in-hand with a denunciation of human relationships considered in terms of money only. Freedom for him meant the highest possible development of human creativeness. That is why today we should not jump uncritically on to the bandwagon of "permissiveness" rolled out by the bourgeois mass media.

One of the unexpected and, for the bourgeoisie, unwanted effects of release from old restraints is the protest movement among students. In the uprush of demand for higher education, young people have stumbled against aspects of the educational system that were hitherto barely noticed, especially the autocratic remoteness of governing bodies composed to a large degree of big business representatives and conservative, upgraded academics, some, like Lord Robbins, with a substantial foot in both camps. As with every recent generation of enquiring young people, students and young workers are struck by the hypocrisy and lies of a Labour Government, who have thrown overboard all their most important electoral promises, as well as the open

[1] See the *Sunday Times* (owned by Lord Thomson!), 3rd August 1969.

[2] *Report of the Committee on Broadcasting 1960* (Cmd. 1753), ch. XIV.

defence of privilege and reaction by their "opponents", the Tories. In rejecting the capitalist system, however, students may be affected, first, by their lack of contact with the industrial workers and, secondly, by their disappointment at the mistakes and disasters in the socialist world. But their protest activities are yeast to the general dissatisfaction among the working population. Even this élite of Britain's youth finds aspects of the system, and some the system as a whole, hateful; and their place in the socialist movement, which is important and complex, will be discussed in the next chapter.

9

END THE SYSTEM

"A large class, like a great nation, never learns better or quicker than by undergoing the consequences of its own mistakes." (Engels.)

1. Our long analysis of post-war British society stressed two basic aspects. First that, strictly from the point of view of the division of the national product, our society remains unquestionably capitalist; that is to say, most of the country's wealth is owned by a very small part of the population. This minority also controls industry and wields the main economic and political power. Those who argued that it was no longer so based themselves on statistics derived from taxation of incomes, which appeared to show a drastic reduction in the wealth and incomes of top taxpayers and, at the other end, the almost total disappearance of very low incomes. In place of pre-war society, depicted as a pyramid, intoxicated enthusiasts of the "new society" regarded it as egg-shaped, bulging in the middle and tapering top and bottom. Many left-wingers felt this picture to be slightly phoney; but it was not until the 'sixties that Titmuss and his co-researchers at the London School of Economics tore it apart. They showed that the distribution of wealth (including income) remained as wide as, if not wider than, pre-war and that the numbers of poorest, redefined as those living at or below National Assistance level, was staggeringly large and getting larger.

Secondly, studies show that, far from moving towards a state of "classlessness", society in Britain is still stratified in much the same basic way as pre-war; that is to say, there is the capitalist class, with its royal figureheads and its fusion of landed aristocracy and business interests, and the working class. In one respect the picture has altered significantly, not only as compared with Marx's time but even relative to pre-World War II, and it continues to alter in the same direction. For Marx the middle "class", consisting of shopkeepers, self-employed artisans and some professional people, was relatively unimportant. Today, however, there are vast numbers of non-manual—professional, technical, administrative and clerical—workers, whose upper ranges reach into the ruling class and whose lower groupings stretch down economically and socially into the (manual) working class. But in those sociological aspects which bourgeois sociologists stress, "style of life", network of relationships, attitude to work, class consciousness, status, type of education, voting behaviour—the bulk of the middle strata are still largely distinguishable from the manual workers (wage-earners). However, at both the upper and the lower ends a process of convergence is taking place. The ruling class is creaming off an upper-middle-class élite to help it govern British neo-capitalism more effectively; at the lower end the non-manual workers are "converging" towards the upper working class, not merely economically (i.e. income-wise) but in those sociological characteristics which previously sharply separated them from the workers. This convergence is strong in the newer, or most developing, industries and services, weak in the older and declining ones.

As for the Welfare State, it is absolutely true that the growth of public welfare has brought very real gains to all working people by way of educational opportunity, a national health service, unemployment and sickness benefits and retirement pensions. The Welfare State is, however, paid for largely by the bulk of wage-earning and salaried workers; and rising costs, of which private profit constitutes a large part, coupled with restriction of expenditure, are bringing about a double, and doubly dangerous, situation. On the one hand, the burden of contributions is becoming too heavy for people to bear; on the other hand, fundamental sectors of public welfare are getting very much worse through an alarming staff shortage and totally inadequate funds. All the time, private profit and private wealth go up by leaps and bounds. Nor has the Welfare State altered the fundamental class relations.

Reformism, the philosophy of right-wing Social-Democracy, has certain common themes, which Crosland brought up-to-date and summarised.[1] They were: the appropriation of property incomes, co-operation, workers' control, social welfare and full employment. Examining the situation in the nineteen-fifties, he came to the conclusion that property incomes were being heavily eaten into, partly by nationalisation but even more by taxation; co-operation was steadily growing as class antagonism decreased; workers' control was irrelevant, but workers' participation in management was growing; social welfare had been largely achieved; and full employment was here to stay. All that remained to be done was to abolish the last patches of poverty and squalor in our big cities, eliminate the remaining areas of "social antagonism and class resentment", reduce the vast inequality of rewards and increase opportunities of rising to the top.

[1] *The Future of Socialism*, pp. 103–5.

In actual fact, the examination we have made, based on factual material, shows that in every one of these aims, what has been achieved has, since the late nineteen-fifties, been under attack and this attack has, though in different forms and to different degrees, gone on under both Tory and Labour rule. The revisionist, Bernstein, invented the famous epigram, "The ultimate aim of socialism is nothing, but the movement is everything." All the reforms that socialists could wish for could be achieved, without a revolution. In post-1945 phraseology capitalism could be, and was being, transformed out of all recognition: Bernstein would have approved the new description, "post-capitalism". But the high tide of British reformism has come and passed; and is not likely to return. For a Labour Government which returned to power with a parliamentary majority of 100 has not merely failed to keep up the momentum of reform of the first decade after 1945; it has gone backwards. Reformism is in process of committing suicide.

Possibly the fundamental misconception of all who, for whatever reason, followed the flag of reformism, was that in a capitalist democracy any changes could be made simply by voting in a parliamentary majority which believed in social and economic reform and which would appoint a government to carry out popular wishes. One after the other, each citadel of capitalist power could be taken over, not by force but by simple acts of the legislature. It would all be very reasonable. But, as Marx once pointed out, this reasonableness, this rationality, is only the bourgeois mind idealised.

This is not to say that democracy is to be sneered at. On the contrary, Britain's tradition of parliamentary democracy is a tremendous asset; and there will be many battles to preserve it. The same goes for other areas of democracy, for freedom to dissent as well as to consent. One such area is the freedom of collective bargaining, now under attack; another, the right to dissent, which is being fought for in the universities, has hardly touched that entrenched machinery of bourgeois ideology, the mass media. But, when all is said and done, Karl Kautsky had possibly the last words on democracy under capitalism; and they are worth repeating in full.

> "I do not wish to be understood as holding democracy to be superfluous," he wrote, "or to take the position that cooperatives, unions, the entrance of social democracy into municipalities and parliaments, or the attainment of single reforms, are worthless. Nothing would be more incorrect. On the contrary, all these are of incalculable value

to the proletariat. They are only insignificant as means to avoid a revolution.

"This conquest of political power by the proletariat is of the highest value exactly because it makes possible a higher form of the revolutionary struggle . . . the elections are a means to count ourselves and the enemy, and they grant thereby a clear view of the relative strength of the classes and parties, their advance and their retreat. They prevent premature outbreaks and they guard against defeats. . . .

"Neither are the political acquisitions that are gained through democracy and the application of its freedom and rights to be undervalued. They are much too insignificant really to restrict the dominion of capitalism and bring about its imperceptible transition into socialism. The slightest reform or organisation may be of great significance for the physical or intellectual *rebirth of the proletariat*, which without them would be surrendered helpless to capitalism and left alone in the misery that continuously threatens it. But it is not alone the relief of the proletariat from its misery that makes the activity of the proletariat in Parliament and the operation of the proletarian organisations indispensable. They are also of value as a means of practically familiarising the proletariat with the problems and methods of national and municipal government and of great industries, as well as to the attainment of that intellectual maturity which the proletariat needs if it is to supplant the bourgeoisie as ruling class.

". . . Democracy is to the proletariat what light and air are to the organism; without them it cannot develop its powers. But we must not be so occupied with observing the growth of one class that we cannot see the simultaneous growth of its opponent. Democracy does not hinder the development of capital, whose organisation and economic and political powers increase at the same time as does the power of the proletariat. To be sure, the cooperatives are increasing; but simultaneously and yet faster grows the accumulation of capital. To be sure, the unions are growing; but simultaneously and faster grows the concentration of capital and its organisation in gigantic monopolies. To be sure, the socialist press is growing . . . , but simultaneously grows the partyless and characterless press, which poisons and unnerves ever wider popular circles. To be sure, wages are rising, but still faster rises the mass of profits. Certainly the number of socialist representatives in Parliament is growing; but still more sinks the significance and efficaciousness of this institution, while simultaneously Parliamentary majorities, like the government, fall into ever greater dependence on the powers of high finance.

"So beside the resources of the proletariat develop also those of capital, and the end of this development can be nothing less than a great decisive battle which cannot end until the proletariat has attained the victory.

". . . Social peace inside of the capitalist system is a utopia which has grown out of the real needs of the intellectual classes, but has no foundation in reality for its development. And no less of a utopia is the imperceptible growth of capitalism into socialism. We have not the slightest ground to admit that things will end differently from the way they began. Neither the economic nor the political development indicates that the era of revolution which characterises the capitalist system is closed. Social reform and the strengthening of the proletarian organisations cannot hinder it. They can at the most operate to the end that the class struggle in the higher developed grades of the battling proletariat will be transformed from a battle for the first conditions of existence to a battle for the possession of dominion."[1]

The purpose of reformist ideology is two-fold. In boom periods it can secure concessions which the ruling class are prepared to give; in periods of growing crisis it abandons its aims in practice and in practice reformism becomes partner to vicious reaction. Long ago Rosa Luxemburg, one of the great leaders of German socialism, put her finger on the main consequence of reformist theory.

"Either revisionism is correct in its position on the course of capitalist development, and therefore the socialist transformation of society is only a utopia, or socialism is not utopia and the theory of 'means of adaptation' is false."[2]

In other words, if you believe in reformism or revisionism, you give up the idea of socialism and instead adapt capitalism. But it follows from what we have said that, in trying to adapt capitalism, reformists are forced to adapt themselves *to* capitalism; capitalism itself triumphs; they have to go along with it, all the way. So, as the behaviour of the Wilson government has shown, the "reformers" rush to help the

[1] Kautsky: *The Social Revolution* (1902) passim. Reprinted from C. Wright Mills: *The Marxists* pp., 171–3.

[2] Written in 1899; quoted in Mills, p. 192.

capitalist giants to become bigger through mergers, encourage profits (because "industry" has to be "encouraged"), suppress or restrain wage rises, reduce consumption by the masses, create and maintain a pool of unemployed, and use State power to try and hobble the trade unions. In the *end*, "reformists" following this road finish up, as in Nazi Germany and fascist Italy, advocates of force and terror. But force is getting ever more difficult to use, because popular resistance is on the increase.

One of the arguments used to justify the Labour Government's right turn between the 1964 and 1966 General Elections was its tiny parliamentary majority. Even left-wing members of the Labour Party argued that Wilson was a left-winger at heart (didn't he, after all, resign with Bevan over prescription charges?) and that all he needed was a really big parliamentary majority to bring in really tough left-wing measures. That Labour's massive victory in 1966 brought about a much tougher *right*-wing policy is now, unhappily, only too well known.

Bourgeois sociology in the 'fifties was reformist ideology in an academic gown. It persistently ignored or attacked the Marxist interpretation of society. It went much further than Weber, who appreciated perfectly well both the importance of property-ownership as a determinant of class and that class and status-position often overlapped. His modern followers, ignoring this, also distorted the meaning of social class, arguing, because the data seemed on their side, that both capitalist and working classes were dissolving and that property ownership was unimportant. To a lesser extent other theories, old and new, were brought in to keep Marxism out: cyclical (like Pareto's), managerial (Burnham), élitist (Pareto and others), all trying to raise secondary features of contemporary capitalist and socialist societies to first place. Above all, Talcott Parsons and his followers produced the theory that all members of a society (and particularly "Western" society) agreed on basic norms and values. As a group of British left-wing intellectuals point out, this is one of the fundamental ideas which the propagandists of our ruling classes have tried to put over in the past twenty years.

> "The political aim of the new capitalism, and of the governments which sustain it, is clear. It is to muffle real conflict, to dissolve it into a false political consensus; to build, not a genuine and radical community of life and interest, but a bogus conviviality between every social group. Consensus politics, integral to the

success of the new capitalism, is in its essence manipulative politics, the politics of man-management, and as such deeply undemocratic. Governments are still elected, M.P.s assert the supremacy of the House of Commons. But the real business of government is the management of consensus between the most powerful and organised élites."[1]

Raymond Williams and his colleagues go on to emphasise this matter of manipulation. Certainly manipulation is preferable to the use of force but, particularly in a crisis of capitalism, the ruling class and its managers tend to forget the lessons of contemporary history. If manipulation or man-management fails, then they are always ready to use force, even if it is the relatively non-violent force of sending their opponents to jail. I foresee an increasing trend towards coercion, which will however provoke greater and greater opposition.

In fact, this dual trend has been visible for some years. The Labour Government's action from about 1965 onward show that the *real* meaning of the "consensual society" is what the newspaper linguists call the "credibility gap", that is, a growing divergence between stated aims and actual governmental performance. As the writers of the May Day Manifesto tell us, the "consensual society" myth is the outward brass face of a huge confidence trick.

Into the credibility gap between consensus theory and political reality stepped conflict theory. Conflict theory contended that all modern industrial societies consisted of conflict groups. At first it rejected the Marxist view that the basis of conflict today was, as in all class societies, economic. Its most influential early spokesman, Ralf Dahrendorf, argued that class conflict was only a particular type of conflict over *authority*. Writing in the late 'fifties, Dahrendorf swallowed the current idea of growing classlessness hook, line and sinker. Inventing (I believe) the label "post-capitalist" for our post-war societies in the "West", Dahrendorf committed such huge blunders as that the individual who stays in his father's occupation all his life has become a rarity; and he accepted unquestioningly the general bourgeois dogma that the extremes of wealth and poverty have been abolished. Classes, therefore, probably didn't exist any longer! Instead there were "conflict groups", each pursuing its own "interest". There was always conflict and conflict always led to change. It followed, wrote Dahrendorf, that a "classless" society was impossible, because in every

[1] *May Day Manifesto 1968*, ed. R. Williams, p. 143.

society there was always a distribution of authority. But, he added, in modern, post-capitalist society industrial conflict was lessening; it was becoming "institutionalised" through the numerous machineries of negotiation, conciliation and arbitration, as well as through increasing worker participation in industry. The ruling class, too, was no longer of the type described by Marx as the "executive committee of the capitalist class". Condescendingly adapting the various élitist theories, Dahrendorf described the ruling class of the post-capitalist state, whether communist or "western", as composed of the administrative staff of the state, the governmental élites at its head and the interested parties represented by the governmental élite. In this way, Dahrendorf expunged *economic* classes from neo-capitalist societies, mis-appropriated the word class for his own type of grouping and obliterated not merely capitalism itself in the world today but the distinction between capitalism and socialism, except that in communist societies political conflict was repressed and (a wishful thought) there would be increasing violence. But, cleverly, by allowing "discussion", the communist rulers were able to reduce conflict. Hence Dahrendorf arrived at the crazy conclusion that communist societies were utterly wrong, because they aimed to reduce conflict! "Totalitarian monism (i.e. socialism—H.F.) is founded on the idea that conflict can and should be eliminated, that a homogeneous and uniform social and political order is the desirable state of affairs. . . . The pluralism of free societies, on the other hand, is based on recognition and acceptance of social conflict."[1]

2. Dahrendorf's outlook reflected a trend which, appearing in the late 'fifties, exploded both theoretically and in practice during the present decade. A number of notable left-wing books appeared criticising our present society and stressing the relevance of Marxism. In academic writings in the social sciences Marx's ideas took an increasingly important place. For a time, even after the election of the Labour Government in 1964, socialists of widely-differing views began to draw nearer to each other. As the Labour Government stumbled from one right-wing blunder to another, the Left took heart and campaigned for their alternatives.

3. The left-intellectual critique of the "affluent society" (so-called) went along two lines. The "affluent society" was a grossly materialistic society; money was the be-all and end-all; and this was as true of the working class as of the capitalist class. The car, the TV and the washing machine had become the new symbols of working-class affluence;

[1] Dahrendorf: *Class and Class Conflict in Industrial Society*, p. 318.

while for the capitalists the pursuit of financial gain stood above everything else. The second line of thought and action, following the revelations of poverty amid increasing wealth, was what could be done about it—in other words, how, since social-democratic reformism had quite obviously failed, could we bring about the social revolution?

Exploration of this second question came up against two major queries. First, could the revolutions which established communist regimes elsewhere be models for those in Western capitalist societies? Secondly, have the present communist countries genuinely socialist regimes which can be regarded as attractive alternatives to affluent, western capitalism? As regards the first, Marx, Engels and western Communist Parties were, it seemed, quite wrong in thinking that the industrial proletariat were necessarily the spearhead of the revolution. Without the peasants, how far would the tiny Russian proletariat have got during both the Revolution and the Civil War? It was the Chinese peasants who formed the mass of the Red Army; here too there was only a handful of industrial workers. East Europe was socialist (or communist) only because Stalin had imposed communism on it. Finally, Cuba, too, was a largely peasant country. In Britain, the working class seem unable to understand what socialism is, do not want a revolution and vote in a Tory or a right-wing Labour Government. Membership of and votes for the revolutionary socialism of British and U.S. communist parties are pitifully small. It was obvious, these left writers declared, that reliance upon the working class of the West was useless.

Such an interpretation of twentieth-century developments is extremely one-sided. The Russian Revolution *was* led by the industrial proletariat, but the Chinese and Cuban revolutions involved peasants, intellectuals and urban proletariat.[1] As Marxists have come to recognise again, socialist revolutions may be inextricably interwoven with national uprisings against foreign oppression and colonial status; and the way the revolution goes on depends upon the balance of socialist and other forces. A strong industrial base and a class-conscious proletariat can, even if small, provide the right foundations: without them

[1] The particular way the Chinese revolution has gone is due, as several commentators have pointed out, to several factors. Although the Red Army began in the cities, it was driven (the Long March) into remote rural China, where the soldiers were isolated from the urban proletariat and became peasant-oriented. The main opposition to the adventurist "cultural revolution" came from the industrial workers; and it is they, in alliance with the more politically experienced peasants and intellectuals, who will eventually correct the Maoist mistakes.

all sorts of wrong turnings may be taken (although a class-conscious proletariat can also make terrible mistakes). But there is no peasantry in Britain, only a highly-organised industrial proletariat in the classical Marxist sense, plus a large white-collar proletaroid. Does that mean Marx was so wrong that we have, in fact, to turn him upside-down again, to say that the revolution is *least* likely in a highly industrialised state with a large, class-conscious proletariat? Or should we rather say that Kautsky hit the nail on the head when he argued that as the western proletariat got stronger, so did the western bourgeoisie get even stronger; but that, when the climax is reached—and it would take longer to arrive—the revolution would be swifter, the building of socialism better, more efficient and more successful? This view doesn't go down well with the extreme left: there is still no sign of revolutionary spirit among the industrial proletariat, the perspective is too long, the revolution in this way too slow in coming, if it ever comes at all. The ultra-left cannot see that the existence of mass revolutionary parties in France and Italy, based on the industrial proletariat but also widely supported by white-collar workers, peasants and intelligentsia, invalidates their argument that the Western industrial workers are not revolutionary, but rather supports the communist claim that the British case is no different, only that, because of the uniqueness of British imperialism, it is likely to take longer here than elsewhere. In their lack of hope—the sort of hope expressed by Engels' famous remark about the return of socialism to England—the ultra-left look for a quicker way forward.

Then there is the problem of Stalinism. Was all the effort along classic communist lines simply to result in a bureaucratic state, where the leadership could maintain itself only by terror and where all freedom and opposition were suppressed? Hungary made this view very common and it was confirmed by the invasion of Czechoslovakia. The countries beyond threat, specifically China, Yugoslavia and Cuba, offered the only hope: they provided backing for the theory of peasant-led revolutions and for a type of "non-Soviet" socialism.

Academic intellectuals and students are prone to distrust the Soviet Union and its socialist allies. Less realistic than the working class, they tend to think of socialism coming like Venus pure out of the sea. Socialism cannot be sullied; and the terrible crimes pervading the history of the U.S.S.R., from Stalin's rejection of world revolution in favour of "socialism in one country", his ruthless collectivisation of agriculture, the Moscow trials, up to the use of Soviet tanks against

Hungarian "freedom fighters" and the Czechoslovaks, not to mention the economic inegalitarianism and the massive bureaucracy, confirm their view that the U.S.S.R. cannot be socialist; and all who regard her as socialist are tools of the Kremlin bureaucrats.

Theoretically, many left-wing intellectuals go back to those whom Wright Mills included under the umbrella title of critics of Stalinism. They look to Rosa Luxemburg's criticism of Bolshevik dictatorship under Lenin and Trotsky and to the later Trotsky himself. One may reject Trotsky's conclusion that the Soviet Union was, under Stalin, a state half-way between socialism and capitalism, while still regarding his analysis of how the Soviet Union managed to get into the condition where the Stalinist crimes (and successes) were possible as profoundly true.[1] One may believe that Rosa Luxemburg's criticism of early Soviet rule was too idealistic, and still insist that it raised important questions about freedom. The danger in being anti-Soviet today is two-fold; the critic may associate only with a narrow ultra-left clique, or he may end up throwing in the sponge. But this does not mean we should not speak up when we believe that the Soviet Union, or any other socialist country, is doing wrong.

The ultra-left tends also to over-value the middle-class intellectual. Stressing the number of middle-class intellectuals who have led socialist revolutionary movements, from Marx to Che Guevara, the exponents of this viewpoint, by implication, under-estimate the working-class. To them the workers are passive, even lumpen, and only the intellectuals, bringing the ideas of revolution and socialism, can lead. Such people are fond of quoting a certain passage from Lenin's *What is to be done?*, a book-length pamphlet Lenin wrote against the idea current in Russia at the turn of the century that the masses could be left *spontaneously* to bring about the revolution. In it Lenin stressed the absolute need for a revolutionary theory and the important role of intellectuals.

> "We said that there could not yet be *Social-Democratic*[2] consciousness among the workers. This consciousness could only be brought to them from without. The history of all countries shows that the working class, exclusively by its own effort, is able to develop only trade union consciousness.... The theory of Socialism, however, grew

[1] Trotsky: *The Revolution Betrayed*. A valuable extract is given in C. Wright Mills, *The Marxists*, pp. 300–23.

[2] Social-Democratic here means, of course, revolutionary socialist. The party in Russia was then called the Social-Democratic Party.

out of the philosophic, historical and economic theories that were elaborated by the educated representatives of the propertied classes, the intellectuals. According to their social status, the founders of modern scientific Socialism, Marx and Engels, themselves belonged to the bourgeois intelligentsia. Similarly, in Russia, the theoretical doctrine of Social-Democracy arose quite independently of the spontaneous growth of the labour movement; it arose as a natural and inevitable outcome of the development of ideas among the revolutionary Socialist intelligentsia."[1]

To read this passage as an affirmation of the idea that the intellectuals necessarily lead the workers to the revolution makes two mistakes. First, it ignores the fact that Lenin was writing in the earliest period of the revolutionary movement, when the intellectuals had an overwhelming superiority in knowledge and understanding. Secondly, it assumes (wrongly) that Lenin regarded the working class as passive and lumpen. On the contrary, Lenin's whole career demonstrated his unshakable belief that, once the workers had grasped the ideas of socialism, nothing could stop them ultimately carrying through the revolution.[2] Today, with the considerable help given by middle-class intellectuals, the working classes of several countries have established socialist states and built mass revolutionary parties. While it is true that Castro, Guevara and many of the Chinese leaders are intellectuals of middle-status origin, the socialist states of Eastern Europe, including Yugoslavia, are led by men mainly of working-class origin. So are the mass communist parties of France and Italy.

It is particularly interesting that Marcuse, the doyen of intellectuals of the extreme left, himself avoids this mistaken notion. He certainly holds the view that the workers of the industrially advanced countries are no longer capable of revolt; the capitalist system has neutralised them with affluence and by incorporating the labour movement into its structure. Who then, he asks, can make the revolution?

"Can we say that the intelligentsia is the agent of historical change? Can we say that the intelligentsia today is a revolutionary

[1] *Selected Works of Lenin* (Lawrence and Wishart 1947), Vol. I, pp. 167–8.

[2] Four years before *What is to be done?* Lenin, in the pamphlet *The tasks of the Russian Social-Democrats*, emphasised that the working class were the vanguard of the Revolution, while the intelligentsia, most of whom were tied materially to the capitalist system, exhibited that political inconsistency mentioned in the *Communist Manifesto*.

class? The answer I would give is: No, we cannot say that. But we can say, and I think we must say, that the intelligentsia has a decisive preparatory function, not more; and I suggest that this is plenty. By itself it is not and cannot be a revolutionary class, but it can become the catalyst. . . ."

Further on, he explains why.

"This class, this intelligentsia (employed by the largest concerns) has been called the new working class. I believe that this term is at best premature. They are—and this we should not forget—today the pet beneficiaries of the present system. But they are also at the very source of the glaring contradictions between the liberating capacity of science and its repressing and enslaving use."[1]

But, having condemned the industrial workers to political sterility, and written off the Communists and Left-Labour as "revisionists", to whom does he look for salvation? The answer is, to the outcasts and outsiders of capitalist society, the coloured, the unemployed and the unemployable (including all the varieties of drop-outs). Unfortunately, any socialist with his feet on the ground can only shake his head at this impractical idea. Of all these groups only the coloured people are fighting in an organised way, but, like the Jews in the 1930s, they fight in the main only for equality with the rest of the population. Only the best go from there to socialism.

4. The political development of the British people clearly points to one road, and only one road, out of capitalism, however long it may be. Britain has perhaps the capitalist world's most highly organised working class. This class is, of course, divided within itself; the most skilled workers came to socialism first and it has since spread to the less skilled. The special, privileged position of the British working class due to the material superiority of British imperialism is disappearing. The extremes to which "reformism" is moving today—legislative control of wages and salaries and, next, of the trade unions—powerfully indicate that "reformism" is crumbling, that the State is being used more and more to bolster what is now an historically obsolete system and that socialist, not merely trade union, consciousness is increasing, particularly among the industrial workers. Still more, the old, clear separation

[1] Article: "Liberation from the Affluent Society" in *The Dialectics of Liberation*, ed. D. Cooper (Pelican 1967).

between skilled and unskilled is becoming clouded as "unskilled" work comes to require greater effort and skill and old craft skills are replaced by new techniques, creating a bigger and bigger wedge of intermediate "semi-skilled". Finally, the white-collar "proletaroid" are being increasingly drawn into militant activity against the system that threatens to drag them down; and this proletaroid includes not only the lowest paid clerical workers but a substantial and growing section of professional workers, most of whom are in any case salaried employees subject to the same ruling-class policies as the manual workers (heavier work burdens, rising prices, the rising cost plus the inadequacies of the social and public services, taxation), as well as that new force, the students. That the intelligentsia have an important preparatory function is absolutely true: they produce information and ideas and, as students, provide leadership and the largest part of the protest movement. But, as even student leaders like Cohn-Bendit have pointed out, the social revolution can only be made in the industrial "West" by an alliance, led by the industrial workers, of workers, salariat and intellectuals.

Sociology came into existence in a continuous attempt to counter the growing influence of socialism. Today it has become another academic discipline, and as such offers help to train students in social work, education and business management. To the extent that it does this it has succeeded in adapting people to the system. But it has also produced its opposite, valuable factual and ideological ammunition *for* socialism. This new material, which has been extensively quoted in the present work, bears out the conclusion that the capitalist system is over-ripe for overthrow and that the most scientific sociological theory to help bring this transformation is Marxism.

Those features of capitalism which the sociologists assert belong to all industrial societies and which a scientific sociology must take into account—bureaucracy, managerialism, élitism, authoritarianism, status striving, alienation and over-concern with money, aspects of "mass society" (apathy, anomie, criminal deviation on a large scale) and internal conflict—all these will, more or less, remain problems for us during the socialist phase of history, the phase which is likely to last until the whole world is socialist. But for tens of millions of the people of this country socialism will be an immediate blessing over and above any distorting features. Tens of millions will begin to live under a new system, in which the private accumulation of enormous wealth and mass poverty will cease, where equality of opportunity will really begin, where the needs of the people in housing, transport, old age, sickness and health will be put before private profit. Above all, the whole quality of living will begin to change and, with the resources made available through the scientific and technological revolution, British people will begin to lead fuller and better lives than they have ever lived before.

INDEX